OUR FUTURE

Also by Steven Shafarman

Basic Income Imperative: For Peace, Justice, Liberty, and Personal Dignity

Peaceful, Positive Revolution: Economic Security for Every American

We the People: Healing Our Democracy and Saving Our World

Healing Politics: Citizen Policies and the Pursuit of Happiness

Healing Americans: A New Vision for Politics, Economics, and Pursuing Happiness

Awareness Heals: The Feldenkrais Method for Dynamic Health

OUR FUTURE

The Basic Income Plan

for Peace, Justice, Liberty, Democracy, and Personal Dignity

STEVEN SHAFARMAN

RealClear
PUBLISHING

Our Future: The Basic Income Plan for Peace, Justice, Liberty, Democracy, and Personal Dignity

For more information, please contact:
Amplify Publishing
620 Herndon Parkway, Suite 320
Herndon, VA 20170
info@amplifypublishing.com

For information about bulk purchases, please contact:
info@amplifypublishing.com or 703-437-3584.

Library of Congress Control Number: 2019917058

CPSIA Code: PRV0420A
ISBN-13: 978-1-64543-216-6

Printed in the United States

For true citizens of all lands

Contents

To the Reader   1

1   We the People   5

2   The Plan   13

3   To Make Taxes Fair and Simple   29

4   To Reform and Shrink Government   41

5   To Produce Smart Economic Growth   51

6   To Promote Justice and Personal Dignity   63

7   To Enhance Liberty and Democracy   73

8   To Respect and Protect Our Environment   83

9   To Nurture Peace and Security for All   97

10   We the People Renewed   113

11   Our Strategy   125

12   Now   133

From the Author   143

Appendix 1   Related Ideas and Efforts   149

Appendix 2   Financial Matters   219

Appendix 3   International Activities   225

Appendix 4   For More Information   235

Endnotes   237

Acknowledgments   269

Index   273

To the Reader

The central person in this book is you. Your dreams and goals are core concerns, what you want for yourself, your family, your community, and your country. And what you want from our government and for it as a citizen.

Please pretend we're friends. Imagine that you're excited to see me – we haven't been in touch since high school, when we were close – and I'm eager to hear about you. The best way for us to reconnect, I suggest, is for you to read this book. It's short and sincere, and I worked hard to make it pleasant reading.

You might also pretend it was inspired by our shared concerns, and that I wrote it to renew our friendship. It was, in effect, and I did, with questions in every chapter to help us connect. Pause and think about your answers, please.

Even better, think aloud. Talk with friends and family, and tell them what you would tell me. What do you like? What would you change? Do you want to work together on the next steps?

I began talking and writing about these ideas in the mid 1980s, and I've been active with the U.S. Basic Income Guarantee Network since 2000, soon after it was founded. I'm also a life member of the Basic Income Earth Network, and I presented talks at their meetings in Geneva in 2002, Dublin in 2008, and Montreal in 2014. I published my first book about basic income in 1998, while enrolled in a doctoral program in human development, then three more books over the following decade as my thinking evolved.

The big ideas in this book are: (1) We can have peace, justice, liberty, democracy, and personal dignity *for everyone*. (2) Basic income is the key. And (3) regular folks have to lead.

You'll find more about me, my thinking, and my dreams in From the Author, and that section concludes the main part of this book. Appendix 1 is very long; I compiled it over twenty years, and crafted it to provide a comprehensive, enduring resource for academics and activists. Endnotes are fairly elaborate, to keep the main text simple.

In the 1980s and until today, while talking with thousands of people about basic income, I've noticed that people's initial responses tend to reflect their politics, significant differences between liberals and conservatives. Yet I also found fundamental commonalities. Appreciating both the differences and the commonalities kept me motivated.

Over the past few years, a growing number of people have heard of basic income, also called Universal Basic Income or UBI, Citizen Dividends, guaranteed income, negative income tax, or Freedom Dividend. Though many interpretations are inaccurate or incomplete, so I'm often frustrated. My primary goal with this book is to inspire informed discussions leading to action.

Every day brings more news of real threats to our safety and happiness, and more evidence that our government is broken. Even so, most of us still believe in traditional American ideals: Free citizens. Life, liberty, and the pursuit of happiness. Equal rights and equal opportunities. Government of the people, by the people, for the people. Liberty and justice for all.

I still have a lot to learn – from you, I hope – yet I now believe this plan is good for everyone: poor and rich, old and young, women and men, rural and suburban and urban. Specifically, I believe it will be good for you and your family.

So let's talk about our dreams and goals, and what we can do to achieve them. Let's talk about how to make a better world for our children, our grandchildren, and their great-grandchildren — a better world for everyone.

And let's make history.

★　★　★　★　★

For readers around the world,

This book is for you, too, though it mainly refers to the United States. You'll find parallels with the political situation where you live, plus prospects for modifying this plan and making it your own. Your country, your plan.

In a democracy, your plan can be a platform for the next election. In a country going through a political transition, you can help ease and speed the passage to a true democracy. In a country with an autocratic ruler or dictator, activists can use these ideas to discreetly attract allies and build support. Your time will come, and you'll be prepared to organize actively, mobilize politically, and succeed quickly.

You and your friends can lead. If your country acts before the United States, I'll thank you. Your efforts could be the catalyst that dissolves the dysfunction in U.S. politics. In our interconnected world, progress anywhere helps people everywhere.

CHAPTER 1

We the People

What do I want?
How should I live?
What's best for my family?

These questions lead to thinking about where we live or want to live, the place and the people, our friends and neighbors. Also to thinking about how we earn or want to earn money, and therefore to considering our coworkers, customers, and clients, our employers and perhaps employees. These personal questions connect us to countless people.

As we pursue happiness throughout our lives, we rely on government for our personal safety and our national security. Government issues our money, maintains our police and military, builds roads and other public assets, fosters commerce, and administers justice. Government is necessary. Politics, too, necessary because politics is the process we use to select and direct the people who manage our government, and to hold officials accountable.

What do I want? How should I live? That's for me to decide, me and my family; you and your family, other folks and their families. Our decisions ought to be truly *ours*.

What's best for a neighborhood or community? Who decides? The residents or members, ideally, the folks who are most directly involved or influenced by the consequences.

Who decides for your town or city? Your state? Our country? America's Founders gave us an answer: we decide, we individuals acting together as *We the People*.

> We hold these truths to be self-evident, that all men are created equal, that they are endowed by their creator with certain unalienable rights, that among these are life, liberty, and the pursuit of happiness, — that to secure these rights, governments are instituted among men, deriving their just powers from the consent of the governed, — that whenever any form of government becomes destructive of these ends, it is the right of the people to alter or to abolish it, and to institute new government, laying its foundations on such principles, and organizing its powers in such form, as to them shall seem most likely to effect their safety and happiness.[1]

And

> We the People of the United States, in order to form a more perfect union, establish justice, insure domestic tranquility, provide for the common defense, promote the general welfare, and secure the blessings of liberty to ourselves and our posterity, do ordain and establish this Constitution.

Individual citizens are *We the People* — when we choose to act as such, together.

We the People are sovereign. We, as equals, institute government to secure our rights. We decide our government's roles, duties, powers, and limits. We consent to it and it serves us, each and all of us. Direct relationships, with reciprocity, between individual citizens and our government.

The Founders' ideals, however, are missing from our everyday experience. Today, inequality is irrefutable. Reciprocity is only a theory. Consent is passive, partial, transitory, or conditional. Or consent is coerced.

Our government is broken. Most of us are struggling with debt, worrying about our retirement prospects, worrying about our kids and how they'll manage. Most of us are upset or angry about crime, taxes, healthcare, education, immigration, global warming, national security, and other matters. Government wastes untold billions of our tax dollars, while generating nonstop noise, nonsense, and negativity.

Our political system is failing, paralyzed by partisan conflicts. Like rival teams in a serious sport, Democrats and Republicans do and say whatever it takes to win. Campaign events are pep rallies. Pundits are coaches, scorekeepers, and cheerleaders.

The two parties are also like rival cliques in a big high school. Each clique is a small gang of leaders and insiders, a posse of wannabes jockeying to become insiders, and a large mass of passive followers. Members use colors, code words, and culture signals to define and identify themselves, to keep the cliques distinct. The two cliques rule, sharing power at times or passing it from one to the other. Independent groups and individuals – 40 percent of us, more than either party – are generally excluded, occasionally bribed or bullied.

Our elections are mostly marketing. Politicians and policies are sold like toothpaste and breakfast cereal, and political marketing is a multibillion-dollar industry. But unlike toothpaste and cereal, which are tested, regulated, and come with a list of ingredients, political products lack disclosures and can be noxious or toxic.

Our elected officials are, no surprise, politicians. Did something good happen? They'll take credit. Anything bad? Their opponent's fault entirely. Ask a question, and they respond by restating carefully-crafted talking points. If they say something often enough, they seem to believe, it must be true, will somehow become true, or will somehow be perceived as true. They claim to know what's best for everyone, and promise to do what's best, as our champions, heroes, and saviors. Novice politicians are normally sincere, but most are then infected with a virus that kills courage, supplants sincerity, and replicates careerism, self-righteousness, and a sense of entitlement.

Our laws are tainted by pay-offs and trade-offs. Wealthy elites fund campaigns, hire former officials as lobbyists, and sometimes draft the bills that become our laws. Laws, rules, and regulations can be hundreds or thousands of pages, dense legal and technical jargon, incomprehensible to anyone who's not an expert. The complications help politicians conceal their collusion with the elites, and help the elites conceal their roles and the rewards they'll reap.

Our political discourse is polluted, a mess of tweets, slogans, buzzwords, sound bites, talking points, name-calling, platitudes, and euphemisms. *Liberal* has become a synonym for pro-government. *Conservative* now means anti-government, pro-market, pro-business, pro-private enterprise. These redefinitions are recent, yet rarely examined and routinely expanded. Some liberals seem to believe that every problem requires a government program. Some conservatives insist that private is good, public is bad, and government should be privatized. Politicians wear labels as logos, and wield them as swords and shields.

What went wrong? Why is the system so dysfunctional?

Many of us blame special interests. That sounds persuasive, and there's plenty of evidence to support it. But it's not the whole story; it can't be. Special interests have been wielding power throughout America's history. Our Constitution contains blatant concessions to a wealthy special interest: slave-owners.

Special interest has no formal definition; the meaning is set by the speaker. Ask a liberal Democrat, and it refers to Wall Street, the N.R.A., oil companies, and evangelicals. Conservative Republicans are likely to list Hollywood, trial lawyers, environmentalists, gays and lesbians. Independents cite from both sides, and often indict the Democratic and Republican parties. *Special interest*, for most of us, is a proxy for "powerful groups I dislike or oppose." One exception is widely praised, envied, and celebrated, an extra-special special interest: the superrich.

Many blame the news media. A free press is necessary to hold politicians and government accountable, and freedom of the press is protected by the First Amendment. Today, though, "the press" and "the media" are, mainly, big companies that seek profits first, truth second. They highlight conflicts, controversies, personalities, and drama, presenting politics as a reality TV show. Democrats and Republicans share power, and the news media habitually report two sides to each issue, those two sides, while dismissing or discounting other perspectives. Big media companies tout themselves even when reporting on their failures, stories about "news" and "fake news." Big media companies are a uniquely privileged special interest.

Many blame social media (Facebook, Twitter, Instagram, et al.), and often extend the blame to include Google, Apple, Microsoft, and Amazon. The internet has severely disrupted our lives, our culture, and our politics. Before, people on the street made eye contact and said "Hi." Now many of us wear earbuds and stare at smartphones. We're constantly in contact with friends, "friends," and newsfeeds filled with gossip, rumors, and ads, including political ads and lies. Big internet companies are a special interest with unknown, maybe unknowable, influence.

But blaming is misleading. Special interests exacerbate political dysfunction and profit from it, though they're not the primary cause.

Public withdrawal is more fundamental. Regular folks – feeling, believing, or knowing that we're powerless – turned off and turned away from politics. Special interests moved into the gap, expanding their access, increasing their influence, procuring funds and favors, providing further reasons for folks to withdraw. Withdrawal, apathy, and low voter turn-out are now normal and expected. Pundits lament that and academics try to explain it, while politicians count on it and exploit it, with negative campaign tactics designed deliberately to drive people away.

We're also angry. Anger ignited the Tea Party in 2009, Occupy Wall Street in 2011, Black Lives Matter in 2013, and #MeToo in 2017, each with a surge of rage at the status quo. Anger is healthy, even necessary, and can be the spark and the fuel for our efforts to repair our broken government.

Anger, however, is only part of the answer. Tea Party Republicans shut down the federal government for sixteen days in 2013. Occupy activists emphasized income inequality, and emboldened liberal Democrats. Black Lives Matter is demanding changes from both parties. #MeToo is confronting abusers in all sectors of society. Distinct movements – different folks, goals, strategies, and tactics – though a common or cumulative outcome, normally, is further political paralysis.

In the presidential election of 2016, angry "populists" attacked entrenched establishments. Bernie Sanders nearly won the Democratic nomination. Donald Trump seized and stoked public anger, and was elected. Trump promised to "drain the swamp," to end decades of bloat, failure, corruption, and special interest dealing. But while people are eager to flush something down the drain, we disagree about what, or who, is "the swamp."

The 2018 elections were marked by acute anger on both sides, aggravated by the Trump administration, Supreme Court confirmations, and Robert Mueller's investigation. The partisan divides are now like distinct tribes. Leaders of the two parties – Donald Trump and Senate Majority Leader Mitch McConnell on one side, Speaker of the House Nancy Pelosi and Senate Minority Leader Chuck Schumer on the other – routinely refuse to compromise. They're citing different facts, proclaiming different values, presenting different policies, and speaking to different voters — as if America is two countries, not one.

Political paralysis persists, in part, as a byproduct of multiple groups competing for attention, privileges, and public funds. Men vs. women, seniors vs. youth, rich vs. middle-class vs. poor, urban vs. suburban vs. rural. Some conflicts concern race or ethnic or religious identity: Whites vs. Blacks or Latinos or Asians; evangelicals vs. Catholics or Jews or Muslims or atheists. Some conflicts involve a single issue, often guns or abortion, though issues and groups are mostly a muddle: tax-cutters vs. environmentalists vs. education reformers vs. healthcare activists vs. supporters or opponents of whatever's in the news at the moment.

If one group wins anything, other groups fight on, and sometimes win the next round. In nearly all political conflicts, consequently, the real winner is the status quo. The superrich get richer and more super.

Politicians promise to reach across the aisle, find the center, work together, and unite Americans. Nice sentiments, but only rhetoric. The conflicts, competitions, and conventional assumptions have us trapped. Regular folks and politicians – the superrich, too; all of us – are trapped in a dysfunctional system.

The trap is partly from disregarding differences in the meaning of *we*. Among friends, when someone says "We should ... ," for example, listeners can agree, "Yes, good idea." Or decline, "No, I'd rather not." Or propose an alternative, "Instead, let's ... ." The personal *we* is voluntary and requires consent. True consent requires freedom to dissent or withdraw.

In political discourse, *we* is one-sided. Speakers assert "we" and assume consent. Speakers say "*we* are," "*we* know," "*we* must," etc., as if listeners already agree. Speakers presume or pretend to represent an unspecified group, *we*, as if the group is united and unanimous. Consent is contrived or passive — or partial, transitory, conditional, or entirely imaginary.

The one-sided *we* is widespread, normally unnoticed.

When regular folks use *we* this way, as an assertion or assumption, *we* is mere chatter or utter conjecture; in most cases, nothing happens. But *we* has a different meaning when spoken by politicians, CEOs, billionaires, and other prominent personalities. Their assertions and assumptions are compelling. Their *we* can include or affect us without our consent, without our knowledge, and despite our dissent. Their *we* can be deceptive, coercive, self-serving, a fraud.

We is truly valid only when it's voluntary. Consent is only true when it's active and affirmed. Every included individual must have meaningful opportunities to agree or decline or propose an alternative — or there is no *we*.

Elections are supposed to express or produce a valid *we*. But elections are blunt instruments, and recent elections have been awfully blunt. Many of us don't vote. Some voters select for a single issue only. Some voters are strictly against the other party or candidate. Some voters ignore issues, and choose candidates based on race, gender, religion, appearance, name recognition, or likability. Voters are deceived or misinformed. Voters and nonvoters have heard, and are influenced by, claims and lawsuits alleging fraud, suppression, mismanagement, and meddling by partisan officials.

A valid *we* often emerges during disasters and tragedies, but the feeling is fleeting. Then people revert to familiar assertions, assumptions, attitudes, and behaviors.

Real progress requires a *we* that's meaningful, voluntary, and enduring: *meaningful* for all citizens as equals; *voluntary,* with active consent from a true majority; and *enduring* through disasters and tragedies and quiet times as well.

A meaningful, voluntary, enduring *we* is the key to *We the People.*

CHAPTER 2

The Plan

Politics is personal, unique individuals pursuing dreams, goals, and happiness.

Politics is also social, obviously. Government is fundamentally social.

This plan respects the personal and the social. This is a way to attract, engage, and encourage individuals to actively think of ourselves as citizens. Also a way to inspire, motivate, and mobilize us to act together as *We the People*.

Starting with individuals, regular folks – not elites or experts, not groups or statistics or abstract concepts – this plan creates conditions for rapid progress toward realizing our ideals. Personal dreams and goals are the keys. The engines are our choices and actions.

Warning

This plan is bold. More than bold; it's radical, it goes to the roots. Some people will object without saying why. When ideas are unfamiliar, unproved, risky, or radical, many of us react emotionally and swiftly say "No."

If a knee-jerk objection is your first response, please pause and exhale. We're steeped in the status quo. It colors our thoughts, feelings, and assumptions about politics and economics; we tend to defend it, even though we know it's dysfunctional. Knee-jerk responses impair our ability to think. Special interests are specialists at jerking our knees and chains.

Bold and radical, though this plan has many precedents. Thomas Jefferson and Thomas Paine proposed related ideas, as did Abraham Lincoln, economist Milton Friedman, and Martin Luther King Jr. In 1970, moderate Democrats and moderate Republicans supported a prior version, the Family Assistance Plan. Most Americans favored it, opinion polls showed, and the House of Representatives passed it, twice, with majorities of nearly two-to-one. In the Senate, however, extremes of both parties voted against it, for different reasons, and blocked it.

Another precedent is Alaska, the Permanent Fund Dividend. Since 1982, every resident has received a cash payment each year, a share of oil royalties. Ask any Alaskan. They love it.*

The Plan

- Set an amount, say $500 or $750 or $1,000, and have government provide that amount each month to every adult citizen. The same amount for everyone: homeless veterans, recent graduates, working parents, retired grandparents, and the rest of us. Universal and unconditional, added to and independent of what one earns. Direct payments or factored into our taxes. A basic income, guaranteed. Citizen Dividends.[†2]

- Cut or eliminate programs that basic income makes superfluous: welfare, corporate welfare, and everything else that goes to a special interest or segment of the population. Many programs operate

---

* A history of related ideas, proposals, advocates, and efforts – from the Bible, Thomas Jefferson, and Thomas Paine, to the Family Assistance Plan and Permanent Fund Dividend and through 2019 – is in Appendix 1. Current supporters include Nobel laureate economists, prominent authors, and Silicon Valley billionaires. International activities are in Appendix 3.

† Other names include Universal or Unconditional Basic Income, UBI, and Basic Income Grant or Guarantee, BIG. Also Citizen's Income, Freedom Dividend, and Social Security for All. And guaranteed income and negative income tax, the familiar terms from the 1960s.

through the tax code, as credits, deductions, or exemptions, so taxes will instantly be fairer and simpler.

- Adjust the amount occasionally to relieve or prevent recessions, inflation, or other troubles, and to produce smart economic growth.

- Let state and local governments supplement this income using local revenues.

Citizen Dividends will ensure that everyone has the means to participate in markets and in politics. All of us will be on the playing field. The field will be more level, the games more fair, and the outcomes more satisfying.

Basic income is the key to unlocking our political system and repairing our broken government. It opens the doors to the back rooms where special interests and political operatives hide in the shadows. When the doors are open, we can turn on the lights to see what's really going on, and why. It's also the key to restarting the engines of citizenship and moving forward on issues that matter to us. Every American will have meaningful incentives to work together, *We the People* renewed.

★　★　★　★　★

Some will say it's socialism. This will be a big government program that serves all of us equally; that's the definition of socialism, some say. For most folks, though, socialism is only harmful when it's oppressive or autocratic.

This plan shrinks government. Compared with today, our government will be smaller, less oppressive, and more democratic.

Everyone will be free to work where we want and to earn as much as we can. Free to participate in markets as we choose, to spend, save, and invest as we like.

Basic income is a way to repair capitalism, to resolve or remedy the flaws, failures, and excesses. This is humane capitalism, inclusive capitalism, democratic capitalism — *free enterprise for everyone.*

Some will insist it's unaffordable, a budget buster. Our national government is deeply in debt, with huge budget deficits, and the total cost of this plan could be two or three trillion dollars a year.

Yet numerous programs will be superfluous and, unlike today, every American will have a personal stake in working together for real reforms. We'll cut welfare, end corporate welfare, close tax loopholes, and slash bureaucracies.

We can positively afford a basic income. With prudent cuts and reforms, there could be a surplus.

Are we serious about balanced budgets and fiscal responsibility? Many of us say "Yes!" We can achieve it with this plan.*

Some will disapprove of "something for nothing" — people getting money without working and earning it. Welfare programs have work requirements, or require recipients to seek jobs or do job-training, and that seems sensible. Citizen Dividends will go to full-time workers and the wealthy as well, so work requirements are unworkable.

Before work, and before seeking or training for work, people need food, clothes, and shelter. These are necessities, work prerequisites, and we need money to pay for them. Basic income is boots and bootstraps. Everyone will be able to lift themselves up — to live with dignity, contribute to society, and climb the ladder of opportunity.

Work prerequisites, not "something for nothing." This is something for being a citizen. Also something that advances our society as a whole.

Do people want a work exchange? We can create one. National service is an idea that many politicians endorse, liberal Democrats, moderates, and conservative Republicans. A majority of Americans might welcome a national service program, possibly universal citizen service.

---

* Financial matters are in Appendix 2 — with budget numbers for suggested cuts, reforms, and taxes. The numbers show the potential for a large surplus, which we can use to pay down the national debt.

Some will oppose giving money to drug addicts, alcoholics, "losers," "takers," "failures," "parasites." There are such people today, have been throughout history, and will be tomorrow, too, regardless of whether we enact basic income.

Like today, some addicts, etc., will reform on their own or with help from family, friends, faith, or therapy. Unlike today, everyone will have assured means and motives for personal responsibility. Folks who want to reform will be more likely to succeed.

Most important: Whatever anyone does or doesn't do, *the rest of us will be better off.*

Personal responsibility is central to this plan, and we can promote it by linking basic income to the justice system. When anyone breaks the law and gets caught – whether a drug addict, a car thief, a con artist, or a corrupt CEO – courts can redirect the money to pay fines, penalties, jail fees, child support, and victim restitution. Society will have an added instrument to punish and deter wrongdoers. Individuals will have added incentives to be responsible and do what's right.

Some will seek to exclude millionaires and billionaires. It might seem foolish to give money to the wealthy, but excluding them would require rules, regulations, and bureaucracy, with endless disputes about where and how to draw the lines. Including everyone makes sense and will save dollars. Plus, we'll reform the tax code, eliminating loopholes, deductions, and exemptions. Millionaires and billionaires will pay more taxes than today.

The main reason to include everyone: Citizen Dividends will continuously affirm that all of us are full citizens, with equal rights, equal dignity, equal liberty, and equal responsibilities.

Some will denounce it as a redistribution of wealth. Redistribution is socialism, some say, wrong and unfair.

But government redistributes money through most of its activities: when it collects taxes, spends on defense, invests in infrastructure, makes Social

Security payments, provides healthcare for disabled veterans, and so on. Our task as citizens is to insist that the taxing, spending, investing, etc., are prudent and appropriate. This plan empowers us to make government efficient, effective, and accountable.

Basic income is distribution, more fundamental than redistribution. And this distribution will be equal, honest, and open.

At the same time, and long overdue, we'll end the redistribution from regular working folks to wealthy special interests; that's rampant today, mostly hidden. And that's beyond wrong and unfair; it's absurd.

Some will question the impact on work ethics and incentives. Basic income is just that: basic. It's a floor. Everyone will still have myriad incentives to work and earn: to buy a home, save for retirement, do more for their kids, enjoy a romance or vacation, experience community with coworkers, and to pursue other dreams or goals.

Work is – and will continue to be – a source of pride, meaning, and dignity.

This plan rewards work. As we spend our basic income dollars, hard-working folks will gain and profit. Strong work ethics are rewarded.

When people are motivated by fear – or facts – of hunger, homelessness, or other hardships, that's not a work ethic. That's a *coercion* ethic. Basic income will reduce coercion, and reduce or remove the coercion ethic. Our work ethics will be healthier, less tainted by the indignity of coercion.

Everyone will be free to seek or create work that's meaningful and satisfying. Meaningful work naturally motivates us to work harder and longer. Meaningful work is a true incentive for strong work ethics.

Some will call it an "entitlement," like Social Security, Medicare, and Medicaid. Those programs were established in 1935 and 1965, and they're very different from basic income.

This is about our unalienable rights – entitlements endowed by our creator – to life, liberty, and the pursuit of happiness. Life requires food, clothes, and shelter (at the very least), and therefore money to pay for these necessities. Without an income, life is precarious, liberty imperiled, and happiness elusive. Citizen Dividends will secure every American's unalienable rights.

We are created equal, the Founders declared, and this plan enhances equality. They instituted our government to secure our basic rights, and this plan has government do that directly, efficiently. This is a plan to fulfill their ideals.*

Some will worry about people being dependent on government. Welfare causes dependency, supposedly, and some say dependency is demeaning or degrading. Dependency is definitely a concern with corporate welfare; recipients can be parasites, living mainly on or for government handouts.

These worries are reasons to welcome Citizen Dividends.

Welfare is necessary, today, and so is corporate welfare. There are no alternatives. Without existing programs, many millions of us could not get by, and countless businesses would fail. There would be far more hunger, homelessness, unemployment, unrest, and crime.

Basic income is the alternative. Welfare and corporate welfare will become superfluous — at least partly, perhaps completely.

Everyone – each of us, all of us – depends on government. We rely on it every day for our personal safety and national security. We are mutually interdependent.

Our mutual interdependence is a source of meaning and happiness, and this is self-evident in families. We experience healthy interdependence

---

* Thomas Jefferson, before writing the Declaration of Independence, proposed giving land to propertyless individuals to secure their subsistence and their rights. John Adams asserted that "Every member of society" should be "possessed of small estates" as the basis for "equal liberty." James Madison endorsed laws to "Raise extreme indigence toward a state of comfort." (Jefferson, Adams, and Madison are in Appendix 1.)

Endnote 1 reviews the self-evident truths in the Declaration. Jefferson wrote with editing assistance from Adams, Benjamin Franklin, Robert R. Livingston, and Roger Sherman, the drafting committee appointed by the Continental Congress. They worked on it for two-and-a-half weeks, and presumably had candid debates about the rights of people and the role of government.

in sports, especially among teammates, and while cheering for our country in the Olympics and the World Cup. Also when we come together during disasters and tragedies. Interdependence is the soul of patriotism. When we salute the flag and celebrate the Fourth of July, we're proclaiming our independence *and* our interdependence.

Citizen Dividends will reinvigorate our sense of patriotism. Our interdependence will become more meaningful, more voluntary, and more enduring.

Some will look at the size and scope, and see the makings of massive waste, fraud, and abuse. With basic income, size is a virtue; bigger really is better. An added virtue is simplicity, the fact that it's universal and unconditional.

Small programs are seldom examined. Complicated programs provide multiple opportunities to rig and exploit the system. Most programs are complicated by design, devised by special interests that lobby legislators and capture regulators. These concerns are compounded by the proliferation of national, state, and local programs, with their confusing and often conflicting goals, rules, regulations, procedures, and jurisdictions. Waste is widespread, fraud frequent, and abuse unavoidable.

Size invites scrutiny, and simplicity expedites it. Concerned citizens will be watching closely, continuously, checking to be sure everything is efficient and trustworthy.

If we really want to eliminate waste, fraud, and abuse, basic income is imperative.

Some will focus on what it might mean for recessions, inflation, unemployment, and economic growth. As we get close to enacting any version of basic income, we'll have budgets, forecasts, and other analyses for various situations. Economic principles affirm this plan. Many prominent economists have endorsed similar plans.*

---

* More than 1,200 economists signed a letter in 1968 declaring that "As economists we offer the professional opinion that income guarantees and supplements are feasible and compatible with our economic system. As citizens we feel strongly that the time for action is now."

To end recessions, standard models and practices call for putting more dollars into circulation, increasing the money supply. Our national government can cut taxes or increase spending: fiscal policy. The Federal Reserve can cut interest rates, print more money, adjust bank reserve requirements, or buy government securities: monetary policy. With both approaches, the effects are delayed, uneven, and uncertain. Today, though, these are the only available tools. Current policy is a two-legged stool; often unsteady, sometimes falling.

Basic income gives us a third option, a third leg so the stool is stable. We'll end or prevent recessions by increasing the amount. People will spend the money, demanding goods and services — and our demands will drive a rapid, reliable recovery.

Inflation won't be an obstacle. We'll be cutting other programs, so total spending is under control. After we enact this plan, if there's any inflation – any time, from any cause – individuals and families, *all* of us, will have a cushion that protects us from rising prices.

Unemployed citizens will have money for necessities, the means to live with dignity and participate in society. Politicians and economists won't be so worried about the unemployment rate.

Economic growth will be faster and smarter.

Some will object without saying why; no reasons, no explanations. And no alternatives — only the status quo.

When anyone objects to this plan without presenting alternatives – or calls it socialism, or says we can't afford it, or expresses any other knee-jerk notion – a prudent response is to question their motives. Is the objection self-serving? Motives matter. Objections are opportunities for special interests; delays bring in dollars.

Many of us are zealous about a specific cause, issue, or policy, and might object that this plan doesn't address that concern directly, explicitly. But our political system has been failing for decades, our government is broken in multiple ways. This plan is a first step.

★ ★ ★ ★ ★

This plan, for now, is just an outline. That's on purpose. We start with dreams, values, and goals, while seeking consensus on core concepts.

With consensus on the core, we'll be prepared to discuss details. Compromise will be fairly straightforward. The common sense of this plan invites compromise by reminding us that politics is personal and compromise is in everyone's self-interest.

The sooner we act, the greater the gains. Any basic income amount – and any details regarding program cuts, tax reforms, and so on – will free us from the dysfunctional status quo. Let's enact some version promptly and see how it works. Then we'll revise and refine it.

How Much Should Citizen Dividends Be?

Our views will vary with our values, lifestyles, and circumstances; whether we're poor or rich, young or old, single or married, working or unemployed, urban or suburban or rural, parents or not, in debt or not, generous or not. The initial amount might seem too small or too large; we'll debate it in the next election, then maybe adjust it. State and local governments can supplement it.

Suppose it's $500 a month. This is a floor; solid, stable, and sturdy. No holes, no loopholes, no cracks to fall through. Each of us will get this amount every month *in addition to what we earn*; money we can count on no matter what happens with our jobs, our health, our families, or overall economic conditions. Our lives will be less stressful, so we'll be healthier; less precarious, so we'll be freer and happier.

Citizen Dividends of $1,000 a month per person would be $24,000 a year for a couple. That's nearly the official national poverty line for a family of four. This amount, therefore, will dramatically reduce extreme poverty, as defined by our government, and possibly end hunger and homelessness. No other program or policy can accomplish this, not even close.

Which Programs Should We Cut? How Deeply? How Quickly?

With welfare – food stamps, Temporary Assistance for Needy Families (TANF), housing assistance, and so on – deciding may be fairly simple. Apply a classic principle, *do no harm,* to ensure that no one is worse off. We should be extra careful with children, because child poverty is appallingly high, and with seniors and people with disabilities and special needs. A larger amount will facilitate deeper, faster cuts.

With corporate welfare – tax credits, subsidies, loan guarantees, and so on – we'll face real obstacles. That money mostly goes to big companies, and they routinely claim that any cuts will cause a loss of jobs, or lead to higher prices, or hurt the economy, or impair economic growth, or hinder the creation of new jobs. Corporations tout themselves as "job creators," and politicians gain votes by promising jobs. The main obstacle, therefore, is our dependence on jobs.

That will change. When every adult has a secure income, unemployed folks will be able to get by, so corporations will lose most of their leverage. Thus, instead of trying to cut corporate welfare bit by bit, this plan removes the primary pretext for all of it.

Cutting corporate welfare, if we're honest and thorough, will reduce and potentially eliminate waste in military spending. That's impossible today. Members of Congress use military spending as a cash cow for their districts; a sacred cow that must be constantly fed, while contractors suckle and grow fat. When anyone calls for cuts, contractors hijack the debates, wielding jobs as weapons, holding us and our security hostage. After we enact this plan, debates about defense and security will truly be about *defense and security*, untainted by efforts to create jobs. America will stay safe and strong. And we'll save money.

Three programs we have to cut or reform – have to because they're unsustainable, but currently cannot because of politics – are Social Security, Medicare, and Medicaid. Reform will be far easier than today. Seniors will be more secure, with Citizen Dividends added to Social Security. And with this new financial bond between seniors and young people, everyone will have renewed reasons to compromise. Medicare and Medicaid costs will fall, perhaps substantially, because people will have less stress and fewer stress-related illnesses.

We'll also cut national, state, and local government spending on buildings, equipment, bureaucracy, and everything else. Everyone, including government workers, will have a direct stake in making and keeping our government lean, efficient, effective, and responsive. Our government can be more like a successful private business.

★　★　★　★　★

This plan is a bridge across the divide between liberal Democrats and conservative Republicans. Our bridge, wide and sturdy; everyone will be able to embark from wherever we are. Once we're on the bridge, we'll see that the divide was exaggerated, an artifact of dysfunctional politics. Good people live on both sides. There's common sense on both sides — common concerns and interests as well.

More than a bridge, actually; this plan leads to a better place. Regardless of which side anyone is on or from, we'll all be moving forward to a place that's better for everyone.

Politicians promise to unite us, and this plan does: liberal Democrats with conservative Republicans, the Tea Party with Occupy activists; also moderates, independents, conservatives who are not Republicans, Democrats who are not liberals, Greens and Libertarians and members of other "third" parties, and people who were apolitical or anti-political. We'll dissolve the old divisions, definitions, and identities, and transcend the politics of us vs. them. With this plan there's only *us* — each of us and all of us. Everyone will have incentives to act together as *We the People*.

When we discuss the details, we should shed and avoid the usual labels. Ideally, we won't ask, won't tell, and won't care about partisan identities or political ideologies.

We'll have to compromise, and that'll be easier when we speak as, for, and about ourselves, simply stating personal preferences. What do I want? A large basic income, or fairly small? Deep cuts to welfare, or extra cautious? Wholesale reform of other programs, or gradual and limited?

Real leaders will expedite compromise while crafting effective ways to educate folks. Elected officials who endorse this plan will be displaying true courage, risking loss of support from the special interests that helped them get elected.

"I promise to put people first," many politicians proclaim. "My goal is to empower people." This plan does both, putting us first and empowering us directly, concretely, with cash. Politicians who campaign for basic income will show that they sincerely care about regular folks. And that they trust us, real people, unique individuals — not "people" as a rhetorical device or a euphemism for special interests.

On nearly every issue – unemployment, education, global warming, healthcare, and so on – Republicans say the market has to provide solutions, while Democrats seek or propose government action. Both sides ignore obvious facts: markets and government are created by, and consist of, individuals. *Individuals are first.*

With this plan, individuals gain economic security and *We the People* regain our sovereignty. Security and sovereignty — and synergy, markets and government working harmoniously to enrich all of us.

This plan can:

- End hunger, homelessness, and extreme poverty;

- Make the tax system more fair, simple, and sensible;

- Improve health, bringing better healthcare at lower cost;

- Decrease crime and expedite cost-effective criminal justice;

- Boost market-driven progress on pollution and global warming;

- Enrich cities and towns, making them more distinct and attractive;

- Advance prudent immigration policies, good for citizens and businesses;

- Produce a surge in small businesses forming and growing and creating jobs;

- Promote education reforms that work for students, parents, and communities;

- Lead to enduring national security.

These gains are readily attainable. Basic income, in effect, pays us to participate as citizens. We'll be rewarded for cooperating and compromising. Progress starts with us, our personal dreams and goals.

★　★　★　★　★

What do you think? Would you like a basic income added to what you earn?

Should it be $1,000 a month, or more? Only $500 a month, or less? Maybe $750?

To get the money – every month, guaranteed, for the rest of your life – here are three things to do:

1. Agree to the same amount for *every* adult citizen — unless a court redirects funds for some purpose, such as to pay a fine or child support.

2. Tell friends, neighbors, coworkers, and other people about this plan. Ask them to join you in attracting and educating more supporters. Spread the word.

3. Demand that politicians make this a top priority and that they compromise on the basic income amount, program cuts, tax reforms, and other details

Imagine what you could do with the added income. If it's $1,000 a month, that's $12,000 a year. For you and a spouse, $24,000. Consider the possibilities, your dreams, goals, values, and quality of life.

Are you unhappy at your job? Many of us are, or say we are. Are you unemployed, underemployed, or unable to advance your life goals? You'll have a secure income while you pursue happiness. If you don't know what you want to do, or you need specific skills or a degree, you'll be able to get by while you decide and take the next steps. Is there work you'd enjoy, such as teaching, but the pay is too low? You might view basic income as a salary supplement. Is your job okay, but only okay? You'll have leverage, a dependable outside income, when you talk with your employer. Want to start your own business? You'll have a launch pad.

You might choose to be a full-time parent. Choose to work part-time or a temporary job while you pursue creative interests as an artist, writer, musician, filmmaker, or inventor. Travel. Enjoy hobbies. Volunteer in your church or with a community group.

Do you have a spouse or parent with Alzheimer's, MS, cancer, or other illness? A child who's autistic or has cerebral palsy? A partner who was wounded in Iraq or Afghanistan? You might be living with a disease or disability. Imagine how this added income, maybe $2,000 a month for you and your spouse or other loved one, will enhance your quality of life.

If you worry about people wasting or misusing the money, are you picturing anyone in particular? An alcoholic cousin, a neighbor who's hooked on opioids, a nephew who's always online playing games, a stranger on the street asking for a handout? Yes, some will use the money in ways you would not approve. Yet they'll have reasons to hope their lives will improve, and resources they can use to change if they choose. Yes, too, some will require extra help. You might offer to assist someone you care about.

Have you ever dreamed about doing something significant? Are you willing to actively serve your community and country? You can join or start a group that's working to enact Citizen Dividends, maybe run for public office. You can help make history.

Our Future

As you pursue your dreams and goals, other people will be pursuing theirs. From our personal actions, a unified outcome — a freer, stronger, healthier, and more democratic America. And a more peaceful world.

CHAPTER 3

To Make Taxes Fair and Simple

With basic income, we can have a tax system that's fair and simple. Also inclusive, progressive, and positive; taxes that affirm our values and benefit our whole society.

Taxes today are an abomination. That's a consensus opinion, one of the few points of political consensus, and it's more than an opinion. According to the Taxpayer Advocate Service, an independent organization within the Internal Revenue Service, taxes are "a significant, even unconscionable, burden." Individuals and businesses spend 6.1 billion hours every year filing tax returns, and that's equivalent to more than three million people working full-time, year-round.[3]

Every taxpayer loses a few of those 6.1 billion hours – some lose dozens of hours – and many of us have to spend money on tax preparation software or an accountant. That's our time and our money, and government is taking them from us. What are we getting in return? What does the tax code produce? Anger and resentment, fraud or temptation to commit fraud, slower economic growth, struggling or failing businesses, and a bloated, dysfunctional government.

The tax code is terrible for obvious reasons; it was designed by and for special interests. Every complication is a confection, a load of sugar that keeps certain groups fat and happy, though sometimes hyperactive. Any hint of reform, and special interests transform into black-belt defenders of the status quo.

Politicians promise to simplify the tax code; they sound sincere, and maybe they are. But their top priority is getting elected or reelected. Most "reforms" are only rhetoric or campaign fodder, red flags to attract attention, red meat to reward their donors. "Tax reform" is a racket.

The racket rests on two tenets: taxes are bad, tax cuts always good. Both are flawed. Taxes pay for government services we depend on, and will fund our Citizen Dividends. Tax cuts mainly go to special interests; good for them, obviously, and good for the politicians who tout themselves as tax-cutters and reformers. Too often, however, government is left without funds for essential services — and that's bad for everyone.

Let's end the politicians' racket. We can take away their toys and stop the games they play with our money.

★   ★   ★   ★   ★

How should we fund our government? What taxes make the most sense? Let's consider some possibilities:

A Flat Income Tax

It's simple. Abolish loopholes, deductions, exemptions, and such, and have everyone pay the same rate. State your income, multiply by the set rate, and that's what you owe. "Tax forms that fit on a postcard." Proponents also want to broaden the tax base, so more folks have a direct stake in our government, "shared sacrifice" and "skin in the game."

But it's not fair. People with low and moderate incomes spend every dollar just to get by, so job losses, accidents, illnesses, and other setbacks can be devastating. The rich have resources to recover from setbacks, and money to invest in their efforts to get richer. A flat tax is a recipe for growing inequality.

The income tax was first enacted in 1913, and it's always been progressive, higher rates on higher incomes. In the 1950s, there were 24 tax brackets and a top marginal rate of 91 percent. Yet that was a time of rising prosperity overall. Poor folks could work hard, make it into the middle class, and possibly get rich. Everyone had a shot at winning the game.

Fair and simple are incompatible, it seems, yet we want both. This dilemma affects every tax policy, every reform proposal, every debate about who pays for our government and who gets help from it — and therefore every issue involving wealth, poverty, and income inequality. These issues have ignited major protests throughout U.S. history, including the Tea Party and Occupy Wall Street.

This dilemma dissolves with a tax-free basic income. Here are four tables with a perfectly flat tax, rates of 15 or 30 percent, and tax-free Citizen Dividends of $6,000 or $12,000 a year:

Pre-tax Income	15% Tax	Citizen Dividends	Net Tax	Net Income	Net Tax Rate
0	—	6,000	-6,000	6,000	—
10,000	1,500	6,000	-4,500	14,500	—
20,000	3,000	6,000	-3,000	23,000	—
40,000	6,000	6,000	0	40,000	0
80,000	12,000	6,000	6,000	74,000	8%
160,000	24,000	6,000	18,000	142,000	11%
320,000	48,000	6,000	42,000	278,000	13%

Pre-tax Income	15% Tax	Citizen Dividends	Net Tax	Net Income	Net Tax Rate
0	—	12,000	-12,000	12,000	—
10,000	1,500	12,000	-10,500	20,500	—
20,000	3,000	12,000	-9,000	29,000	—
40,000	6,000	12,000	-6,000	46,000	—
80,000	12,000	12,000	0	80,000	0
160,000	24,000	12,000	12,000	148,000	8%
320,000	48,000	12,000	36,000	284,000	11%

Pre-tax Income	30% Tax	Citizen Dividends	Net Tax	Net Income	Net Tax Rate
0	—	6,000	-6,000	6,000	—
10,000	3,000	6,000	-3,000	13,000	—
20,000	6,000	6,000	0	20,000	0
40,000	12,000	6,000	6,000	34,000	15%
80,000	24,000	6,000	18,000	62,000	23%
160,000	48,000	6,000	42,000	118,000	26%
320,000	96,000	6,000	90,000	230,000	28%

Pre-tax Income	30% Tax	Citizen Dividends	Net Tax	Net Income	Net Tax Rate
0	—	12,000	-12,000	12,000	—
10,000	3,000	12,000	-9,000	19,000	—
20,000	6,000	12,000	-6,000	26,000	—
40,000	12,000	12,000	0	40,000	0
80,000	24,000	12,000	12,000	68,000	15%
160,000	48,000	12,000	36,000	124,000	23%
320,000	96,000	12,000	84,000	236,000	26%

Calculations by Steven Shafarman

Obviously fair, extremely simple, fully inclusive, and clearly progressive. The same basic income for every citizen, the same tax rate for every taxpayer and every dollar we earn — even while high earners pay a higher percentage of their incomes. People with incomes below the break-even point – in these examples, $40,000, $80,000, $20,000, and $40,000 – get payments from our government, a *negative income tax.**

Easy to understand and easy to calculate. Shared sacrifice with equal treatment. Skin in the game plus money in our hands.

---

* *Negative income tax* is what Milton Friedman, who was awarded the 1976 Nobel Memorial Prize in Economic Sciences, called his proposed basic income. He endorsed it in his 1962 book, *Capitalism and Freedom,* which also called for "a flat-rate tax on income above an exemption." Combine and streamline his proposals, and the results are these tables.

Both variables affect a wide range of concerns, issues, problems, and solutions. Both will be topics for future elections. After elections, because this system is so obviously fair, simple, and inclusive, compromises will be straightforward.

With current efforts to reform the tax code, the burden is entirely on those who are calling for change, and the burden is heavy. This plan lifts the burden and moves it to the other side. If special interests want special treatment, they'll have to explain their priorities and attain popular support.

Are there tax breaks, credits, deductions, or exemptions we should retain?

- A lower rate on capital gains and dividends? In the tax code, that's "unearned income." The chief beneficiaries are wealthy investors and Wall Street brokers.

- Interest on mortgages? Homeowners with bigger loans get bigger deductions, renters get nothing. The deduction indirectly subsidizes the banking and housing industries, and it increases home prices overall.

- Deductions for children? We can help parents and their kids in other ways; perhaps provide all children with healthcare, daycare, or preschool. Another option is to create a parallel program, a universal child benefit, say $200 or $300 a month for each child.[4]

- Charitable contributions? Charity is a virtue, generosity is admired, giving is meaningful and satisfying. We'll continue to support groups and causes we believe in, just because we care.

Some tax breaks, etc., help the poor; others aim to aid the middle class. Most of that money, by far, goes to the wealthy. The existing tax code fuels class warfare. This plan will end class warfare for good.[5]

This plan cuts taxes – *real* cuts, not promises or rhetoric – for nearly everyone. The wealthy will pay more than today, because they'll lose their loopholes. Yet those loopholes incite envy, resentment, or anger, and such feelings will fade. Wealthy citizens might view higher taxes as a smart investment. In return, they'll get a more just, peaceful, prosperous country.

Consumption Taxes

Many economists say we should tax sales, spending, or expenditures – not income – to encourage people to save and invest. Saving and investing are good for individuals, families, and our society as a whole.

One method is to tax consumption directly. Total income, minus savings and investments, equals spending. Then tax that sum, filing tax forms like today. Rates can be flat or progressive.

A value-added tax is a sales tax assessed at each stage in the production of goods and services. A VAT is very efficient, easy to collect and hard to avoid. Most economists recommend it, and Canada, England, Germany, Mexico, Japan, and other market democracies use it as their primary tax on corporations. America is the only major country that doesn't have a VAT, and that's partly because certain politicians claim it leads to bigger government. This plan shrinks government and keeps it small, so a VAT would be smart politics and smart economics.*

A third possibility is a national sales tax. Advocates call it the "Fair Tax," and they estimate a 28 percent rate, paid at the cash register when we buy anything. The Fair Tax would replace income taxes, payroll taxes, estate taxes, gift taxes, capital gains taxes, and corporate taxes. Paychecks would include 100 percent of pay, minus only state income taxes. To protect and provide for the poor, proponents add a "prebate" — a cash payment each month to offset sales taxes on necessities. That prebate is like a basic income, though more complicated because it would vary with household size (single adult, couple with two children, and so on).

---

* "The average VAT in Europe is 20 percent," entrepreneur and Democratic presidential candidate Andrew Yang notes in his 2018 book, *The War on Normal People*. "If we adopted a VAT at half the average European level, we could pay for a universal basic income for all American adults."

Sales taxes can include stocks, bonds, derivatives, and such. Financial transaction taxes would be quite small, maybe 0.1 percent, so there would be minimal impact on long-term investments. Yet the tax would restrain high-frequency trading and could prevent market meltdowns. Financial markets will be more stable, and that's good for entrepreneurs, investors in start-ups, and everyone who's saving long-term. Many jurisdictions tax financial transactions, including Hong Kong, Singapore, and the London Stock Exchange. So did the United States from 1914 to 1966, a "transfer tax."[*]

Carbon Taxes and Land Value Taxes

Carbon taxes – taxes on oil, coal, and natural gas, calculated on the carbon emitted when fuels are burned – have been proposed in several states and nationally, primarily in the context of concerns about climate change. That context, though, conceals the concept. The core concept is compelling.

Oil, coal, and natural gas come from nature. So do metals, minerals, air, water, timber, seafood, and so on. These are – or ought to be, at least partly – our common wealth and shared heritage. When anyone claims, collects, consumes, or degrades what nature provides, some fair market value can be assessed and taxed. Taking from nature, after all, is taking from society and from future generations. Takers should pay us.[†]

---

[*] Financial transaction taxes are sometimes called "Tobin taxes," for economist James Tobin, a Nobel laureate. He also supported guaranteed income.

An expanded version, which entrepreneur Scott Smith calls a "Payments Tax," would include all transactions. He presents it in *The New Operating System for the American Economy* (2017), where he calls for a basic income of $24,000 a year. (See Appendix 2.)

[†] This concept inspired an early call for universal income support. Thomas Paine, in 1797, described land as the "common heritage of mankind." He wanted landowners to pay a "ground rent" into a "national fund." Every citizen would then receive a cash payment at age twenty-one and yearly payments starting at age fifty as "a right, and not a charity."

Similar insights sparked the creation of Alaska's Permanent Fund, which collects a portion of oil royalties, and the Permanent Fund Dividend, which distributes money to every resident. (Appendix 1 has more about Alaska's PFD and Paine's *Agrarian Justice*.)

Land value taxes are property taxes on the land only, not buildings or other improvements. This is simpler than a property tax on buildings, because land is visible and readily measurable, while buildings depreciate and assessments fluctuate. Tax rates, ideally, are based on the full rental value of the land, and can be adjusted to foster compact urban neighborhoods and to preserve farms and open spaces. Because improvements are not taxed, landowners have greater incentives to invest in building or rebuilding, and those investments will create jobs and stimulate local economic activity.

Taxing the land value does not change the amount of land; other taxes suppress whatever is taxed, income, labor, production, consumption, or wealth. That's why Milton Friedman called this "the least bad tax." Joseph Stiglitz – a Nobel laureate in economics, like Friedman – endorses land value taxes to reduce inequality. Wealthy people and corporations own most of the land, vastly more than regular citizens, so they'd pay the largest share of taxes. The wealth gap is much wider than the income gap, Stiglitz notes, and this tax can shrink both.

Carbon taxes and land value taxes are like users' fees for consuming or exploiting nature. They're also like sales taxes, though assessed upstream, at the source or site of taking from nature, as distinct from any sales tax at the gas pump, utility bill, or cash register. Upstream is far more efficient.

These are taxes on takings, and will expedite market-based efforts to protect our environment. Raw materials are more expensive, an incentive to innovate and conserve. Reused materials are not taxed, so re-use, recycling, and redesign are rewarded. Thus, this is a way to promote sustainability and private enterprise at the same time.

Payroll Taxes, Estate Taxes, Corporate Income Taxes

These are substantial and we have to reevaluate each of them — *after* we implement this plan, so special interests don't dominate debates or dictate decisions.

With payroll taxes for Social Security, Medicare, and Medicaid, reasons to wait are obvious. Multiple special interests have been preparing for years and are spoiling for a fight. When we have Citizen Dividends, seniors will be more secure. And most people will have less stress and better health, therefore lower costs for Medicare and Medicaid. Reform and compromise will be much easier than today.

Estate taxes are only on multimillion dollar estates, about 1,700 estates each year, after the owner's death; some call it the "death tax." Under a 2001 law, the rate gradually fell to zero in 2010, for one year only, then jumped back to 35 percent on estates larger than $5 million. The Trump-Republican tax cut in 2017 lifted the exclusion to above $11 million, and the superrich are again seeking total repeal. Class warfare? The superrich versus the rest of us? Ceasefire, please, until after we reform other taxes and policies.

Corporate taxes are complicated, and the 2017 tax cut created huge new loopholes. Big corporations have big budgets for lawyers, accountants, and lobbyists who are experts at minimizing their taxes. They also have big budgets for public relations, to persuade us that we should cut their taxes. Conflicts about corporate taxes are major barriers when negotiating foreign trade and tariffs. Trade agreements and corporate tax reforms can wait. Basic income first.

Initial Suggestions

A smart tax system has to respect regular citizens and our everyday lives. Tax concerns should never dictate our choices about marriage, kids, jobs, careers, where to live, or when to retire. Our choices should be truly ours and truly free, and this should be true for everyone equally, the poor, middle class, rich, and superrich.

- Tax income: Let's start with a simple flat tax / negative income tax. We'll probably want to adjust the tax rate or basic income after a year or two, and that'll be a time to reconsider – and perhaps restore – prudent tax credits, deductions, and such.

- Tax spending: Consumption taxes make sense, and we should phase them in, perhaps while cutting income taxes or boosting the basic income.

- Tax takings: We should increase taxes on oil, coal, timber, metals, minerals, and other natural materials, for revenue and to discourage consumption. Let's shift property taxes off buildings and onto land values. Because land is local and natural materials have local origins, these taxes ought to be the main source of funds for local governments.

- Reexamine payroll taxes, estate taxes, corporate taxes, and all other current or proposed taxes — after we enact this plan.

This tax system has distinct elements, predictable dynamics, and ready options for revisions. When we have reasons for reforms, the debates will be more honest and straightforward than today.

Taxes can be fair and simple, also inclusive, efficient, and non-intrusive. Taxes can fund current activities while advancing our long-term interests. We just have to start with a tax-free basic income.

★   ★   ★   ★   ★

Do you think a flat tax makes sense? Would you support a VAT? Fossil fuel taxes? Land value taxes? Financial transaction taxes?

Suppose the basic income is $1,000 a month, tax-free, and income taxes are perfectly flat. If you earn less than $80,000 a year and the tax rate is 15 percent, you'll get money from our government; a negative income tax. If the rate is 30 percent, you'll be getting money if you earn less than $40,000 a year. That money will be in your paycheck, through lower withholding, or deposited directly into your bank account or to a debit card.

Your paycheck will be larger than today and your taxes lower (unless you have a very large income, and currently gain from loopholes and deductions).

Filing your taxes might be unnecessary — government can generate the form, and if it's accurate, you'll sign it.

What tax rate would you agree to? Maybe 30 percent? How about 40 percent, if that's what it takes to balance the federal budget and reduce the debt? Or should it be lower, say 20 or 25 percent, while using other taxes to provide additional funds?

Are there tax credits or deductions you want to preserve? For children, say, or contributing to charities? Talk with friends, neighbors, and other people; tell them what you think and why. If a majority agrees, we'll demand action through our elected officials to keep or restore those deductions.

Now suppose we also have a VAT. And financial transaction taxes. And higher taxes on fossil fuels. And land value taxes.

You can avoid the VAT by spending wisely. Avoid financial transaction taxes by investing long-term. Avoid fossil fuel taxes by working from home, moving closer to your work, making your home more energy efficient, commuting by bicycle or public transit. You might welcome fuel taxes as a way to foster sustainability without new laws, rules, or regulations, simply through the self-interested actions of individuals and businesses.

Do you own your home? If you remodel – adding a room for an aging parent, say, or an apartment over the garage to rent out – your taxes won't go up because the property tax is on the land only. If you move, you'll be less constrained by concerns about property taxes, and more free to choose the home you want, the location, size, style, and whether to buy or rent.

Are you an employer? Self-employed? Working multiple jobs, gigs, or contracts? Tax-filing and record-keeping will be easier than today, with fewer worries and lower costs for accounting and compliance. You'll be able to invest more time and money in building your business.

Want to start a business? You'll have plenty of options. We'll see rising demand for various goods and services, with certain rewards for innovating to become more efficient. That means demand for planners, designers, consultants, inventors, architects, engineers, plumbers, carpenters, electricians, and general contractors. These companies and industries will also be opportunities if you are, or want to be, an investor.

Are you concerned about local taxes, how to pay for schools, parks, transit, public safety, and so on? You and your neighbors will have greater opportunities to influence local government. And local officials are likely to be more responsive to residents' concerns.

Real tax reforms are possible, local, state, and national — when *We the People* enforce our demands.

CHAPTER 4

To Reform and Shrink Government

Start with basic income and tax reform, and further cuts and reforms will be inevitable.

The key to success when seeking to cut programs – a key most would-be reformers forget, misplace, or never consider – is to first make programs superfluous. We do that with Citizen Dividends. Doors open, cuts and reforms welcome.

Welfare for Individuals and Families

Welfare is a safety net, supposedly. But the holes are large and irregular, the fabric tattered, and millions of citizens are tangled in the net or trapped beneath it. Welfare is a hodgepodge of national, state, and local programs with onerous requirements and big, costly bureaucracies.

Basic income is a floor. Solid, stable, and sturdy, with no holes and no cracks. There's room on the floor for every citizen — no barriers or obstacles, no waiting in line, no one left outside or locked in the basement. Because it's universal and unconditional, there's minimal bureaucracy and minimal administrative cost.

As we consider what to cut, we can be guided by the ethical imperative to *do no harm*. With a large basic income, we'll cut programs deeply and quickly, abolishing whole agencies. A smaller amount, and we'll have to preserve programs – at least partly – to protect kids, seniors, single parents, and people with disabilities and special needs.

If it's $1,000 a month, a couple will get $24,000 a year. That's far more than current programs provide for typical poor families, and it's close to the national poverty line for a family of four, two parents with two kids. For single parents, a portion of the absent parent's basic income might be redirected, voluntarily or by court order: guaranteed child support.

Whether deeply and quickly or slowly and extra carefully, we'll cut, reform, or eliminate:

- TANF, the program people call "welfare." Temporary Assistance for Needy Families is federal, though administered by the states. Because it's temporary and only helps "needy" families – and because states set rules, regulations, and restrictions, and it's not adjusted for inflation – there are constant problems and stresses for recipients, social workers, and government officials.

- Food stamps, the common name for the Supplemental Nutrition Assistance Program. SNAP has eligibility requirements, restrictions on purchases, and other complications. More than 40 million Americans live with the stigma and hassles.

- Housing assistance. Local, state, and national agencies own buildings, pay or subsidize people's rent, and impose restrictions on bankers, realtors, and developers. Current policies distort housing markets, with higher costs for everyone.

- Unemployment benefits. Job-training, money to pay bills, and related support, though the benefits cease after specified periods.

- Medicaid and associated assistance, national, state, and local.

Some welfare programs are part of the tax code, "tax expenditures," such as the Earned Income Tax Credit, cash assistance for low-wage workers, added to their tax refunds. At $63 billion a year, the EITC is larger than TANF or food stamps, though it does nothing for the unemployed. With Citizen Dividends and tax reform, the EITC will probably disappear. Most states and many cities have local versions, and those might also disappear.[6]

Another reason to enact this plan: Current programs are "poverty traps." Recipients can lose their benefits, permanently, if they take part-time or temporary jobs, or earn more than a specified amount, so many people are afraid or unable to reenter the labor force. Residency requirements are actual traps; people are stuck where they are and can't move to places where living costs are lower, job opportunities better, or family nearby. With basic income, everyone will be free to pursue all opportunities.

Corporate Welfare

Corporate welfare – tax credits, subsidies, loan guarantees, zoning variances, and such – is mainly from state and local governments; an estimated $90 billion a year. Taxpayer money mostly goes to big companies, including Walmart, Boeing, and Amazon. The stated purposes, always, are to create jobs and stimulate economic growth — and consequently to generate tax revenues, so government has funds for healthcare, education, and other public purposes, including welfare for the poor. That's the theory. Corporate welfare is supposed to help everyone, indirectly. The money is supposed to spill over, spread around, and trickle down.[7]

A direct route is basic income. No waiting for money to trickle down, no praying for CEOs to spread it around. Instead, regular folks get money and we'll spend it around. We'll demand goods and services, which companies will compete to supply. Jobs and economic growth will be demand-driven.

Another form of corporate welfare, or a close relative, involves contracting or outsourcing to private companies. Such practices can be smart, sensible, and cost-effective — when the process is open and truly competitive, and when government is vigilant in supervising procedures and outcomes. But flaws, frauds, and failures are far too frequent. Companies lobby officials and donate to political campaigns. Contracts often appear to be, and sometimes prove to be, "pay-to-play" or "crony capitalism."

Corporate welfare and crony capitalism are cancers. Nearly all national, state, and local agencies – including public safety, national security, and other essential activities – are afflicted.

These cancers require surgery. With this plan, regular folks will be the doctors, locating the cancerous tumors so our elected officials, the surgeons, can operate. We'll also be the nurses and therapists, expediting full recovery. After decades of decay and disease, America's body politic will again be strong and healthy.

Social Security

Social Security was enacted in 1935, the middle of the Great Depression. Over the next several decades, poverty among seniors declined significantly. But no longer. Today, millions of seniors are poor, anxious, insecure, and delaying retirement or unable to afford it. Individual retirement accounts are inadequate, private pensions underfunded. Many workers lost their pensions, or had them stolen, when employers went bankrupt. Fewer young workers are paying into Social Security. Americans are living longer.*

Proposed reforms would increase payroll taxes, or raise the retirement age, or change the way payments are calculated, or lift the cap and collect more from wealthy folks, or introduce private investment options. Each proposal has champions and opponents. Special interests on every side have been preparing for years, recruiting allies, sharpening their rhetoric, and launching guerrilla attacks in Congress and through the media. The battles will be fierce, costly, and prolonged. Countless seniors will be casualties.

---

* The political pressure to enact Social Security came from two mass movements for guaranteed income. More than two million people supported the Townsend Plan to give everyone age sixty and over a monthly payment of $200 (about $3,500 in today's dollars). Share Our Wealth claimed to have 7.5 million members, and they were demanding a guaranteed annual income for every family of $2,500 ($44,000 today).

Or we can enact this plan.

With Citizen Dividends added to Social Security, seniors will be more secure. And everyone will have real incentives to compromise.

Basic income is like Social Security for all — plus, it's more social and more secure. Instead of payroll taxes taken from our paychecks, money is added to what we earn. Instead of variable returns based on past earnings, payments are equal and unconditional. Instead of dividing us into taxpayers and recipients, we'll be united.

Medicare, Medicaid, and Obamacare

When basic economic security is guaranteed, we'll have less stress and lower rates of stress-related illnesses (back pain, migraine, strokes, heart attacks, depression, sexual disorders, etc.), therefore lower costs for healthcare.

Medicare is for seniors, and savings are sure to be substantial. Savings will increase over time, because citizens will generally be healthier when we become seniors.

Medicaid is for the poor. Even the poorest will be able to afford healthier food and regular fitness activities. We'll see significant declines in diabetes, heart disease, kidney disease, and other conditions that correlate with poverty.

The Affordable Care Act, Obamacare, was designed to increase healthcare access, quality, and affordability. Citizen Dividends will advance all three aims, while expediting prudent reforms. If the amount is adequate, subsidies will be superfluous. Mandates and penalties will probably be superfluous because recent debates have educated all of us, including healthy young folks, about why we should have health insurance. Instead of targeted taxes, funds can come from general revenues. A reformed Affordable Care Act might be fully bipartisan.*

---

* Charles Murray, a renowned libertarian, seeks a basic income of $10,000 a year — plus $3,000 for mandatory health insurance, which he says government can rightly require, like auto insurance. He wants to abolish Medicare, Medicaid, and Obamacare. Everyone would be free to choose from a range of insurance options, comprehensive, employer-provided, health savings accounts, and so on. Through personal choice,

Healthcare is a major concern for a majority of Americans. Citizen Dividends may be the best, or only, route to true consensus and lasting progress.

Waste and Excess in Military Spending

Our government spends an enormous amount on defense, the military, and homeland security. How much is corporate welfare? How much is crony capitalism? How much is political meddling?

Waste is sometimes obvious, but impossible to cut. When military contractors' profits are threatened, they deploy high-energy patriotic rhetoric. Our duty as citizens, they tell us, is to support the troops, salute the flag, and be proud that America is the leading military superpower. *We're #1!* While we're cheering and distracted, contractors lobby Congress, get their requests into the budgets, and get those budgets passed.

Military contractors and their enlisted allies – politicians, pundits, and public relations professionals – have other tactics, too; notably, fear. *Terrorists! Rogue states! Radical Islam! Weapons of mass destruction!* Our massive military is necessary, they insist, and may be inadequate unless we increase spending on drone aircraft, spy satellites, cyberweapons, cyberdefenses, and the next generation of ships, jets, nuclear weapons, and everything else. *Remember 9/11!*

When contractors and politicians are not sowing fear or deploying patriotism, they're talking about jobs. Contractors constantly boast about the jobs they create, or tout the number that would be lost. They play the jobs card, and we allow it to trump other concerns.

With basic income, we won't be so dependent on those jobs. And we'll be better prepared to evaluate our true defense and security needs.

---

he maintains, healthcare costs will decline. (The $3,000 figure is his estimate for catastrophic coverage.)

Medicare for All is gaining support, even among conservatives. Most Americans say healthcare is a right, and many agree that the most humane, efficient, cost-effective way to provide it is a national plan. When we have Citizen Dividends and the associated political reforms, Medicare for All may be broadly popular.

We'll be safer after we cut the waste and excess. Money is only one concern; there's also wasted time and attention. Our security depends on leaders who are focused, vigilant, and thinking strategically about real threats. When we cut excess programs, we'll remove burdens and distractions. Cutting waste and excess, therefore, is a way to support our troops and strengthen our military.

For real national security, we also have to be concerned about budget deficits, the national debt, trade deficits with China, weak global supply chains, decaying infrastructure, the fragile electric grid, dependence on fossil fuels, and dispersed chemical and nuclear plants. Terrorists and hostile nations have countless potential targets, to threaten or worse.

Threats provoke spending; spending causes deficits; and deficits divide us politically and heighten our vulnerability. The dangers increase year-by-year, a vicious cycle fueled by fear, fanaticism, and profit-seeking.

With Citizen Dividends, we'll escape the vicious cycle — and can embark on a virtuous upward spiral. We'll be more secure economically, more united politically, and therefore more ready to respond effectively to any and all threats. We'll also be prepared to focus on our true goals: peace, justice, and liberty. America can lead the world toward enduring peace.

Initial Suggestions

Instead of abstract or arbitrary aims, this plan starts with real people. Every American will have reasons to demand lean, efficient, effective government. We'll eliminate some programs entirely. Other reforms will, and should, be gradual.

- Welfare for individuals and families: Again, with *do no harm* as a guiding principle – and extra care for kids, seniors, single parents, and citizens with special needs – let's cut deeply at the national level, while ensuring that local programs have adequate funds and flexibility.

- Corporate welfare: Efficient government, by definition, eliminates excess jobs. Let's examine every program, checking to be sure they all serve common purposes, not special interests. To end crony capitalism, we should demand open, competitive bidding on government contracts, with strict oversight and penalties for violations, penalizing both the politicians and their corporate cronies.

- Social Security: Let's postpone debates until we have Citizen Dividends. Seniors will be more secure and all Americans more united, so reform will be reasonably straightforward.

- Medicare, Medicaid, and Obamacare: People will be healthier, healthcare costs lower, and everyone will have money for health insurance, copays, health savings accounts, and such. Reform? Repeal? Replace? We should wait for basic income to begin, then decide.

- Waste and excess in military spending: Our national security must always come first, far ahead of efforts to create jobs. Let's work to end military corporate welfare, while we focus on our true defense and security needs.

There's more, of course, much more that we can do to shrink government, at all levels. We'll regularly reexamine every government program, agency, and department, seeking greater efficiencies.

With Citizen Dividends, real tax reforms, and vigorous efforts to cut government, we'll have a peaceful democratic revolution that frees us from special interests and the status quo. It starts with us, our personal dreams and goals.

And we can start now.

★   ★   ★   ★   ★

When you think about cutting government, what are your priorities? Are there programs you want to eliminate promptly? Programs you'd protect, at least partly?

Many of us seek cuts as a matter of principle; we sincerely believe in small government. Many mainly seek lower taxes. What about you? Both reasons? No matter who we elect, however, and no matter how we present our demands, government seems to get bigger and more intrusive.

Basic income, any version or variation, will make many programs superfluous. And everyone will have incentives to work together, demanding and attaining real cuts.

Have you ever used food stamps, TANF, or unemployment benefits? If you've been there and done that, you know what it's like and how it feels. When we debate cuts and reforms, we might ask recipients to recommend ways to protect children and other vulnerable individuals.

How do you feel about corporate welfare and crony capitalism? Frustrated? Angry? You're in good company. Most of us want to eliminate that spending, at least cut it substantially, and with this plan we'll have the power to succeed.

Can you see how Citizen Dividends will help us reform Social Security, Medicare, Medicaid, and Obamacare? Americans of all ages, incomes, and health conditions will have less stress, maybe much less. You'll sleep better at night, probably eat better and healthier, too. You'll also have more opportunities for healthy physical activities. You and everyone else.

Are you a veteran? On active duty? A peace activist? Do you think this plan will keep America safe, perhaps make us more secure than today?

If there are specific programs you want to eliminate – or reform, protect, or expand – you might run for public office. Serving as an elected official is likely to be far more satisfying than today.

You can help make our government efficient, effective, responsive, and fully accountable — government we're pleased with and proud of, at local, state, and national levels.

You can be part of the solution.

CHAPTER 5

To Produce Smart Economic Growth

When every citizen has a basic income, we'll have sensible economic policies that work for *all* of us.

Unemployment

Fear of unemployment is serious, an insidious fact of politics, economics, and everyday life. Most of us are afraid of losing our jobs. The unemployed are afraid they'll never find jobs. The wealthy are afraid of high unemployment causing unrest, instability, and shrinking investment portfolios. Elected officials are afraid of losing the next election, losing their jobs, if unemployment goes up.

Our fears are often tinged or merged with other feelings: shame, scorn, and stigma among or toward the unemployed. Blame and anger, particularly when politicians denounce the unemployed as "losers," "takers," "failures," or "parasites." Also hypocrisy, perhaps, about our judgments.

Basic income will ease our fears and, because it's universal and unconditional, will minimize any shame, scorn, stigma, blame, and anger. We'll be less judgmental and less hypocritical.

Unemployed citizens will be regular folks.

Will people quit their jobs? What if unemployment goes up? These are frequent questions about basic income, though often overstated.

Nearly everyone will want more money. Work will still be a source of pride, meaning, and dignity. People who quit jobs will go back to school, or seek better jobs, or start businesses, or devote more time to raising their kids. Pursuing personal dreams and goals, some will be artists, writers, or inventors, and possibly create something uniquely valuable, even world-changing. People will do what's best for themselves and their families, and their choices will often be good for our whole society.

Yes, some folks will quit jobs, do nothing, be lazy. But the unemployed and underemployed will have money for necessities, at least, so they won't be an added burden on the rest of us.

The unemployment rate, today, is often in the news. It only counts people who are actively looking for jobs. When people aren't looking, they're not counted, and the uncounted are generally ignored or forgotten. Basic income counts *everyone*; no one left out or left behind. The unemployment rate will be merely a number.

Inflation

Ordinarily, inflation is low when unemployment is high; there's a ready supply of people seeking jobs, so workers are wary of asking for higher pay, and businesses rarely raise prices. Inflation is likely when unemployment is low; workers are emboldened to demand higher pay, and many businesses must raise prices. Inflation often fuels further inflation, an accelerating cycle. Then, because politicians are afraid to act, the Federal Reserve intervenes and raises interest rates; inflation comes down, unemployment goes up.

When we have basic income, inflation and unemployment won't be so entangled. The Federal Reserve won't be so empowered.

We'll be cutting current programs as we add Citizen Dividends, so total government spending should be relatively steady. Then, after this is implemented, individuals and families will have a cushion that protects all of us from inflation, no matter the cause, time, or reason.

Our economy will be more stable. Stability helps individuals and families plan our lives and manage our money. Helps businesses, entrepreneurs, and investors anticipate market conditions. And helps government agencies set policies and balance their budgets.

Stability is good for everyone except speculators. Speculators profit from instability, and compound it. When speculators buy or sell stocks, bonds, currencies, companies, commodities, or land, the resulting disruptions can force businesses to close plants, fire workers, or declare bankruptcy. Economic instability often leads to social and political instability, sometimes to protests, riots, and wars.

We can enhance stability, and make our economy more robust and resilient, by partly funding Citizen Dividends through fossil fuel taxes. With small increases at regular intervals, fuel prices will be more predictable than today. Predictable higher prices are preferable to volatile low prices. Today, prices fluctuate, sometimes wildly, and any change – up or down – disrupts markets and affects all economic activity. Predictable prices will facilitate planning, budgeting, investing, and innovating — with sustainable gains for families, businesses, government, and our whole society.

Recession

The correct policy response to recessions, most economists tell us, is to increase the quantity of money being circulated, the "money supply." Today, there are two ways to do that. Fiscal policy uses tax cuts, subsidies, and government spending, like the Bush tax cuts in 2001 and the Obama stimulus in 2009. Monetary policy operates through the Federal Reserve, which can cut interest rates, issue more currency, buy or sell government bonds, and adjust bank reserve requirements.

With both supply-side interventions, CEOs, lobbyists, et al., are paid first – and paid well – before there's any hiring or higher wages. That happened under Bush and Obama. Stock prices went up and Wall Street prospered, while government debt and deficits deepened, income inequality increased, and most Americans were left behind to fend for ourselves.

Basic income gives us a third option. We'll end or prevent recessions by increasing the amount, either one-time or ongoing. Regular folks will spend the money, demanding goods and services, delivering a demand-driven recovery.*

Demand-driven, the converse or counterpart of supply-side policies. Money will flow upward, like from a spring, versus trickle-down from "job creators." Our government will aid citizens directly, rather than indirectly through banks and other big corporations. The Federal Reserve will fine-tune economic conditions, instead of controlling or dominating our economy.

Recent decades have been marked by recurrent recessions, persistent uncertainty, and increasing income inequality — strong evidence, perhaps proof, that supply-side policies are flawed. This demand-driven alternative is overdue, even imperative.

Economic Growth

Growth is good, we're often told (unless it's too fast and triggers inflation). Politicians and economists say it's mandatory.

Economic growth mainly refers to gross domestic product, GDP, the total dollar value of everything that's produced or sold in a country. Add up all the goods and services, and that's GDP. A higher GDP supposedly indicates greater overall prosperity.

But GDP measures quantity only, not quality. It disregards whether products are essential or useless, helpful or harmful, good or bad. It counts war, waste, crime, and pollution as positive line-items, as if more is better. And it spurs excess government spending. Elected officials spend our tax dollars on bridges to nowhere, high-speed trains that never run, and military equip-

---

* This principle has already been tested and proved effective. In the recession of 2001, the first Bush tax cut featured a one-time-only direct distribution, checks for $300 or $600 to every taxpayer. In the recession of 2008-2009, the Obama stimulus put extra money in people's paychecks through a change in Social Security payroll tax withholding; workers got an average of $1,000 a year for two years. Both approaches worked; both recessions were soon ended. (Both are in Appendix 1.)

ment the Pentagon doesn't need or want. Those officials then claim credit for economic growth, and such claims can get them reelected, rewarded for wasting our money.

Indiscriminate economic growth is degrading our society and destroying our planet. It's a cancer. When cancers grow, they're feared, not cheered, yet politicians are cheerleaders for GDP growth.

Another huge flaw: GDP only measures work that's paid. The most meaningful work we do, the most essential for our humanity, is caregiving. Caregiving – raising our kids, especially; also caring for spouses, aging parents, sick friends or neighbors – is mostly unpaid. Caregivers are generally undervalued and underappreciated. Unpaid caregivers save countless lives.

GDP also obscures inequality, and consequently hinders efforts to reduce inequality.

Economists acknowledge these flaws. Economist Simon Kuznets invented GDP as a tool for measuring and comparing national policies, and was honored with a Nobel in economics, yet he stipulated that GDP doesn't indicate well-being, and he objected to using it as a goal. Economists have developed alternatives, counting only what we desire, what's good, while discounting or subtracting the bad and undesirable. Various cities, states, and countries use the alternatives as adjunct indicators. But GDP has a stranglehold over current discourse and policies.[8]

Smart growth is qualitative. And Citizen Dividends will enhance everyone's quality of life. Regular folks will have more money to spend, and our choices will accelerate the transition to smarter, more sustainable policies — while also increasing GDP. Economists can then use GDP as intended: a measuring tool, not a goal.

Private Enterprise

People pursue self-interests. Prices are set by supply and demand. Markets are self-regulating, as if guided by an "invisible hand." Markets are most efficient when free from government interference. These doctrines guide our everyday lives and our national economic policies, and they come from the book that originated modern economics, *The Wealth of Nations* by Adam Smith, published in 1776.

The market Smith praised and promoted was local, like a farmers market or neighborhood craft fair. Choices were limited. Goods and services were mostly produced by the sellers. Buyers and sellers interacted face-to-face. Participants had continuing contact, therefore compelling reasons to be honest. Participants also had comparable and readily-attainable information about other participants and their products.

Today, we shop online, pay with credit cards, and have a seemingly infinite array of choices wherever we live. Faceless corporations make and sell the stuff we buy, using parts and people in multiple countries. Even our food comes from far away, from big corporations that grow, process, transport, and sell it. There's far too much information, and nearly all is biased, marketing.

Smith's invisible hand was a network or system of real people with real hands. People need air, water, food, sleep, shelter, clothing, occasional healthcare, and community with others. We are limited by our innate needs. We are self-regulating.

Corporations seek profits 24/7. They lack innate needs and limits. They don't self-regulate, and can't.

Modern markets – with Walmart, Amazon, Microsoft, Bank of America, et al. – are profoundly different from the markets Smith studied and praised. Modern markets require a hand that's visible and sometimes firm: the hand of democratic government.

For efficient markets – or "fair markets" or "free markets" – government is necessary and government must regulate. When markets are unregulated or badly regulated, they're neither efficient nor fair nor free. Powerful partici-pants can coerce, collude, conspire, fix prices, and form cartels or monopolies. These activities are often dismissed as "market failures," but that's an excuse or euphemism. *Market failures*, in most cases, are signs that government failed to regulate effectively; they're government failures.

Rules and regulations reassure us, promoting trust, consumer confidence, and business confidence. We also need referees. Companies sometimes break the rules, and someone has to step in and blow the whistle. Referees are far more important in business competitions than in football, tennis, and other sports. In business, the outcomes affect people's quality of life — and sometimes life itself, if food, shelter, or healthcare are unavailable or unaffordable.

For several years prior to 2008, the laws, rules, and regulations in the banking and housing industries were flawed, and the referees' eyes were shut or blinded by ideology. Then banks collapsed, stock markets plunged, General Motors and Chrysler filed for bankruptcy, and millions of Americans lost homes, jobs, and savings. We also lost trust in government. Our loss of trust was compounded when government "rescued" Wall Street. Finance companies created the housing bubble and caused the collapse — yet they got an $800 billion bailout from our national government, plus $4.1 trillion from the Federal Reserve. At each stage – the bubble, the collapse, and the bailout – millions of regular folks were harmed or left behind, while a few of the superrich got richer.

Congress responded with the Dodd-Frank law to regulate Wall Street, enacted in 2010. Since then, however, finance companies have become larger and wealthier, and they've been lobbying aggressively to weaken or repeal that law, with a partial success in May 2018. In other industries, too, big companies are getting bigger, hiring lobbyists, and seeking deregulation.

Our government has a duty to protect our personal safety and to promote the general welfare. Therefore, it also has a duty to regulate corporations.

Regulations should be clear, simple, and consistent. We might have distinct levels of regulation based on the size of the entities: minimal for start-ups and small businesses, mid-size when companies cross specified thresholds, and full-on vigorous oversight for corporations that operate internationally. Plus extra supervision and authority over finance companies and the information industry; that's vital because transactions are ephemeral, bits of data exchanged electronically.

One way to cut and simplify regulations is tax reform. Taxes, ideally, are like invisible hands; regulations are like fists. Financial transaction taxes restrain flash traders and speculators, and favor long-term investors; we'll be less worried about Wall Street frauds and excesses. Taxes on raw materials – oil, timber, minerals, land, and so on – increase those costs; markets will reward efficiency, innovation, and conservation.

Private enterprises will be freer.

Economic Discourse

When economic policies fail, the flaws and errors often involve abstract language.

Consider "the market," as in "*the market* tells us" and "let *the market* decide." These phrases disregard differences between participants, particularly the distinction between people and corporations. *The market* is an aggregate, and it mainly represents the actions, desires, interests, and intentions of wealthy people and big companies. Regular citizens are insignificant, except when large numbers act in unison. The poor are excluded almost entirely. *The market* also obscures differences between local shops, multinational corporations, and the New York Stock Exchange.

Consider "the economy." The phrase is a fiction, a full-blown abstraction, an amalgam of GDP, other statistics, and the speaker's biases. "*The economy*" is weak or strong or growing or struggling, economists assert, as if they're talking about something alive, like a person. "We have to do what's best for *the economy*," politicians proclaim, as if this fiction is sovereign. In conventional discourse, *the economy* is a god-like creature we must serve, even worship, or risk being condemned to unemployment, inflation, a recession, or worse.

When sentences start with "*The market*" or "*The economy*," the abstract term is the subject or agent that acts on whatever follows, the object. That object is often us. Such statements imply that people are passive and powerless, uniform and unchangeable.

Abstract language is dangerous. Words can be vague, ambiguous, metaphor, or metonymy, yet we normally assume words have the same meanings for other people as they do for us. We also tend to assume or pretend we understand what people are saying, even though nearly everyone is sometimes ignorant, careless, or lazy with language. Abstract language lulls us into complacency, and often into errors or failures.

We are citizens, although we mostly behave as consumers, customers, clients, critics, spectators, or bystanders. We individuals and *We the People* must remember that it's *our* economy, that we participate in *our* markets, and that we are sovereign over *our* government.

Initial Suggestions

Smart growth is qualitative, and distinct from quantitative GDP growth. Economic policies ought to always focus on regular citizens, seeking to improve our everyday quality of life and our future prospects.

- Unemployment, inflation, and recessions: Let's promptly implement the core plan, a negative income tax/flat tax, like the tables in Chapter 3. Economic conditions will be fairly stable, and stability will expedite further reforms. To enhance economic stability and overall progress, we should occasionally adjust the basic income, the tax rate, or both.

- Economic growth: We have to pursue growth in desired activities only, while reducing or preventing whatever is wasteful, unwanted, or unproductive. We should question GDP and claims based on it, and encourage economists to persist with refining alternative indicators. Let's also insist that politicians and journalists use those alternatives.

- Private enterprise: To protect people, families, and communities, government must regulate big corporations. We should demand regulations that are clear, simple, enforced, and coordinated with smart taxes and other reforms.

- Economic discourse: When politicians use abstract terms, such as *the market, the economy,* and *economic growth,* let's challenge them. And if they can't or won't be concrete and specific, we should vote against them.

With these measures, we'll have fairer markets, freer enterprises, and economic growth that's truly smart.

★ ★ ★ ★ ★

Do you often think or worry about economic issues? Are current policies working for you and your family?

If you're confused, upset, angry, or turned-off, you're not alone and your feelings are valid. Economists and politicians present themselves as experts, and sometimes say these issues are too complicated for regular citizens to understand. They're wrong. If elected officials can't explain issues clearly and accurately, we should elect smarter officials.

Suppose you have a basic income of $1,000 a month, tax-free, and income taxes are totally flat, say 20 or 25 percent. Also suppose fuel prices are predictable, with periodic small tax increases that limit volatility.

Regarding unemployment, you'll have less fear of losing your job, and more freedom to seek or create meaningful work. Regarding inflation, you'll have money to save or invest, plus a direct personal stake in policies that promote stability. Regarding recessions, you'll be more secure and less concerned, because government will have reliable tools for a rapid recovery.

Managing your money will be simpler than today, and you'll be better prepared to make good decisions about college, marriage, careers, jobs, where to live, when to retire. After any setbacks, or if you simply want a change, you'll have multiple options.

Do you have a job you like, or that suits you at least? Your job will be more secure, probably, because economic conditions will be more stable. When it's time for vacation or a break, or when there's a family emergency, your boss will likely be able to find someone who's only looking to fill-in temporarily. If you want higher pay or flexible hours, your independent income will give you more leverage when you negotiate.

Do you own a business? Want to start one? Starting and running a business will be easier than today, because market conditions will be generally predictable. When hiring, you'll have more flexibility, because many folks will prefer part-time work or variable schedules, perhaps as independent contractors. You and prospective employees might agree to trial periods, to see if it's a good fit for both of you.

All of this also applies to your spouse, parents, kids, and friends. Their improved economic opportunities will add to your happiness.

Tired of politicians' empty promises? Turned off by their vague, abstract, or unsupported claims? You might try to educate them. Or shut them up, shut them down, and shut them out by running against them.

And winning.

CHAPTER 6

To Promote Justice and Personal Dignity

Justice and dignity are sacred values, secular goals, and universal ideals — and basic income will make them more real.

Injustices and indignities are widespread today, and impose huge costs on individuals, families, and our whole society. "I feel your pain," politicians tell us, "I want to help. I'm doing my best." Their best, perhaps, but that's not enough.

We can do much better.

Dignity, Equality, and Social Justice

Basic income will be a baseline of dignity and equality. We'll all be on the economic and political playing field; on the social, cultural, and educational playing field as well. The games will be more fair, the outcomes more meaningful.

Many of us are not in the game today, not even on the sidelines. We're spectators, sitting in the stands or watching on TV. Or we're too busy or too tired from working two or three jobs. Meanwhile, fortunate folks are making plays and scoring points. The superrich act like they own the playing field, and some of them do. Big companies have their names on the stadiums.

Inequality leads to injustices and indignities, inevitably, and we've seen a steep rise in income inequality over recent decades. Charts, graphs, and videos show the huge gains made by the top 1 percent and 0.1 percent, and the stagnant or falling incomes of the bottom 90 percent. But statistics are abstract. Personal experience is more persuasive. Each of us knows how much money we have, or how little, and how much we owe on our student loans, credit cards, and mortgages. Most Americans are in debt.*

When we feel poor, insecure, or exploited, a normal impulse is to seek explanations, sometimes to blame other people. Blaming is often biased, typically targeting race, gender, background, or identity. Everyone has biases. We naturally tend to trust and favor those who are most like us, and to be wary of those who are different.

This basic income plan will enrich the poor, end tax breaks for the rich, and expand the middle class. We'll be more equal economically, politically, and socially — and, therefore, almost certainly less biased and less blaming.

Justice must include everyone. This plan won't end racism. Women, Latinos, Muslims, atheists, LGBTQ, Native Americans, and other discriminated groups will still have to demand rights, file lawsuits, mobilize protests, and win elections. Yet all Americans, as equals, will have opportunities to participate in moving our country forward.

Everyone will be on the playing field. Yes, some people start with points on the board – wealthy parents, family connections, elite educations – but those advantages will be less decisive than today. The rewards will more likely go to individuals with real integrity, creativity, and strong work ethics.

We'll see rapid progress on a wide range of issues. Dignity and justice for all.

---

* A National Commission on Income Maintenance Programs studied poverty, inequality, and social justice in 1968 and held hearings around the country. Members were presidents of big corporations, presidents of labor unions, prominent scholars, and politicians from both major parties. Their final report was unanimous, and called for "a universal income supplement program financed and administered by the federal government, making cash payments to all members of the population with income needs."

Crime and Criminal Justice

The motives for most crimes are greed, despair, poverty, and a perceived lack of options. Perpetrators are mostly teens and young adults, and one factor is high youth unemployment. Another is desire for status. In too many places today, the only people with money are drug dealers, gang members, pimps, and other criminals. Dealers and pimps seek susceptible folks, give them drugs to get them hooked, then coerce them to commit crimes and prostitute themselves.

With basic income, teens and young adults everywhere – and children, too – will have meaningful prospects for fulfilling lives. Young adults will have more money for college, job training, to start businesses, to start families, and to buy homes, while children and younger teens look forward to these opportunities. Parents will have added means to protect and guide their kids, and to be good role models. Aunts, uncles, and neighbors will be thoughtful citizens. Thus, the whole culture will nurture children, teens, and young adults to be responsible and to obey all laws.

Judges will be able to redirect basic income money to pay fines, penalties, child support, victim restitution, and any costs for parole, probation, and electronic monitoring. With minors, judges might deduct from the parents' basic income, or defer deductions until the minor becomes an adult. Fines and such will be easy to collect and impossible to evade. Everyone from the extremely poor to the superrich will know that if we commit any crime, and we're caught and convicted, we'll pay for it: effective deterrents and punishment, with minimal administrative costs.

Prison is expensive. It costs $20,000 to $70,000 a year to incarcerate someone. We can withhold inmates' basic incomes to cover some of the costs, then resume payments when the prisoner is released, so returning citizens have reliable means to move forward. Recidivism will plummet. Today, many former prisoners can't find jobs, and they know that an arrest means "three hots and a cot," government-provided food, shelter, and healthcare; in effect, recidivism is rewarded. Instead, former prisoners will have money, dignity, and equality, as long as they obey the law.

Many crimes are victimless, such as possession of drugs for personal use; we'll rewrite those laws. Many prisoners are immigrants, detained because they're undocumented; we'll reform immigration. Many prisoners are mentally ill, an estimated 30 percent; we'll help them instead. (Friends, families, and faith groups can assist the mentally ill with housing, managing their money, and getting appropriate treatments. Social stability is a most effective therapy.)

Local and state governments will save several hundred billion dollars a year nationwide. Direct savings on prisons, police, court costs, and legal fees. Indirect savings involving stress, medical care, and lost productivity — with benefits for everyone who's affected in any way; victims and perpetrators and their families, neighbors, and employers.

Also, because nearly all of us will have a stronger sense of personal and social responsibility, we'll see a significant decline in corporate and white-collar crime. Bank fraud, tax fraud, real estate fraud, and related offenses are difficult to investigate and prosecute; fraudsters expect to get away with it, and many do. When corporations are caught violating laws on public health, worker safety, and environmental protections, fines and penalties are relatively small, factored-into budgets and stock prices. But those crimes have real victims – workers, taxpayers, public trust, and future generations – and must be vigorously enforced. Some CEOs should go to jail. Some corporations should get the death penalty, the revoking of their charters.

Preventing and prosecuting crime is in everyone's interest. This plan aligns our interests, our values, and our capacities to act responsibly and get desired results.

Family Issues and Values

Americans have strong feelings about abortion, teen pregnancy, single parenting, same-sex marriage, and transgender rights. Our feelings confound our politics.

Family, for many of us, evokes a stereotype from the 1950s and early '60s, and the TV shows from or about that era. Men worked and earned money, women were housewives, children did as they were told. Abortion was illegal. Teen pregnancies were hidden, and often led to forced marriages. Immigration was restricted (and most immigrants were Europeans). African-Americans, Hispanics, and Asians were deferential. Gays and lesbians were in the closet. No cell phones and no computers, therefore no sexting, no selfies, no social media.

Modern families, and our values, are more varied.

This plan empowers all of us to live our personal values. Individuals and families will be free to choose what's best today, and to preserve or recover what we value from the past. One parent might stay home with the kids, like in the '50s, perhaps work from home. Or both might work part-time. Parents will have greater opportunities to impart positive values to their children.

Abortions will decline. Teen pregnancies will decline. Men and women will be extra cautious before having sex because we'll know there's no way to avoid paying child support. When a parent leaves, part of the basic income will stay behind for the kids, redirected voluntarily or by court order. If it's $300 a month, that's $64,800 over eighteen years; for multiple kids, it might be $800 or $1,000 a month (so the absent parent gets that much less; potentially nothing).

Kids will benefit immensely.*

Education and the Future

Education reform is a major concern for multiple reasons. It's a family value, a path to personal success, and an investment for the future. Politicians say it's the key to reducing poverty; they're partly right, though they routinely downplay critical facts. Education takes time before outcomes are evident – years, normally, sometimes a generation – and the gains are uncertain, unequal, often transitory.

---

* If we want to do more for children and families, we might create a parallel program of universal child benefits. See Endnote 4.

With this plan, everyone will have money to pursue education for ourselves and our kids. For other kids too, and that's vital. America's future prosperity depends on educating *all* kids to be responsible citizens. No one left behind.

When politicians extol education as a way to reduce poverty, they're mainly talking about jobs, job-training, and preparing people to participate in the labor force. But what if there are no jobs? Or if the available jobs are unsuitable or unsatisfying?

Life is more than working and earning. Education has to include learning how to make good choices about jobs and careers and life in general. A good education develops our capacities to ask questions, solve problems, think creatively, communicate effectively, and continue learning throughout our lives.

Education also involves values. We learn our values mainly from our parents, and most of us believe that's best, though personal values reflect our whole culture. With Citizen Dividends and a shared experience of security and equality, our culture will be healthier, our values more enduring.

Each of us will get a continuing education in personal responsibility. When one wastes or misuses the money, the following month will be an opportunity to learn and do better, perhaps assisted by family and friends. We'll teach our children to budget, save, and invest, with classes in money management, preparing them to use their basic incomes responsibly when they're adults.

Our world is changing rapidly in ways we can't predict. We have to keep learning in order to keep up. We regular citizens must be free to make decisions about how to educate ourselves and our children — *our* decisions, not deferred or defaulted to politicians or self-proclaimed experts. This plan empowers individuals, families, and our whole society to educate ourselves and the people we care about.

Initial Suggestions

Everyone will have the means, and the dignity, to seek justice for ourselves and other folks.

- Dignity, equality, and social justice: All of us – every race, background, and identity – will be on the playing field. Because we tend to ignore injustices to others, and because past injustices persist as present inequities, we should actively seek reconciliation — with remedies, including reparations.

- Crime and criminal justice: We should fully link basic income with the justice system. Let's modify current laws and prior sentences as appropriate, and let's be sure returning citizens can successfully reintegrate into society.

- Family issues and values: Individuals and families, each in our own way, will have greater means to live our values. This baseline of equality can, and should, be a starting line toward mutual respect for people whose lives and values are different from ours.

- Education and the future: We should create multiple, diverse opportunities for children and adults to continue learning throughout our lives, for better jobs and careers, for personal enrichment, and to be skillful citizens.

Dignity fosters decency and respect for diversity. Justice requires us to protect the rights of minorities, including minorities of one. For lasting progress on complex issues, we have to consider facts calmly, reasonably, responsibly, and respectfully — and that'll be easier when everyone's basic economic security is guaranteed.*

★　★　★　★　★

---

* "A host of positive psychological changes inevitably will result from widespread economic security. The dignity of the individual will flourish when the decisions concerning his life are in his own hands, when he has the assurance that his income is stable and certain, and when he knows that he has the means to seek self-improvement." Martin Luther King Jr.

Do you think we have a duty to seek justice? Are you concerned about crime? Racism? Abortion? Education?

Recall injustices you've experienced, witnessed, or heard about, whether blatant or subtle, recent or remote. Most of us can recount numerous incidents.

If you're actively working for justice, you know how hard it is to make lasting progress. Is there one cause or issue you focus on? That's normal, often necessary, to sustain interest and maintain pressure on politicians. Activists are competing to be first in line for funds and attention, each of us insisting that our cause or issue is most worthy. But injustice is injustice.

Imagine an America with basic economic security guaranteed for every citizen, a baseline of equality.

Are you concerned about economic injustice or income inequality? We'll end – at least greatly reduce – hunger, homelessness, and hardships due to debt and financial difficulties. The tax system will be more fair, so the rich pay their share.

Do you seek to end racism? Have you been active on issues involving women, say, or Muslims or immigrants or LGBTQ or people with disabilities? We'll be much closer to achieving a truly just society that values *all* individuals. Elected officials will have to be more willing, prepared, and determined to end injustices — or they'll be former officials.

Have you ever been mugged or assaulted? Do you know, or know of, anyone who had a car stolen or a home burglarized? Or worse, anyone who was raped, shot, or killed?

Pause for a moment, please, and picture a criminal. Maybe recall an incident you read about, saw on TV, or personally experienced. Got it? Did you conjure up an image of a young man?

Now suppose he has a basic income. And so do his friends, parents, neighbors, and every other adult he knows. Also suppose a judge can deduct fines, penalties, and victim restitution if he's convicted of any crime; or, if he's a minor, can order his parents to pay. He'll have added inducements to obey the law and, more important, real prospects for a satisfying future. Do you agree? Can you see how this plan will curtail crime?

Did you or a family member lose a job, home, or retirement savings when Wall Street crashed in 2008? Has your water ever been contaminated with oil, lead, or chemicals? Today, corporations pay fines, normally small ones, and continue with their business. Or they declare bankruptcy, and taxpayers are then stuck with cleaning up the mess. Should corporate charters be revoked? Should CEOs go to jail?

Do you know any single parents? Child support will be guaranteed, redirected from the absent parent's basic income. Unmarried people will have that added reason to be cautious about sex, so there'll be fewer teen pregnancies and fewer abortions.

Consider how an independent income can help anyone – a friend or family member, perhaps, maybe you – who's in an abusive relationship. When victims stay, it's partly or mainly because they can't afford to leave. Right? Folks who are abused will have money to flee if necessary. Couples will be more equal.

Do you have kids in school? Are you concerned, frustrated, or angry about the education they're getting or not getting? You'll have more choices. You might consider private school, a charter school, or homeschooling. You'll also have added opportunities to meet with teachers, attend events, assist with class trips, join the PTA, or serve on the school board.

If you like these possibilities, you can help in many ways. Talk with friends about your concerns and the prospects for progress. Contribute money to causes you care about. Volunteer in community groups. Join a political campaign. Perhaps run for public office. Seek justice.

CHAPTER 7

To Enhance Liberty and Democracy

Liberty demands democracy, democracy defends liberty, and basic income will boost both.

In "life, liberty, and the pursuit of happiness" – and in our everyday experience – life is before liberty. Life requires food, clothes, and shelter, at least; these are prerequisites for liberty and happiness, and people need money to pay for them. With Citizen Dividends, we reaffirm and realize these self-evident truths for every American, as equals. We'll also reaffirm

> — that to secure these rights, governments are instituted among men, deriving their just powers from the consent of the governed, — that whenever any form of government becomes destructive of these ends, it is the right of the people to alter or to abolish it, and to institute new government, laying its foundations on such principles, and organizing its powers in such form, as to them shall seem most likely to effect their safety and happiness.

Liberty and the Pursuit of Happiness

One definition of *liberty* is freedom from government. This seems obvious. Government can be oppressive, undeniably, and it sometimes makes mistakes.

Nearly everyone occasionally – or often – feels abused, coerced, or exploited by government, with valid reasons to be angry about it.

We are most free when government secures our unalienable rights. Good government protects us from crime and terrorism, and prosecutes offenders; it builds and maintains roads, schools, transit, sewers, and such; it issues money and enforces contracts, which are necessary for commerce and justice; it also issues patents, trademarks, and copyrights, inducements to create and innovate. Government is our ally in seeking redress when any business sells unsafe products, defrauds consumers, or pollutes our environment.

Liberty, therefore, is not simply freedom from government. What we want is freedom from abuses, freedom from oppression, freedom from coercion and exploitation, freedom from bad government. Moreover, and most importantly, whenever government is bad, broken, or destructive, we have the right to replace elected officials and to change laws, rules, and regulations "to alter or to abolish it, and to institute new government."

Rights and liberty come with, and require, responsibility. If we disobey laws, society breaks down. If we don't pay taxes, other people have to pay more, and those "other people" include our children and grandchildren.

A second aspect of *liberty* is the freedom to pursue happiness. Liberty involves, perhaps requires, meaningful opportunities to pursue and realize personal dreams and goals.

This definition complements the first, and completes it. Our desire for happiness is what motivates us to free ourselves from bad government. The colonists in 1776 were pursuing happiness when they fought a war and brought forth a new nation.

Both aspects of liberty affirm the importance of Citizen Dividends. Today, when personal liberty is threatened, thwarted, or denied, the causes normally involve money concerns or constraints. Many of us are enslaved by poverty. Basic income means real freedom for all.

Democracy and the Pursuit of Happiness

When we talk about democracy, what it is and why we value it, we tend to restate familiar phrases and formulas: Rule of law. Equal rights. Equal treatment. Equal opportunities. Free speech. Freedom of religion. A free press. Majority rule. One person, one vote. Protections for minorities. Pluralism. An independent judiciary. Due process. Government of the people, by the people, for the people. Liberty and justice for all.[9]

These concepts are useful, significant, and meaningful – obviously – though they're also inadequate. To understand and truly appreciate democracy, we have to consider what it can and should be. In a true democracy, every citizen has equal access to government and viable prospects for influencing it. That requires equal and effective opportunities to define issues, set agendas, select candidates and officials, and shape legislation. The United States is a representative democracy, a republic, so access is mostly indirect. Yet equality is fundamental. Democracy must respect and protect true political equality.

Today, inequality is irrefutable. The elite few – the superrich, celebrities, CEOs of big companies, leaders of special interests – have direct access and influence, far beyond regular folks. At political events and public forums, the elites speak first, loudest, longest, and last. They also use the news media to ratify and reinforce their roles, and to celebrate themselves. After elections, no matter who wins, the elites retain their power and privileges.

The United States, apparently, has devolved into an oligarchy, government by the few. Or a plutocracy, government by the rich.

We have the right to alter our government, but we lack effective means. Elections? Petitions? Mass marches and demonstrations? We've been there, tried that, and our grievances persist. Amend our Constitution? That's far more difficult than winning an election.

To renew our democracy, regular citizens in large numbers must voluntarily act together as *We the People*. Success requires explicit goals and effective strategies, with diverse tactics for attracting allies, educating ourselves, organizing actively, and mobilizing politically. We'll have all of that with our campaign for Citizen Dividends.

The Trouble with Corporations

Corporations influence every aspect of our lives and our government. Yet there's nothing about them in our Constitution, not one word, neither the original document nor any of the amendments.

In America's early decades, state legislatures publicly debated requests for corporate charters, and states only issued charters for corporations that provided a specified public benefit (such as banks, colleges, canals, and toll bridges). States imposed limits on ownership, operations, and duration, and corporations were prohibited from starting or buying other corporations. Charters expired and were sometimes revoked.

As industrial corporations expanded in the 1800s – above all, coal, steel, and railroads – the owners became rich and politically powerful. The Fourteenth Amendment was written after the Civil War, ratified in 1868, to protect the equal rights of all citizens, particularly former slaves.

> All persons born or naturalized in the United States, and subject to the jurisdiction thereof, are citizens of the United States and of the State wherein they reside. No States shall make or enforce any law which shall abridge the privileges or immunities of citizens of the United States; nor shall any State deprive any person of life, liberty, or property, without due process of law; nor deny to any person within its jurisdiction the equal protection of the laws.

Corporations promptly started citing it in lawsuits, claiming that they are "persons." One lawsuit, *Santa Clara County v. Southern Pacific Railroad,* reached the Supreme Court in 1886. The suit was actually about taxes. The railroad had not paid a portion of their property taxes for six years, and argued that the tax violated their right to equal protection under the Fourteenth Amendment. The Court apparently agreed, though did not explain why, and it conceived a new legal doctrine: *corporate personhood.* That was never debated publicly, not even by the Court, and never enacted by elected representatives. Lawyers and judges invented it, a blatant example of "judge-made law." Yet current laws apply and rely on it, a precedent.[10]

The Court reaffirmed and extended corporate personhood in 2010 with *Citizens United v. Federal Election Commission.* Citing the First Amendment and freedom of speech, the Court ruled that government cannot prohibit corporations from spending on political communications.

But corporations are not people. They're artificial entities, created by people, not by nature or God. They don't have natural rights. They only have the privileges we gave them through our government, and we can take away those privileges.

Corporations are tools, like hammers and computers. Hammers can build homes or smash skulls, and sometimes we accidentally hit our thumbs. Computers spread viruses, hate speech, child pornography, and stolen credit card numbers. Corporations are tools for doing business. People create corporations, and investors use them, to limit liability and protect their assets. When corporations fail or fold, typically, founders and investors retain their wealth — even while workers lose their jobs, sometimes also their homes and retirement hopes.

Some corporations have immense wealth and power. A few have tacit or overt government support, and have been called "too big to fail" and "too big to jail." Many are experts at extorting money from government, primarily by saying they'll create jobs if they get the money, or that they'll cut or export jobs if they don't. Many are involved with political campaigns.

We the People have to restrict or reverse corporate personhood — even if that requires us to amend state constitutions and our U. S. Constitution.

Restricting or reversing corporate personhood must include nonprofit corporations. Numerous nonprofits operate as special interests, or represent special interests, or were created to influence elections or public policies. The Democratic and Republican parties are nonprofit corporations; each is multiple corporations, with coordinated staff, purposes, and fundraising. Some nonprofit executives are paid more than a million dollars a year.

When corporations engage in politics – through lobbying, funding campaigns, running issue ads, or exhorting workers about how to vote – they're acting as proxies for their CEOs and directors. Nonprofits are proxies of their major donors. In order to assert our sovereignty over corporations, we may have to focus our attention – and our anger – on the individuals who own or run them.

At the same time, however, we want to remember that CEOs are people like us, with spouses, children, friends, neighbors, and dreams of a better world for their grandchildren and great-grandchildren. Countless CEOs are likely to join the campaign for Citizen Dividends.

The Problem with "Jobs"

The word *jobs*, like *corporations,* is not in the Declaration nor our Constitution. Now it's everywhere in political discourse. Politicians are full of it.

Government got busy with creating jobs in the 1930s, during the Great Depression, when President Franklin Roosevelt's administration declared government to be "the employer of last resort." With the goal of putting Americans back to work, the federal government built dams, schools, roads, bridges, and other structures around the country. It also hired artists, actors, writers, musicians, and photographers, and paid them to make art.

Today, government is the promoter of the private sector. Its stated role is to stimulate, facilitate, or expedite private companies that create jobs. That's the rationale for corporate welfare. That's also why tax cuts are so often directed toward rich folks and corporations, the self-proclaimed "job creators."

Politicians routinely promise to create jobs, though they usually skip the details. Who gets the jobs? When? Where? What do the jobs pay? Why is government involved? And how, specifically, will taxpayers benefit? Details are vague or lacking because the claims and promises are mainly the rhetoric of wishful thinking, rooted in ideology. Or worse, and often, politicians are soliciting or rewarding donors.

Every employer, large and small, especially start-ups, knows that hiring is expensive and workers are a recurring cost. Companies constantly seek higher productivity from fewer workers. Companies that fire workers – "downsizing," "rightsizing," or "rationalizing production" – are rewarded with higher profits and rising stock prices. Instead of hiring people, companies use robots, computers, voice recognition, artificial intelligence, and related technologies. Jobs are disappearing or threatened even for lawyers, doctors, accountants, and journalists, the work performed by software or outsourced to places where professionals are paid less than in the United States.

When government promotes private sector jobs, CEOs and other executives are paid first, and paid well, before they create any new jobs. Job-creating policies invariably increase income inequality.

The problem with "jobs" has only one true solution: basic income. Everyone who's unemployed will have boots and bootstraps, money to live on and to lift ourselves up. We – the unemployed, underemployed, and fully employed; as individuals and as a society – won't expect or rely on government to create jobs for us, neither directly nor indirectly. Creating jobs, in other words, will no longer be government's job.

Regular folks will be the job creators. We'll spend our basic income dollars, demanding goods and services, thereby stimulating economic activity while creating jobs for ourselves and others.

Employers will benefit in numerous ways. Many employers, especially start-ups and small businesses, can only afford or simply prefer part-time workers or independent contractors. Many workers will want part-time jobs while they pursue other dreams or goals. Workers who choose full-time jobs will truly be choosing, and are more likely to be loyal, productive, and motivated. Business conditions are constantly changing, and employers will have greater freedom to adopt, and adapt to, new technologies and strategies.

Initial Suggestions

For most Americans today, liberty and democracy are impaired by economic insecurity. Radical reforms are required.*

---

* "True individual freedom cannot exist without economic security and independence," Franklin Roosevelt declared in his State of the Union on January 11, 1944. He proposed "a second Bill of Rights under which a new basis of security and prosperity can be established for all."

- Liberty and the pursuit of happiness: To enhance liberty, equality, and happiness for all Americans, we should be sure local governments can enact versions of basic income, funded with local revenues.

- Democracy and the pursuit of happiness: One way to strengthen our democracy is to upgrade our political practices. Let's ban gerrymandering, reform election procedures, and demand full disclosure of funding and spending. (See the first section of Chapter 10.)

- The trouble with corporations: We have to restrict corporate personhood, at a minimum to ban corporations from political activities. Does that require amending state constitutions? Amending our U. S. Constitution? We should start immediately.

- The problem with "jobs": Let's tell politicians to stop talking about jobs, and to just *do* their jobs. Their jobs are to serve all of us, including future generations, and they can do that by enacting this plan.

Liberty is never fully secure. We have to be vigilant, alert for violations by corporations, special interests, and government. Regular citizens must be prepared to resist abuses, harms, and threats, even when the offenders are our employers.

Democracy succeeds only when citizens participate actively and consistently. Citizen Dividends, in effect, will pay everyone to participate.

This is a plan to liberate all of us, to "secure the blessings of liberty to ourselves and our posterity."

★　★　★　★　★

What do you think about our democracy? How do you feel about your personal liberty?

Liberty and democracy are central to our national identity, and Citizen Dividends make these ideals personal. You'll have greater liberty to pursue happiness, with an independent income that's guaranteed and unconditional, unlike a paycheck. You'll also have meaningful opportunities to participate as a citizen.

Are you concerned about government infringing on your liberty? Have you experienced any abuse or violation? Perhaps your taxes were wrongly assessed, or you had an upsetting encounter with federal agents, or your business was harmed by arbitrary regulations or capricious enforcement. Errors, abuses, and excesses happen. When your income is more secure and larger, and our democracy is stronger, you'll be better able to seek redress for any grievances.

Has a bank raised the rate on your credit card? Did your health insurance provider refuse to cover a necessary procedure? Does your phone or cable company charge you for services you don't want and don't use? Most of us have been abused or exploited by a big corporation, and many of us have sought assistance from our elected representatives or government agencies. With this basic income plan, corporate power will be diminished, and you'll have more power to demand accountability.

What about your employer? Were you due for a raise or promotion, but didn't get it? Have they refused to give you time off for a family matter, or altered the terms of your healthcare? You'll have more freedom to look for a better job, if that's what you want. Also more leverage to negotiate with a current or future boss about your pay, hours, vacation, retirement, and other conditions.

Do you vote? Do you sometimes donate to causes or candidates? Have you ever volunteered for a political campaign?

If you're like most folks, you vote in presidential elections, though sometimes skip midterms, primaries, and runoffs. Maybe you occasionally sign petitions, email or phone elected officials, go to rallies, donate a few dollars. Though you probably have reasons for not being more involved. Why bother? Has an election ever produced the changes you desire?

With this plan, your relationship with government will be more reciprocal than today. You'll be paying taxes to, and getting money from, our national government. Elected officials are likely to be more responsive.

Does this make sense? Will you be more active as a citizen, do you think? You can start now.

CHAPTER 8

To Respect and Protect Our Environment

Basic income will bring rapid progress on environmental issues, with sustainable success.

The obstacles are obvious, clichés, "jobs versus the environment" and "the economy versus the environment." More accurate, though not a cliché, "special interests versus the environment." However, these three phrases distract us from a crucial fact: the real obstacle is *us*. We demand jobs, and therefore we depend on economic growth to create jobs. Special interests promise both, jobs and growth, so we let them exploit and despoil our environment. In these statements, "we" is the conventional consensus, the bipartisan status quo.

When we talk about our environment, how to protect it and why we must, many of us use the words *prudent, cautious, restrained,* and *traditional,* and these are synonyms for *conservative. Conservative* is the root of *conservationist,* a synonym for *environmentalist.* Protecting our environment ought to be nonpartisan or transpartisan.[11]

Our environment is *ours,* everyone's. Clean air and clean water are human *needs*, literally, and we rely on government to keep them clean, safe, and healthy. On matters of public health and public safety, anti-government is anti-self-interest.

Global Warming and Climate Change

Agents of the status quo, including elected officials, deny or distort evidence of global warming, and tout every doubt, dispute, and disagreement. "I'm not a scientist," they proclaim. "No one really knows."

But global warming is not waiting. We're seeing more frequent and more destructive droughts, heat waves, wildfires, storms, floods, and mudslides; glaciers are melting and coastlines are eroding. The Trump administration released a National Climate Assessment in November 2018, produced by thirteen government agencies. Climate change is costing us many billions of dollars a year. If we stay on the current path, costs will rise to more than $100 billion a year, while projected GDP falls by 10 percent. It's an economic catastrophe. Wherever we live, we'll soon be paying higher prices for food, fuel, housing, and insurance.

People can doubt, dispute, or deny the science – some will, undoubtedly – yet the prudent response is to act promptly. Everyone will benefit directly, personally, as we enact reforms.

A sensible first step is central to this plan: end corporate welfare. Specifically, end the tax breaks and subsidies – direct and indirect, national, state, and local – for producing and consuming fossil fuels. Companies will compete to become more efficient, innovating and developing new products, services, technologies, and business strategies, in many cases leading to higher profits.

Next, the most effective and cost-effective approach – according to economists and environmentalists, liberals and conservatives – is to tax oil, coal, and natural gas: a carbon tax. Fuel prices go up, consumption falls. Some jobs disappear, others are created. Each of us will make our own decisions about what to change or not change, when, where, why, and how. Personal choices, not government decrees.* [12]

---

* Most politicians, in both parties, are afraid to talk about carbon taxes, though a growing number support "tax-and-dividend." With the basic income first, this plan is dividend-then-tax.

Current efforts to slow global warming mainly call for investing in clean energy and infrastructure, the Green New Deal, though opponents say that's unnecessary and unaffordable. Dividend-then-tax will greatly accelerate Green New Deal efforts.

Small taxes can produce big gains. If we periodically increase the taxes, everyone will have escalating incentives to demand efficient cars, homes, appliances, and lifestyles. Fossil fuel taxes will function as invisible hands, guiding people and companies to do what's best for all of us, and for future generations.

To maximize market efficacy and efficiency, and to minimize government involvement, we should assess taxes where the fuel first enters the economic stream, at the mine, well-head, border, or port. A wholesale tax, in other words, not a retail tax at the gas pump, utility bill, or cash register.

Fossil fuel taxes will:

- Make fuel prices more predictable;

- Reduce pollution of all types, from all sources;

- Enhance national security by conserving fuel supplies;

- Protect nature and save uncountable endangered species;

- Drive American companies to innovate and become more efficient;

- Promote organic farming, through higher costs for synthetic chemicals;

- Reward re-use, recycling, redesign, and other environmentally-positive practices.

All these gains will come through market forces.

Our economy demands fossil fuels, depends on them, is addicted to them. Fuel taxes will reduce our demands and dependency, and help end our addiction.

Global warming is global, obviously, and this fact is central to the Paris Agreement, which was signed by 195 countries, including the United States. President Trump announced that America is withdrawing (and he initiated that process, which takes a few years), but state and local governments and major companies are operating as if the agreement will remain in effect. With realistic fuel taxes, we can exceed the goals our government agreed to in Paris.

As we reverse course, we have to confront conventional notions. Consider water. Clean water is a human need; we can't live without it. Corporations don't have needs; they're artificial entities. Various industries use water; "fracking" for example, hydraulic fracturing, which pollutes water with toxic chemicals and injects it deep underground to release natural gas. But fossil fuel companies can exist, and profit, without fracking. Using water for profit is different from needing it for survival.

Basic income will free us to focus on real human needs, and free us from the artificial "need" for jobs. We'll also be freed from flawed notions about corporations, and therefore better prepared to regulate them appropriately.

Oil, coal, and natural gas are created by nature, so everyone ought to have a share. *Everyone* includes our grandchildren and their grandchildren, our posterity and all of humanity. By taxing fossil fuels and reducing consumption – while providing a basic income for all – we'll promote social justice, economic justice, and environmental justice. (*Agrarian Justice,* too, as Thomas Paine taught us.)

Cities and Suburbs

Our environment is also the built environment. Roads, bridges, sewers, etc., are public works, built and maintained mainly by government. They're also public assets, necessary for local and national prosperity. Yet we often hear or read about – and are sometimes harmed by – roads buckling, bridges collapsing, water mains bursting, and transit systems breaking down. Hundreds of communities – most conspicuously Flint, Michigan – have lead in their drinking water.[13]

Urban and suburban communities throughout America are afflicted by crime, poverty, and racial unrest, and pockmarked by vacant lots and empty buildings. Remote special interests fund local political campaigns. Major employers, some of them foreign-owned, have real influence over local officials, local news media, local cultural organizations, and therefore over every resident.

Cities and suburbs will be safer and more prosperous. Every resident will have more money to spend at local businesses, and our spending will create jobs and generate tax revenues. Local governments will have funds to invest in public safety, education, transit, parks, schools, and so on. Residents will have real incentives to demand effective government that's truly responsive to local concerns.

Our national government sends a lot of money to state and local governments, often with strict mandates about how to spend it, local policies dictated from above. Basic income skips the mandates and the middlemen, the bureaucrats, technocrats, lobbyists, and politicians. Local policies will be more truly local, decided by residents.

In Flint, Michigan, the lead poisoning was caused by reckless spending cuts and multiple failures by government officials. Suppose the residents had had Citizen Dividends before that happened. Their local and state governments would have been better funded and more prudent. If or when lead was detected, residents would have been able to mobilize rapidly to get repairs, remedies, investigations, and prosecutions.

Most cities and suburbs have racial disparities in housing, education, employment, amenities, and law enforcement. Protests are common, and sometimes explode into riots. With basic income as a baseline of economic equality, we'll also have a starting line toward greater racial, social, and political equality.*

A related issue is gentrification. Wealthy residents move into prime neighborhoods, housing prices go up, poor residents are squeezed out. The wealthy are White, typically, and they're displacing Blacks and Latinos. When current residents have basic income, they can buy the homes they're living in; they'll be the gentry. Neighborhoods will be more stable.

---

* "We are likely to find that the problems of housing and education, instead of preceding the elimination of poverty, will themselves be affected if poverty is first abolished," Martin Luther King Jr. wrote. "The solution to poverty is to abolish it directly by a now widely discussed measure: the guaranteed income."

Where the cost of living is high – New York City, Miami, Silicon Valley, Hawaii, Washington D.C., and so on – residents can demand supplements, funded from local revenues. Local businesses might also favor supplements to keep their customers from moving away. How much? How to pay for it? Residents will decide.

Residents everywhere will benefit from fossil fuel taxes:

- Cleaner air, and therefore lower rates of asthma;

- Less traffic congestion, so it's easier to get around;

- Walkable neighborhoods, with a greater sense of community;

- More stable economic conditions for locally-owned businesses.

We can magnify these gains by taxing land values. Where property taxes are 100 percent on the value of the land, taxes are the same on a luxury building or a vacant lot. Owners of vacant lots will want to promptly build or rebuild. Even a partial tax shift – 80 percent, say, or 60 percent – will help make cities and suburbs more livable, while also creating jobs. This is another example of using taxes as invisible hands to serve public purposes.

When communities invest in schools, parks, transit, and such, nearby property values increase. With land value taxes, public investments really are *investments*, and the gains are returned directly and dependably. In most places today, those gains are privatized, captured by wealthy landowners, including speculators. Land value taxes deter speculation. These benefits have been demonstrated in America and around the world.[14]

Communities will become more distinct and attractive — a welcome change from the sprawl, strip malls, and sameness that are so widespread today. Progress will be market-driven, through the self-interest of individuals and local businesses. Distinct communities, in turn, are likely to generate new businesses and other innovations, with greater prosperity for everyone.

Small Towns and Rural Areas

Rural communities are beset with troubles:

- Poverty, lack of opportunities, and declining populations;

- Drug abuse – meth, heroin, opioids, etc. – and related crimes;

- Conflicts between long-time residents and recent immigrants;

- Air, water, and land polluted by fracking, oil drilling, and coal mining;

- Boom-and-bust cycles, uncontrolled growth then some buildings abandoned;

- Toxic materials transported by trains or trucks that sometimes crash, or pipelines that sometimes leak.

Small towns will see rapid gains with basic income — on all these issues. Residents will have reasons for hope, and hope is vital for ending drug abuse and addiction. Residents will have more money, and local spending will create jobs. Local governments will have tax revenues to invest in public health and safety. Millions of people will choose to stay, return, or start anew in rural areas, seeking affordable homes, traditional values, and nearby access to open spaces and outdoor recreation.

Rural areas will clearly benefit from taxes on takings. Fossil fuel taxes will reduce the political and economic pressure for drilling, mining, and fracking. Land value taxes are based on the rental value of the land, so landowners have incentives to use land wisely, keeping towns compact and farms intact, while preserving forests, prairies, and wetlands. On these matters and others, local governments will have greater power than today.[15]

In small towns, politics and government are obviously personal. Mayors and council members are neighbors, not just names in the news. Residents see elected officials in coffeeshops and grocery stores, and at their kids' little league games. When big companies try to steamroll local communities – with promises of jobs, economic growth, and "development" – casual contacts among residents and officials can help ensure that local values endure.

Rural areas are also home to a category of citizens who, throughout our history, have been horribly abused, exploited, and impoverished: Native Americans. Many tribes have casinos, but gambling is usually a distraction, not a solution. Basic income will help all Native Americans, on rural reservations and in urban areas. At the same time, importantly, it can remind the rest of us about our ongoing obligations to respect native rights and sovereignty.*

These gains are sure to grow over time, as rural areas retain young folks and attract new residents. Small towns will be increasingly unique, attractive, and prosperous.

Food, Farms, and Agriculture

Our food system is dominated by big agribusiness corporations, and their primary goal is to produce profit. They sow political influence by creating rural jobs and feeding urban folks. And they reap plentiful subsidies, harvesting billions of dollars a year.

Subsidies are almost entirely for major producers of corn, soybeans, wheat, rice, and sorghum. Corn feeds cattle, chickens, and pigs, and is processed into ethanol and high fructose corn syrup. Soybeans are processed into protein supplements and meat substitutes. Sorghum is mostly animal feed. Those subsidies deliver low prices for meat, dairy, eggs, and processed food, leading to unhealthy diets and higher rates of obesity, diabetes, heart disease, and kidney disease — and higher costs for medical care and health insurance.

Small farms are not subsidized. Vegetables are not subsidized. Organic practices are not subsidized. Yet organic produce and farmer's markets are gaining popularity throughout the country, proof that Americans want, and will pay for, healthier foods.

---

* A few tribes distribute casino profits directly as a basic income. One is the Eastern Band of Cherokee Indians in North Carolina, and their program is in Appendix 1.

Public policies should favor agriculture, not agribusiness. Culture cultivates complex, robust, resilient relationships between and among people, communities, and nature. Business mainly seeks short-term profit. Agriculture respects nature and preserves the land. Agribusiness is business first.

We have to protect farms and farmers; that's vital for public health and national security, so it ought to be a top priority. When we reform price supports and subsidies, our main goal must be to ensure that farmers can continue farming. Reforms are necessary, even urgent. Countless farmers lost their land in recent decades, and farmers were seriously harmed by the Trump administration's trade war and tariff policies. Farmers are coping with a warming planet and unstable climate, with floods, droughts, wildfires, fungal infections, insect infestations, and price fluctuations.

One approach is tax reform. Fossil fuel taxes will foster the shift from synthetic chemicals, toward organic practices — and farmers, not government regulators, will make the decisions and drive the changes. Land value taxes preserve farmland. Because the rate is based on the rental value, taxes are low on land that's farmed or fallow. Rates will increase instantly when developers acquire the land, so developers will use land wisely, with homes, shopping, and factories clustered and compact, not sprawling across former farms.

Agriculture reforms can also help slow global warming. One way to remove carbon from the atmosphere – the simplest, fastest, and least expensive way – is to put it back into the soil. Farmers can sequester carbon and enrich the soil by adding biochar, minimizing tillage, through agroecology, permaculture, integrated livestock, holistic resource management, and such. These regenerative practices are similar to, and based on, natural processes that evolved over millions of years. Carbon-rich soil yields more wholesome and abundant crops.

Our Earth and Our Future

Humans have severely altered our planet over the past century, more than we know. Modern industries – fossil fuels, plastics, chemicals, agribusiness, automobiles, aviation, electronics, pharmaceuticals, and nuclear power –

generate huge amounts of waste, much of it toxic. Our air, water, and food are contaminated. Our bodies are contaminated, even newborns.

Corporations synthesize and manufacture materials for their purposes, seeking profit. Each new compound can affect the action of myriad others that are already being used. Chemical actions and interactions vary among species and with changing climate. Testing is limited, and mostly conducted by the corporations. Cumulative impacts are unknowable.

Agribusinesses use massive amounts of herbicides, pesticides, and synthetic fertilizers, and crops have been genetically modified to tolerate the chemicals. Those chemicals are safe, manufacturers tell us, though their claims are mainly based in research they funded.[16]

Genetically-modified crops, GMOs, were introduced in the 1990s, though that was not a response to consumer demand. The "demand" was from Monsanto, seeking higher profit. Monsanto had a weed-killer, glyphosate, marketed as Roundup, and the company modified plant genes to make crops glyphosate-resistant, Roundup-Ready. Glyphosate is made in China, and millions of tons are used every year in the United States.[17]

With the Deepwater Horizon oil drilling disaster of 2010, BP used 1.9 million gallons of oil dispersant, Corexit. That was intended to decrease the damage, though it may have only diminished the immediate disgust, anger, and blame. The Gulf of Mexico is uniquely vital and valuable for seafood, yet BP used Corexit in an untested procedure, injecting it at a depth of 5,000 feet. Scientists now have evidence that Corexit is toxic to marine life, and mixing it with oil increases the toxicity.[18]

Plastic trash in our oceans totals more than 260,000 tons, more than 5 trillion pieces. A lot of that is on the surface, corralled by currents into conspicuous clumps. A lot more is on the ocean floor, or drifting through the depths, or deposited on beaches around the world. A vast amount is invisible or nearly so, including plastic microbeads from cosmetics. Some is consumed by fish and other creatures, and then by humans. Plastic trash also befouls streams, rivers, roadsides, deserts, and forests. Landfills are overflowing. Plastic is forever.[19]

Synthetic chemicals, GMOs, and plastic trash are products of standard practices, policies, and ideologies. Today, the highest priorities are economic growth and consumer convenience. In the battle between special interests and the environment, special interests are winning.

Human activities are causing the extinction of countless species. We humans could go too, possibly with a population crash. Protecting our environment is protecting ourselves. Respecting nature is self-respect.

Initial Suggestions

With Citizen Dividends, we'll be less anxious about our finances, and more prepared to assert our sovereignty over special interests, to stop them from plundering our planet.

- Global warming and climate change: Prompt action is in everyone's self-interest. We should immediately eliminate all subsidies to fossil fuel companies, and then start to raise fuel taxes gradually, periodically. To expedite markets and private enterprise, we should assess taxes at the source, where fuels first enter the economic stream.

- Cities and suburbs: Let's shift property taxes off buildings and onto land, to help make our cities more compact, attractive, and walkable. To further promote local economic activity, we should fund local governments mainly through land value taxes.

- Small towns and rural areas: We should ensure that rural folks have a meaningful voice on the policies that affect them. With taxes on takings (oil, coal, timber, minerals, land, etc.), a portion of the revenues should remain with local governments.

- Food, farms, and agriculture: Farming has changed significantly in recent decades, and countless farmers have gone into debt and lost their farms. Let's redesign subsidies to protect family farms, not big agribusiness. Let's renew or recreate traditional practices that favor small farms, fresh produce, and organic and regenerative methods.

- Our Earth and our future: Our Earth is under assault, and we have a duty to be good stewards. We should demand independent testing of synthetic chemicals and GMOs, with labels that include relevant information. We should also demand plastics that are fully recyclable and recycled, or fully biodegradable. We must apply the *precautionary principle*: when in doubt, be cautious to prevent harm.

These policies are prudent, cautious, restrained, traditional — and truly conservative because they'll help us conserve. They're also urgent. Every delay compounds the cost and the harm.

To protect our environment, we, as individuals and as a species, must reduce our impact. Beyond that, we can and should, perhaps *must*, work to reverse the damage we've inflicted over the past century. Concerned citizens might buy local organic vegetables, embrace zero-waste lifestyles, donate to environmental efforts, become scientists.

Our environment. This plan, by including everyone, can ensure rapid, sustainable progress.

★　★　★　★　★

How do you think about our environment? Are you concerned – or angry – about air pollution, global warming, contaminants in drinking water, or species extinction?

Most of us live in cities or suburbs. We encounter nature primarily as lawns, parks, and gardens. Our food comes from supermarkets and restaurants. Waste and trash are picked up and carried away, or flushed away — *away*, wherever that is. Do you know what happens to your waste and trash?

Imagine that you have an extra $500 a month, perhaps $1,000 a month, added to what you earn. Also suppose fuel prices are higher than today, and predictable, rising gradually through small, periodic tax increases. That means escalating prices for gasoline, plastics, synthetic chemicals, and manufactured goods. Higher shipping costs, too, for products that are made in China, grown in Chile, or from other remote locations.

Your decisions about what, when, and how to change – or not change – will truly be yours. If you view global warming as a serious threat, you'll breathe easier, knowing that we're making real progress. If you believe it's flawed science or a hoax, you'll be less burdened by blaming and shaming from climate activists. The political climate will be relatively calm.

Do you commute? Are you sometimes – or often, or even daily – disturbed by traffic jams, transit breakdowns, or other troubles? You and your neighbors may be more inclined to invest in public assets and infrastructure. After all, when cities and states fail to invest, they are, in effect, choosing inadequate services, lower quality of life, and higher long-term costs. What do you want for your community?

Do you know anyone who was harmed by Hurricane Dorian in 2019, or Florence or Michael in 2018, or Harvey, Irma, or Maria in 2017? Or the vast floods in the spring and summer of 2019? Or the massive wildfires in recent years? With hurricanes, floods, wildfires, and other natural disasters, some people can't afford to prepare or flee, and many don't have adequate insurance. Hurricane Katrina hit New Orleans in 2005, yet countless survivors are still financially underwater. You might consider these facts when you hear about the next natural disaster. Basic income will save lives.

Are you worried about pesticides, herbicides, or GMO foods, possible harm to yourself, your kids, or your grandkids? Local organic foods will be increasingly available and affordable. You might plant a garden and grow some of your own food.

Have you sometimes smelled chemicals in the air or in your tap water? You and your neighbors will have more power to demand appropriate laws and regulations, with vigorous oversight to prevent spills, accidents, and other violations. If anything bad happens, you'll have more power to press elected officials to prosecute CEOs and revoke corporate charters.

Do you enjoy hiking, hunting, fishing, camping, or bird-watching? Vacations at the beach? Over recent decades, these activities have become less accessible and less appealing. If we don't act soon, you might someday talk about outdoor recreation, and your kids will think you're exaggerating. If we don't act soon, your grandkids will assume you're just telling stories.

Act soon.

CHAPTER 9

To Nurture Peace and Security for All

We pray for peace, often, in sacred and secular settings, and basic income may be the answer to our prayers — a true path toward world peace.

Today, "world peace" and "pray for peace" are platitudes. Conventional policies and practices perpetuate conflicts, sometimes provoke conflicts. Underlying resentments persist, undermining our hopes, prayers, and good intentions.

Peace can be the centerpiece of American foreign policy, a core organizing principle. When *We the People* demand this, it will be.

Secure Borders

America's borders are not secure, not from terrorists, illegal drugs, infectious diseases, nor immigrants crossing illegally. The border with Mexico may be impossible to fully secure; it's too teeming with commerce, tourists, and residents who have business on both sides. Airport security everywhere is a problem and a hassle.

We're also vulnerable at our virtual borders. Cyberterrorists can attack from around the world, and some are trained by or work for hostile governments. Cyberterrorists steal credit card and Social Security numbers, empty bank accounts, and encrypt computer files and hold them for ransom paid in untraceable bitcoin. Individuals, businesses, and government agencies – including our election systems and the U.S. military – are targets.

Terrorists troll social media, seeking people who are alienated or dejected, offering solace and a cause to believe in, enticing and exhorting folks to join terrorist groups and attack Americans. Online, people can find instructions for explosives that anyone can build with available materials. One or two terrorists, as we've seen too many times, can cause multiple deaths and mass destruction. Terrorists are nearly unstoppable if they're willing to die.

This plan empowers us in two ways, as citizens and with dividends. Both are necessary. Consider warnings to be vigilant for unattended bags, backpacks, and such: "If you see something, say something." Today, we tend to discount or disregard the warnings; we've heard them so often, we're immune, and most of us are busy with worrying about how to pay our bills. With this plan, everyone will have economic security, plus monthly reminders that we're citizens, with a personal stake in public safety.

We'll also be safer and healthier in any epidemic or pandemic, such as the coronavirus that causes COVID–19. Before the outbreak, most of us went to work when we had a cold or flu; we had no choice, we needed the money. Coworkers, customers, and clients also went to work, so we were exposed to their coughing and sneezing. With the coronavirus, our lives were profoundly disrupted; schools and workplaces closed, we were all told to isolate, many were forced to quarantine. When everyone can afford to stay home while sick, more of us will stay healthy. Basic income will save lives.

Immigration Reform

Immigrants are "taking our jobs," people say, and many of us are anxious or angry. The jobs they're taking, however, are mainly low-paid, low skill, physically hard, or unreliable hours; jobs most Americans don't want and won't take. There are also immigrants who have good jobs, with H-1B visas and employer sponsors.

Citizen Dividends are for citizens only. Americans will be more secure economically and socially, therefore less anxious, less angry, and more ready to consider overdue reforms.

Immigration issues are imposing huge costs – financial, political, social, and emotional – on all Americans. Costs increased significantly when the Trump administration introduced "zero tolerance" for immigrants who are here illegally; with the government shutdown of early 2009, when 800,000 workers were furloughed for 35 days or forced to work without pay; and when President Trump declared a national emergency to build a wall on the southern border. Costs will continue to rise until our government enacts comprehensive immigration reform.

Congress came close in 2013. The Senate passed a bill that was truly bipartisan from the start: the Border Security, Economic Opportunity, and Immigration Modernization Act, S. 744. The vote was 68 to 32. In the House, however, it was never voted on, not even introduced. (Speaker John Boehner, a Republican, yielded to extremists in his party who opposed it.) It would have passed, easily, and would now be the law. Our politics in recent years would have been far more calm, thoughtful, and responsible. And we'd be saving a lot of money. (In 2013, the Congressional Budget Office estimated that it would save $175 billion over ten years. With the huge cost of recent events, total savings would have been far greater.)

Jobs and money are only part of the story. Immigration issues also involve or express core values of love, faith, family, community, and compassion. Apart from pure Native Americans, all of us are descended from, or are, immigrants, and all of us have close or distant relatives in other countries. Americans historically described our country as "a nation of immigrants," and we were proud of that identity.

At the southern border, immigrants and asylum-seekers are mostly from Honduras, Guatemala, and El Salvador, and desperately poor. In the summer of 2018, we all saw photos and videos of crying children separated from their parents, and kids placed in camps where several died. In 2014, 68,000 unaccompanied children crossed the border, seeking to reunite with parents in the United States, or sent by parents or grandparents who feared for their kids' safety at home. That influx was incited by a steep rise in gangs, drugs, rape, and murder. Those troubles continue, pushing Central Americans to seek asylum in the United States.*

Perhaps people in Honduras, etc., would like a basic income. Residents will have money, the means to live with dignity. They'll stay home. And they'll demand that their governments stop illegal drugs, prosecute gangs, and keep people safe and secure. When those governments are more effective, asylum-seekers in the United States will have reasons to return to their home countries.

Let's ask them. We might offer to help fund their programs, perhaps also to help in other ways as residents reform their governments. This may be the most cost-effective way to secure our southern border, possibly the only way. And it will save countless lives. Plus, as those countries become more stable and peaceful, costs will fall while benefits multiply.

Americans will be safer at the border, throughout our country, and when we travel abroad. Plus, in sharp contrast with today, we'll be united on these issues and proud of our government.

Pursuing Peace

To make peace the centerpiece in American policy, we have to resolve four interconnected concerns:

- Millions of us have jobs that depend on military spending.

- Preparing for wars and fighting them are lucrative for military contractors.

---

* Mexicans have been returning to Mexico voluntarily over the past two decades, a net outflow from the United States. One reason is that Mexico gives money directly to the poor, "conditional cash transfers." The benefits are well documented. Brazil, Colombia, Peru, and Chile also have conditional cash programs with proven success. (See Appendix 3.)

- Contractors spend huge sums on lobbying, public relations, and campaign donations.

- Politicians are afraid of being portrayed as weak, soft, or indecisive on terrorism and national security.

When we have Citizen Dividends, regular folks won't be so constrained by our jobs, and politicians won't be so controlled by special interests. Everyone, including people who work for military contractors, even the CEOs, will be prepared to pursue peace.

We can start by cutting the waste and excess from military spending. Contractors and their allies will try to stop the cuts, deploying their usual two-pronged tactics: jobs on one side, fear on the other. The jobs card won't be a trump, so they'll double-down on fear: fear of Russia and/or China; fear of terrorism, Islamic fundamentalism, and other ill-defined abstractions; fear of nuclear weapons in Iran, Pakistan, North Korea, and further proliferation; fear that terrorists will get hold of a nuclear bomb, or material for a dirty bomb, or chemical or biological weapons; and fear of cyberattacks.

We have to be ready for real threats, of course, and prepared to respond forcefully. Always. But Russia's military budget is a tenth of what we spend, their GDP less than a tenth of ours. Their government is corrupt, extreme poverty is increasing, lifespans are declining, and wealthy Russians are buying homes in New York and London. China has billions of reasons to maintain peace with us. Its economy depends on trade with the United States, and the same big corporations operate in both countries. More than 300,000 Chinese, sons and daughters of the wealthy elite, attend American colleges and universities.

Regarding terrorism, Islamic fundamentalism, nuclear proliferation, dirty bombs, chemical and biological weapons, and cyberattacks: our security depends on "soft power," diplomacy. Our best, often only, options are to impose sanctions, freeze foreign assets, and stop the transfer of weapons and funds. To succeed with any of these actions, we need allies. And we can't rely on military force. Every U.S. airstrike, even when properly targeted and perfectly executed, is a recruiting event for terrorists.

As we cut the waste and excess, we also have to reassess. How many F-35s are we building, and why? Do we need another aircraft carrier? Next-generation nuclear weapons? These programs and others, the whole panoply of military hardware, display a 20th century Cold War mindset, and may be useless in the 21st century. Future wars will be, at least partly, cyber — fought mainly with software, computer hacking, artificial intelligence, and such, including propaganda and disinformation. Cyberwars cannot be won with F-35s or nuclear weapons.

We'll be safer. Military leaders and policymakers won't be distracted by efforts to create jobs, and won't be burdened by bloated bureaucracies. The U.S. military will still be, by far, the world's largest and most powerful.

We'll be more prosperous. With the money we save, we can cut taxes, pay down the national debt, rebuild public assets, or increase our Citizen Dividends. America's economy will be stronger.

We'll be more united. If any country threatens us, we'll have the political will to respond effectively and appropriately, whether through sanctions, cyberdefenses, cyberattacks, or with our military. Even if the threat is from Russia or China, or Iran or Saudi Arabia and our response leads to higher fuel prices.

To achieve peace, we have to curtail or eliminate weapon sales and exports. Leading exporters are America, France, Russia, China, Sweden, Italy, and Germany. The purposes, our government and others insist, are to support allies, deter wars, and defeat terrorists. In every exporting country, however, politicians are most concerned with domestic matters, particularly jobs and economic growth. And countries don't simply "sell weapons." Governments subsidize military contractors, contractors lobby or bribe politicians, and countries compete for customers. Exports are evidence that jobs, profits, and economic growth, today, are higher priorities than peace.[20]

In effect, through who we elect, every American will have a choice: A bigger military, with more F-35s and such, or more money in our hands? Export weapons or nurture peace?

People around the world will be asking similar questions. Do I want basic income? Do I want my country to cut military spending? What can I do to promote peace?

Ending Wars and Terrorism

In most conflicts today, U.S. policy is to look for a responsible partner, normally a government, and provide support. First send food, medicine, other supplies, and money, sometimes loads of cash. Then small arms, while training and advising local forces. Then, if fighting crosses an undefined line, deploy drones, airstrikes, and U.S. special forces. Worst-case scenario, "boots on the ground."

When governments falter or fail, even briefly, terrorists and militants can arise or infiltrate, and cause governments to fail faster. Where militants hold territory, they impose order. Residents tend to accept the regime, even welcome it, tolerating tyranny or theocracy rather than suffering the chaos of war. That's how the Taliban reclaimed large parts of Afghanistan. The Taliban, ISIS, Boko Haram, al-Qaida, al-Nusra, al-Shabab, et al., pay their soldiers. Those paychecks are recruiting tools.

Suppose we offer to help war-torn regions by providing residents with basic income. We'll recruit people for peace. This is a strategy to win hearts and minds and hands.

In every ongoing or recent war, and everywhere there's terrorism, recent or threatened, the victims are mainly civilians. Civilian victims include the children, spouses, parents, and neighbors of the tiny fraction who are or become militants or terrorists. The prospect of a basic income – even just the promise, if the distribution is delayed by fighting, factions, or other factors – will give people concrete incentives to demand peace. Residents will work together to create stable governments with laws, courts, and police that can arrest and prosecute suspected militants, terrorists, and other criminals.

Three factors are major features of ongoing and recent wars: the resource curse, extreme nationalism, and militant Islam. Basic income is a remedy for all three.

Resource curse is the term social scientists use to describe a tragic, well-documented fact. Countries with plentiful natural wealth – oil, gold, diamonds, and so on – are often afflicted by war, terrorism, autocratic rulers, or environmental devastation; all of these in many cases. Rulers or factions plunder nature to increase their wealth and power. Russia, Iraq, Iran, Libya, Syria, Nigeria, Congo, Angola, Saudi Arabia, Turkmenistan, Uzbekistan, Myanmar, Malaysia, and other countries — different settings, the same underlying pathology.

An alternative is Alaska, with the Permanent Fund Dividend. Another is Norway, where oil revenues fund universal social programs, education, medical care, and more. Natural wealth should be a blessing — and it will be when countries tax what people take from nature, and use that money to fund dividends for everyone. For resource-cursed countries, this is an escape plan.

Extreme nationalism is distinct from the healthy form. Extremists exploit patriotism, wielding it as a weapon to silence critics, attack opponents, and aggrandize themselves. Where extremists hold power, they sometimes start wars to divert attention from domestic troubles. Vladimir Putin, for example, and Russia's incursions into Ukraine.

Healthy nationalism was when Ukrainians overthrew corrupt regimes in the nonviolent Orange Revolution of 2004 and the Maidan "Revolution of Dignity" in early 2014. After Maidan, however, there was escalating unrest in the eastern provinces; Russia incited that unrest, then cited it as a pretext for annexing Crimea and sending troops across the border. Suppose Ukraine enacts a basic income. Ukrainians throughout the country will have real incentives to seek peace and national unity. Individuals, families, and communities will be free to choose the best from east and west.

Militant Islam is the ideology of ISIS, al-Qaida, et al., groups that have declared war on the west. Tactics include suicide bombings, mass kidnappings, raping and selling women as sex slaves, beheading people or burning them alive. Asymmetric warfare, low-cost yet terrifying, weapons and tactics that we cannot defeat with drone strikes and cruise missiles.

The real danger, though, is not Islam, not fundamentalism, not "radical Islamic terrorism." The real danger is militancy, the use of violence to impose an ideology or way of living. That's coercion, not religion. Coercion defiles religion. True faith cannot be coerced. Militant Islamists use religion as a pretext, smokescreen, or weapon while they rape, kill, kidnap, and plunder. An answer to militancy, and an antidote, is true religion. True Islam is a religion of peace.

Two or three factors typically combine. Iraq was cursed with oil when the country was founded after World War I, and cursed by extreme nationalism under both Saddam Hussein and the Shia-led government that followed. ISIS is all three: extreme nationalist militant Sunnis funded by oil revenues.

Imagine Iraq — if basic income had commenced soon after Saddam Hussein was ousted in April, 2003. Dividends from oil revenues would have united Shias, Sunnis, and Kurds. Every Iraqi would have had money to rebuild their homes, businesses, and communities, plus concrete reasons to create responsible, representative government, local and national. Saving thousands of American lives, saving trillions of U.S. taxpayer dollars, saving more than five hundred thousand Iraqi lives.*

This would have precluded the rise of ISIS and prevented numerous incidents of terrorism in America and around the world. Peace and democracy would have spread rapidly throughout the region and beyond.

Peace and Security for All

The United States, by enacting Citizen Dividends, can lead the world toward enduring peace. Other countries will be eager to join us.

---

* This nearly happened. In the summer of 2003, Senators Lisa Murkowski, a Republican from Alaska, and Mary Landrieu, a Democrat from Louisiana, introduced a resolution calling for an "Iraqi Freedom Fund," modeled on Alaska's Permanent Fund Dividend. The Senate held hearings and debated the idea, and Secretary of State Colin Powell expressed his support. (See Appendix 3.)

We can actively encourage other countries. Perhaps put basic income on the agenda for trade negotiations, or make it a precondition. Perhaps rescind trade agreements, such as preferred status, until countries implement their programs. Perhaps put aid money in escrow, particularly military aid, until after a country acts.

If we delay, another country will lead. The first will be uniquely honored.

Brazil? Under a law that passed their Senate unanimously in 2004, every Brazilian has a right to a minimum income. They're implementing that gradually through the Bolsa Familia, conditional cash transfers. More than 60 million people received payments in 2018, 30 percent of the population of 200 million. They might expand it to create a full basic income.

Namibia? Namibians know about basic income, thanks to a privately-funded local pilot project from late 2007 through 2009. A majority want it nationwide, opinion polls indicate, and elected officials have said they support it. But Namibia is a poor country, and any version would require outside funding.*

Tunisia? The "Arab Spring" began there in 2011, after a fruit vendor's suicide sparked the Jasmine Revolution. The 2015 Nobel Peace Prize was awarded to the National Dialogue Quartet, a coalition of labor, business, legal, and human rights groups. But ISIS terrorists are now active. Tunisians might lead again, with a version of basic income. Other countries are likely to follow again, Algeria, Libya, Egypt, Bahrain, and so on, this time with lasting success.

- Perhaps Greece, to reverse the austerity policies that have burdened their society.

- Or Cuba, to secure their egalitarian values as they welcome further trade and tourists.

---

* The project was in Otjivero-Omitara, a rural village, and 930 people received unconditional monthly payments of N$100, equal to about U.S. $13. There were significant gains in health, education, social equality, and entrepreneurship. (See Appendix 3.)

- Or South Africa, where labor unions and religious groups already endorse Basic Income Grants.

- Or East Timor, an island nation that gained independence in 2002, and may want to lead on global warming.

- Or Venezuela, after years of social, political, and economic decline – and massive suffering – using their vast oil reserves to restore stability and democracy.

- Or ...

Finland, Holland, Scotland, and India are planning or conducting – or recently concluded – pilot projects, and one of them might be first. Elected officials in Germany, Italy, and France have endorsed the idea. Public campaigns are underway in South Korea, Australia, New Zealand, Japan, and other countries.

When any country enacts any version, their neighbors will know — and may be motivated to follow, possibly to overthrow a bad government. Basic income in Namibia could help liberate Congo and Angola. Ukrainians might trigger a transformation of Russia. A program in Jordan, Turkey, Iraq, or Lebanon may be the key to peace in Syria — an indirect strategy to end that tragedy, and maybe the quickest way to eliminate ISIS, oust Bashar al-Assad, and entice Syrian refugees to return home and rebuild their country.

We might soon see peace in the Middle East. In Israel, income inequality is increasing; basic income would promote prosperity, political unity, and national security. A Palestinian program might be funded by Arab countries, and will likely lead to a responsible government that can reduce the number of terrorist attacks and speed the transition to a peaceful Palestinian state. Israelis and Palestinians, the citizens and their governments, will have a firm foundation to negotiate and move forward toward an enduring peace.

In time, maybe just a few years, many nations will have their own variations.

Initial Suggestions

We're dreaming, imagining, and fantasizing, boldly and unashamedly. This is how new ideas emerge. Dreams and fantasies first, playful conjecture, followed by public discussions and debates that lead to definite plans. Then, ideally, to action and success and a better world.

- Secure borders: America is vulnerable, so let's act promptly. We'll be more united and more vigilant, and therefore more secure at borders, seaports, airports, and virtual borders.

- Immigration reform: With Citizen Dividends for citizens only, we'll resolve the political impasse, so we can calmly consider our options. We should also offer to help Honduras, Guatemala, El Salvador, and other countries implement their own programs.

- Pursuing peace: Let's get serious about eliminating waste and excess in military spending, while we also reassess our needs. Let's reduce or stop exporting weapons, while urging other exporters to follow our lead, and perhaps also to enact basic income, cut their militaries, and actively pursue peace. As we enact cuts, we'll gain leverage; when other countries cut their militaries, we'll be safer — a virtuous upward spiral.

- Ending war and terrorism: Where war or terrorism is ongoing or seems imminent, our first response should be to propose a basic income for residents of the region. Offer funds. Offer logistical support. Put money in escrow if the local government is unable or unwilling to distribute it. And be sure the residents know it's there for them.

- Peace and security for all: Let's tell the world that this is what America stands for. Economic security for people everywhere. Personal dignity for people everywhere. Peace everywhere. Tell the world, and act to make it so.

When America helps other countries enact basic income programs, our support will truly be an investment. Those countries will be on track to become self-sufficient.

Countries might include people at age 14, 18, or 21, maybe with some added amount or a parallel program for children. The basic income might be $30 a month in Afghanistan, Yemen, Haiti, and other extremely poor places. Perhaps $40 in Honduras, Guatemala, and El Salvador. Perhaps $60 or $80 in countries with oil wealth, such as Iraq, Libya, Nigeria, and Venezuela, though starting smaller, then increasing as they enact reforms and escape the resource curse.*

We'll save a huge amount of money. Every bomb, drone, or cruise missile costs tens or hundreds of thousands of dollars. Every hour of flight time in an F-16 or F-35 costs tens of thousands of dollars, even testing and training flights. Wars are horribly expensive. Peace is happily economical.

This pro-peace strategy will also bring rapid progress to reduce global warming. The U.S. military consumes huge quantities of fossil fuels, mostly in routine operations, training troops, building weapons, and transporting troops and equipment. War increases fuel consumption immensely, along with fuel waste, oil burned or spilled in attacks on wells, pipelines, refineries, terminals, tankers, and trucks. Fires are sometimes set deliberately to delay or distract enemy troops, and to deprive people, companies, and governments of revenue. War also destroys huge quantities of steel, copper, rare earth elements, and other materials.

Every war, regardless of who, when, where, why, or how, is a war against the Earth. Every war, therefore – no matter how it's fought, no matter the apparent outcome, and no matter where we live – harms our children and grandchildren and great-grandchildren.

Peace must be our goal, a core principle of foreign and domestic policies. America can lead the world.

---

* Extreme poverty, as defined by the World Bank and other institutions, is living on U.S. $2 a day or less. A basic income of half that amount would be around $30 a month. Yet the Namibia experiment provided only $13 a month, and the gains were immediate and significant.

★　★　★　★　★

Do you dream about, or pray for, world peace? Do you think we can achieve it?

Are you concerned about border security to stop terrorists, illegal immigrants, and dangerous drugs?

What would you have America do about the fighting in Iraq, Afghanistan, Syria, and elsewhere?

Imagine that you have a basic income of $500, $750 or $1,000 a month added to what you earn. And that your spouse, friends, neighbors, and all adult Americans have that as well. Consider how this might affect your feelings and opinions about these issues. Also consider our country as a whole, our sense of unity and patriotism, our national identity.

Recall a time when you were told to be alert for suspicious people or packages. "If you see something, say something." Did you ignore it? Did you feel anxious? When economic security is guaranteed and everyone has a stronger sense of citizenship, more folks are likely to act and all of us will be safer.

How have you been affected by the coronavirus? Work disruptions, school closures, isolation, quarantine? Have you lost income? Do you know anyone who contracted COVID–19 or died from it? Do you see how you and your family will be safer and healthier when everyone has a basic income?

When you hear about immigrants taking American jobs, are you anxious about your own job? Only citizens get Citizen Dividends. You'll have more options for your job, your family, and your future.

Consider immigrants you know, maybe your parents or grandparents, maybe friends, neighbors, coworkers, or the cooks at your favorite restaurant. They came to America seeking better lives, pursuing happiness. Are they citizens? If not, do you think they should be able to apply for citizenship?

When you hear people speaking Spanish, do you sometimes wonder where they're from? Do you ever ask them why they left? You might talk with them about basic income, and invite them to imagine a version in their home country. Would they have stayed home? Might they return home?

How do you feel about the situation in Iraq and Afghanistan, and about ISIS proliferating to Syria, Libya, and beyond? Are you sad? Frustrated? Furious?

Have you visited Israel? Have you been to France, England, India, Pakistan, Nigeria, Congo, or another country that's suffered a recent terrorist attack?

Recall a few experiences from your travels, particular people and places, sights and sounds. If you've never been outside the United States, select somewhere you might want to visit. Now, whether you've been there or not, picture that country with a basic income. Consider what it could mean and do for the residents. Is that something you'd like to see?

If you believe this plan makes sense, you might join the movement to make it happen. You can help save countless lives.

CHAPTER 10

We the People Renewed

With the Declaration of Independence, the Founders asserted our rights and reasons to govern ourselves. With our Constitution, they conceived, ordained, and established our national government. With the Bill of Rights, they defined the rights of individual citizens, and limited the powers of our national government.

We'll reaffirm the Founders' ideals and values, and make them our own, with Citizen Dividends. Each of us, as equals, will have the means to assert our rights, participate as citizens, and act together as *We the People*.

We the People of the United States, in Order to Form a More Perfect Union

When the Founders convened in Philadelphia in the summer of 1787, there were armed rebellions within states, economic conflicts between states, and mounting disputes with foreign countries. The national government was a confederation, with no power to resolve these challenges. It was too small, too poor, too weak.

Today, our federal government is too big, too powerful, too bound to special interests, and too broken to serve public interests.

Our union will be more perfect. Every American will have a real sense of reciprocity with our government — reasons and resources to make it the right size, with the right powers only, and then to keep it right.

We also have to renew our political practices. Initial suggestions:

- Real people only: A core principle of democracy is one person, one vote, and this is why we have to get corporations out of politics. When corporations are active politically, owners and CEOs have inflated influence — two votes, in effect, or hundreds or thousands of votes.

- Local focus: Electoral districts should be compact, uniting neighbors and neighborhoods to strengthen democracy at all levels, local, state, and national. Gerrymandering is antidemocratic.[21]

- Full disclosure: For a healthy democracy, citizens have to know who's funding parties, candidates, and issue campaigns. Today, huge sums are from wealthy individuals and corporations, and they can hide their identities; it's called "dark money."[22]

- Citizen-funded campaigns: Funding can be fair, open, and truly democratic – while protecting everyone's rights to free speech – with small-donor matching funds. Or every citizen might get vouchers for each election cycle, say $50 or $100, to donate as we choose.[23]

- Voting reform: Elections can be more democratic and more decisive – also less divisive, less negative, and less expensive – with Ranked Choice Voting. Voters indicate a first choice, second choice, third choice, and so on. The first choices are counted. If no one has more than 50 percent, the candidate with the fewest votes is eliminated, and those voters have their second choices counted; the process repeats until someone surpasses 50 percent. Winners have real mandates to govern. Plus, because every candidate wants to be at least the second or third choice, RCV fosters positive, issue-focused campaigns.[24]

- Pragmatic primaries: One option is to have all candidates and parties on a single ballot, an "open" or "blanket" primary, then advance the top four to the general election and use RCV. California and a few other states have open primaries, but advance only the top two, even when they're in the same party. The top four are sure to include both major parties and maybe third party or independent candidates.[25]

- Impartial procedures: Recent elections have been tainted by charges of fraud, voter suppression, mismanagement, and partisan meddling. To restore trust, we should enact stricter laws and standards, and employ nonpartisan professionals.[26]

More ideas: vote-at-home or vote-by-mail, weekend voting, mandatory voting, making election day a holiday; automatic universal voter registration or same-day registration; fully affirm the right to vote, a constitutional amendment; proportional representation with multimember districts; abolish the electoral college with a constitutional amendment, or bypass it with an interstate compact, the National Popular Vote.[27]

Let's experiment in local and state governments, the "laboratories of democracy." We'll see what works and what doesn't, where, how, and why. Then we can take and improve the best practices, applying them where we live and for our national elections.

Another suggestion is to expand the House of Representatives. It was increased periodically over America's first century, but has been fixed at 435 members since 1913. Then, each member represented 200,000 citizens; now it's 750,000. And our society is far more diverse. A larger House would better represent all of us — and could help resolve the political paralysis.[28]

We the People want, and we can form, a more perfect union.

Establish Justice

The Founders sought justice, and fought and sacrificed to achieve it. But they were White men. And many were slave-owners. Their doubts and disputes over slavery are documented, yet they allowed it to continue with a contrived compromise in the Constitution. Ending slavery required the Civil War and the Thirteenth, Fourteenth, and Fifteenth Amendments.

They didn't even question the status of women. Women also accepted it. At the first women's rights convention – in Seneca Falls, New York, in 1848 – only one-third of the attendees signed the Declaration of Sentiments. Women organized, protested, and mobilized for decades, and several states and territories enacted suffrage in the late 1800s. Women won the right to vote in 1920 with the Nineteenth Amendment.

Another original mass injustice was the removal of Native Americans. Most of the Founders viewed natives as "savages," and the U.S. government waged wars against the tribes throughout the 1800s. The Supreme Court ruled in 1846 that Native Americans were not protected by the Constitution. That ruling established the "plenary power doctrine," which government then cited as granting the authority to violate treaties, to relocate and confine tribes, and to take native children from their parents.[29]

This history conveys vital lessons. First, we normally default to whatever is familiar, customary, or conventional. When ideas are unfamiliar, unproved, risky, or radical, most of us refuse to act, leaving the status quo intact.

Second, justice requires time and effort. Individuals have to commit and work together, often in large groups, sometimes over decades or centuries.

Third, justice requires truly democratic government. Partly because we default to the familiar, and partly because we naturally pursue perceived self-interests, we tend to discount or disregard other people's needs, rights, and concerns; the voiceless and powerless, normally, are left out or left behind. Good government – with equal access, responsible legislatures, and honorable courts – is necessary for justice. Everyone must have equal and effective opportunities to participate.

Blacks, women, and Native Americans experience ongoing injustices and inequities. So do Latinos and Asians. And Muslims and atheists. And people who are gay, lesbian, bisexual, transgender, and queer. And immigrants, documented and undocumented. And people with disabilities. And poor people of all backgrounds and identities.

We have work to do – sacred, serious work – to fully establish justice.

Insure Domestic Tranquility

After winning independence from Britain, Americans were not tranquil. Myriad veterans were wounded or disabled, myriad families impoverished by years of sacrifice. Veterans in Massachusetts, Pennsylvania, and other states took up arms against the new government, demanding redress for their grievances.

Domestic tranquility is not ensured today, not even close. Our tranquility can be disrupted at any moment by a mass shooting, targeted or terrorism or totally random. Columbine, Virginia Tech, DeKalb, Fort Hood, Tucson, Aurora, Newtown, Washington Navy Yard, Isla Vista, Charleston, Oregon, San Bernardino, Orlando, Dallas, Parkland, Santa Fe High School, Annapolis, Jacksonville, Cincinnati, Bakersfield, Pittsburgh, Thousand Oaks, Chicago, Virginia Beach, Gilroy, El Paso, Dayton, Odessa, Jersey City, … . This list, though long, is incomplete. Incidents are increasing, often left off the national headlines. Schools and workplaces have "active-shooter drills." Many of us are numb. Numb is not tranquil.

Basic income may be the key to preventing mass shootings. After each incident, in hindsight, folks who knew the shooter tend to recall signs of mental illness, alienation, or repressed rage. Family and friends and neighbors will have the means to seek and provide preventive help — for other folks and ourselves.

In similar ways, for similar reasons, this will reduce suicide. That includes "suicide by cop," people who threaten or commit crimes, including mass shootings, to get themselves killed. When folks are depressed, desperate, at-risk, help is likely to be available. And hope will be universal. Each of us will have something to look forward to, a secure income next month, the month after, and every month, along with the opportunities that income provides.

Our tranquility has also been disrupted, also repeatedly, by protests and riots after Black men (and a few women) died in encounters with police, Black men killed with guns, Tasers, chokeholds, or beatings. Racial bias and excess force have been reported throughout U.S. history – countless reports, in countless places – though most reports were ignored, dismissed, or hushed-up. Today, bystanders have cell phone cameras. And social media amplifies anger and accelerates organizing. Soon after Michael Brown Jr. was shot in Ferguson, Missouri, on August 9, 2014, Black Lives Matter protesters around the country were marching with their hands in the air, chanting "Hands up. Don't shoot."

Our chant might be "Hands out. Let's connect." Hands out for handshakes, high fives, fist bumps, hugs. Let's connect Black and White and Brown, poor and rich, cops and regular folks and elected officials. Then we may truly know domestic tranquility.

Provide for the Common Defense

Our Constitution was written by veterans. Many, most prominently George Washington, were veterans of the battlefields; others of the political and diplomatic struggles. They defined the military's role, powers, and limits. And they decided to have no standing army.

Today, U.S. military spending surpasses the next seven countries combined, and most of those are allies or customers for U.S. weapons. Our military maintains more than 700 overseas bases; all other countries have a total of 30.[30]

The war in Afghanistan began in October 2001; it continues, and the Taliban again control large areas. In Iraq, the Bush administration unleashed "shock and awe" in March 2003; that war and the U.S. occupation led to a surge in terrorism around the world, and to ISIS, the war in Syria, and fighting in Yemen, Sudan, Somalia, Libya, Nigeria, Congo, and other countries. American forces, today, are active in multiple locations. After every U.S. airstrike anywhere, militant Islamists escalate their efforts and recruit more followers. Our government is preparing for, and perhaps provoking, perpetual war.

Instead, we should promote basic income abroad. Let's ask residents of Afghanistan, Iraq, Syria, etc., if it's something they might want. Perhaps offer funds. Residents are the only ones who can fully pacify a place, and residents will demand effective governments that attain and maintain peace, with laws, police, courts, schools, and commerce. In regions where there's active fighting, it can be implemented in one town, city, or province at a time.

With peace as our priority – truly, not rhetorically – we can deploy our economic might, pressing other countries to enact basic income programs: cancel military aid, redirect foreign aid, maybe put aid money in escrow; impose trade sanctions, offer to remove existing sanctions, renegotiate trade agreements, withhold or rescind preferred status.

Americans will benefit directly, immediately.

Consider these possibilities:

- Iran, to prod them to end support for Shia militants, particularly Hamas and Hezbollah.

- Saudi Arabia, to prod them to end support for Sunni militants and Wahhabi extremists.

- Pakistan, to promote their efforts to eliminate terrorism and safeguard nuclear materials.

- Turkey, to protect Kurds and other minorities, and to prevent a collapse of their flawed democracy.

- Russia, to press for full withdrawal from Ukraine, and to preclude incursions into any other country.

- China, to prevent further military expansion in the South China Sea. Also to prod them to press North Korea to eliminate missiles and nuclear weapons.

The Middle East, too, the United States pressing both sides. With basic income, Israelis will be more secure, while Palestinians gain new incentives to end terrorism and to create a trustworthy state. Residents and governments will be prepared to work actively toward enduring peace.

Boldly pursue peace everywhere, to provide for the common defense.

Promote the General Welfare

The Founders' phrase has been redefined. It now represents relentless efforts to create jobs and promote economic growth.

Our government mainly promotes the *specific* welfare, through programs that help special interests and selected individuals. Special interests get tax credits, subsidies, loan guarantees, and government contracts. Selected individuals, the poor get food stamps, TANF, and such; the rich get special privileges. The rest of us – the middle class, the majority – get only promises and rhetoric.

Our Constitution does not mention *jobs* or *economic growth*.

Let's uphold our Constitution and enact Citizen Dividends — a simple, direct, efficient plan to promote the general welfare.

And Secure the Blessings of Liberty to Ourselves and Our Posterity

Liberty is an unalienable right, the Founders declared, a blessing, though they also recognized that securing it requires a democratic government. They looked to the future and dedicated their lives to creating a great nation.

Contemporary politicians often talk about the future, but their rhetoric is refuted by a readiness to do whatever it takes to win the next election. Our liberty is waning, and may soon be totally eclipsed.

As individuals and together, *We the People* have to restore effective government for ourselves and our posterity.

★　★　★　★　★

The Bill of Rights Renewed

When the Founders sent the Constitution to the states to be ratified, people were dissatisfied. After decades of British rule and despotism, Americans were wary, worried that the new national government might abuse its powers. State conventions instructed representatives to add "further declaratory and restrictive clauses." Congress authorized twelve amendments, ten were soon ratified by three-fourths of the states, and we got the Bill of Rights.[31]

The First Amendment protects our freedom of religion, free speech, a free press, and our right to assemble and protest peacefully. But rights are mere theories when people lack the means to assert and defend them. Too many of us are struggling to pay our bills, busy and distracted with urgent concerns. Too often, consequently, our rights can be threatened or violated, and we're powerless to respond effectively.

The Second Amendment is a constant controversy, with countless disputes and lawsuits about its meaning, history, and consequences. What was a "well-regulated militia," and is that phrase still meaningful? Who should be allowed to carry guns, openly or concealed? Should some guns be banned entirely? Kids are shot every day. Children find guns and shoot friends, siblings, or themselves. Guns are often used in suicides. When Americans are more united with Citizen Dividends, we might soon reach consensus on sensible gun policies.

The Third Amendment reminds us of the abuses people suffered during the colonial period. British soldiers would commandeer homes and demand to be fed and quartered. Today, in many countries, innocent people's homes can be destroyed in an instant by drones, grenades, or missiles. This amendment, therefore, might induce us to call for basic income wherever there is war or terrorism.

The Fourth Amendment has renewed relevance due to modern information technologies. Government has immense powers to conduct surveillance, search our data, and invade our privacy. It also has a reason or pretext: terrorism. When people are afraid, privacy can seem like a luxury; many of us accept surveillance, even invite it, while urging or demanding obedience by other folks. Personal privacy is valuable. We have to be vigilant. Vigilance requires effort and costs money.

The Fifth Amendment protects us from abuses by government prosecutors. It mandates a grand jury before charging anyone with a capital crime, and it prohibits charging anyone twice for the same offense. We cannot be compelled to testify against ourselves. Government cannot seize property without due process, and must pay compensation. But these protections are often inadequate; preparing and presenting a defense is expensive.

The Sixth Amendment concerns judicial practices, our rights to a speedy trial by an impartial jury, to confront witnesses, to present a defense, and to have counsel. Getting charged with a crime can be financially, emotionally, and socially devastating — particularly when one is innocent. And officials sometimes make mistakes.

The Seventh Amendment addresses civil matters, and preserves our right to a trial by jury. But corporations regularly ask us to sign agreements for binding arbitration; most of us sign, sometimes without reading. Arbitration sounds fair, and in theory it is, but the playing field is not level. Corporations have in-house counsel, big tax-deductible budgets for legal matters, and continuing relationships with arbitration providers. Regular citizens are mostly on our own.

The Eighth Amendment prohibits excessive bail and fines, and bans cruel and unusual punishment. But people can be stuck in jail because they're poor and can't afford bail. That's cruel, though not unusual, and it violates basic precepts of equal justice. It's also expensive. When every citizen has money for bail, fines, and penalties, justice will be more equal.

The Ninth Amendment says the people retain rights that are not explicitly enumerated in the Constitution. Our rights shall not be denied or disparaged.

The Tenth Amendment reserves to the states, or the people, the powers that are neither prohibited by the Constitution nor assigned by it to the United States.

The Ninth and Tenth Amendments express colonists' core concerns: people are primary, states are sovereign, and the federal government is strictly limited. Throughout the 20th century and continuing in the 21st, the federal government grew larger, costlier, and more intrusive, imposing rules and regulations through an array of agencies, an "administrative state." Are these amendments still significant? What is the ideal blend or balance of powers between individuals, state governments, and our federal government? Conditions change and so must our answers. Citizen Dividends will expedite thoughtful debates and overdue reforms.

★　★　★　★　★

Neither our Constitution nor the Bill of Rights says anything about corporations. That silence, though, was not from ignorance. Most colonies were founded by or as corporations, and British corporations were everywhere seeking profits.

The Boston Tea Party was partly a protest against a global corporation, the East India Company, which owned the tea. Protests occurred throughout the colonies, though less dramatic and less remembered. Colonists were enraged by taxes levied to subsidize British companies: corporate welfare. Shareholders included King George III and members of Parliament: crony capitalism. British troops protected company property and profits: public-private partnerships.[32]

The Founders decided to leave corporate charters to the states. In the nation's early decades, state legislatures publicly debated charter requests, only issued charters that served public purposes, and imposed strict limits on ownership, operations, and duration. *We the People* were sovereign.

As America industrialized in the 1800s, owners of corporations gained wealth and political power, and that accelerated with the Civil War. The Fourteenth Amendment was written to protect the equal rights of all citizens, ratified in 1868. Corporations promptly began citing it in lawsuits, claiming that they are "persons."

One case, *Santa Clara County v. Southern Pacific Railroad,* reached the Supreme Court in 1886, and the Court created a new legal doctrine: *corporate personhood.* Congress never authorized that. *We the People* never debated it. Yet the Court has reaffirmed it repeatedly, as a precedent, and expanded it in 2010, with its ruling in *Citizens United v. Federal Election Commission.*[33]

Perhaps we should admit that our republic is lost, our democracy a pretense — that we are ruled by the rich, a plutocracy, and by big corporations, a corporatocracy.

Admit and accept it?

Or *change* it! We can wage – and win – a peaceful democratic revolution to rediscover, revitalize, and realize America's founding ideals and values: *We the People* renewed.

CHAPTER 11

Our Strategy

Are you ready for basic income; for a thoughtful debate, at least? Or do you have more questions first?

A leap of faith may be required. This plan affects all aspects of our lives, our culture, our society, and our government, so it's beyond the scope of standard analyses. But nearly everyone seems to agree that our political system is dysfunctional, and that current policies are flawed or inadequate, sometimes counterproductive. Multiple problems are serious, getting worse, and causing irreversible harm to millions of people in the United States and billions around the world. We can leap or we will suffer.

One question is whether a state or city can enact a version. The answer is *yes*.

Alaskans have a small basic income, the Permanent Fund Dividend, since 1982. Every resident gets an equal cash payment every year, a variable amount between $1,000 and $2,100. They love it. The outcomes have been studied, the benefits verified. Income inequality is lower in Alaska than any other state, and the PFD is the main reason. Maybe they'll expand it, increasing the amount with additional revenue sources: PFD Plus.*

---

* The money is from oil royalties and investments; that's why it varies. Investments are diversified to outlast the oil; that's what makes it permanent. Recipients must reside in the state for more than six months of the year, and it includes children. The PFD was $1,606 in 2019. It was $2,072 in 2015, a record; that's $8,288 for a family of four.

Local programs were tested in a series of Income Maintenance Experiments between 1967 and 1974, funded by the federal Office of Economic Opportunity. In urban, suburban, and rural communities around the country, a total of 8,500 people received guaranteed monthly payments. Researchers tracked work hours, incomes, family status, and other variables. Total work hours declined — though the details were good news. Women chose to stay home with young children; teens stayed in, or went back to, school; men left bad jobs and were temporarily out of work while seeking better jobs. People did what was best for themselves and their families, and their choices were good for society.

Americans work more hours today than in the 1970s. In most families, both parents have to work, and parents with young kids rely on daycare. With basic income, everyone will have opportunities to seek better jobs, be full-time parents, stay in school or return to school, or just get more sleep. A voluntary decline will end involuntary unemployment.

Another local program has been ongoing since 1997. The Eastern Band of Cherokee Indians in North Carolina distributes casino profits to all members of the tribe, including children. Researchers from Duke University have been studying the outcomes and comparing recipients with residents of nearby communities. The evidence "strongly suggests that on the whole, universal basic income works."

A local experiment in Canada included a whole town, Dauphin, Manitoba. Between 1974 and 1979, poor residents received unconditional funds to cover basic expenses. The results: a steep drop in poverty, better education outcomes, and significant gains in people's health. Local programs have also been tested in Namibia, India, Kenya, Finland, and other countries — with positive outcomes in every case. *

Local campaigns will be rather straightforward. Most folks generally understand local issues, policies, and politics, and local officials are often accessible. Activists can attract allies by citing specific programs to cut or

---

* The Permanent Fund Dividend, Income Maintenance Experiments, and Eastern Cherokee program are in Appendix 1. International activities are in Appendix 3.

reform, identifying specific sources for additional revenues, and calculating the potential basic income. Talk with friends, neighbors, coworkers, and other people, and suggest a choice: Are you content with the status quo? Or would you rather have the money?

Local campaigns will be necessary even after we have a national program. Where the cost of living is high, residents will want or need additional funds. Local businesses will also want that, to keep their customers from moving away.

Every local effort helps move these ideas forward. Cities and states that act quickly are likely to be policy models and tourist magnets.

Politics is Personal

Democracy, when it's truly healthy, includes everyone as equals. Regular citizens decide what we want for our cities, our states, and our country. Then we select representatives to help us get what we want. Elected officials are public servants.

Our political system is "inverted." Elected officials are VIPs, often acting like, and getting treated like, celebrities. Politics today is reality TV. Politicians are the stars, performing roles that are mostly or entirely scripted. Special interests are the writers, directors, producers, and advertisers. Regular folks are the audience. Our only input, and only at specified intervals, is to give a thumbs up or thumbs down.[34]

We individuals and *We the People* have to reclaim our proper role. We are, and must be, the real executive producers. We have the power to hire – and fire – elected officials and special interests, and to direct them to serve our interests. Citizen Dividends will be regular reminders of our role and our power.

Liberal? Conservative? The best of both!

Before we're liberals or conservatives, and before we're Democrats or Republicans or members of another party or group, we're Americans. More fundamentally, we're human beings. Our humanity defines and unites us. Political labels distract and divide us.

In current discourse, *liberal* is pro-government, while *conservative* means anti-government and pro-market, pro-business, pro-private enterprise. But everyone knows, from personal experience, that government is necessary. And that it's sometimes ineffective, intrusive, oppressive, or abusive. The labels' flaws are obvious when we consider Social Security and Medicare. "Liberals" are fighting to preserve the status quo, so they're conservative on these issues. "Conservatives" want to privatize the programs; that's not conservative, it's retrograde or reactionary.

Recent policies are predominantly *neoliberal* or *neoconservative*. Neoliberal economic policies favor government support for private companies; that's how we got corporate welfare, corporate tax cuts, deregulation, privatization, and globalization. Neoconservative foreign policies aim to impose markets and expand opportunities for American companies, especially for investors; that's why our government backs autocrats and military rulers, and why our government botched the wars in Afghanistan and Iraq. Neoliberal is not liberal. Neoconservative is not conservative. Both sets of policies enrich big corporations – CEOs, shareholders, lobbyists, et al. – while exploiting people and our planet. Both ideologies view regular folks as consumers primarily, and both dissuade or deter us from thinking and acting as citizens.

Political labels, however, ought to be extraneous. When we discuss the plan's details, let's speak for ourselves, as individuals, and simply state our preferences.

You might want a large basic income to maximize personal liberty, to cut government deeply and quickly, or to ensure that all parents can provide for their children. You might prefer a smaller amount to keep taxes low, to reduce budget deficits, or to preserve incentives to work and earn. There may be specific programs you'd eliminate immediately, others you'd reform carefully, gradually.

Start with stating personal preferences, concerns, values, and goals. Shed and avoid abstract labels. We'll be more ready to compromise, more likely to succeed.

The best of both, liberal and conservative, working together to achieve common interests.

We the People Versus the Status Quo

Our broken government is mired in the politics of left vs. right, liberals vs. conservatives, Democrats vs. Republicans. This plan shifts the dynamics. It's regular folks, *We the People,* vs. special interests and the status quo.

Imagine a primary election, Democratic or Republican, for a local, state, or national office. Suppose one candidate campaigns for Citizen Dividends, while others push their usual policies. Proponents can claim, accurately, that they represent the party's core values.

Democrats can quote Franklin Roosevelt's call for "a second Bill of Rights" that establishes "a new basis of security and prosperity ... for all — regardless of station, race, or creed." Cite Lyndon Johnson on civil rights, the Great Society, and the War on Poverty, and show how basic income will advance these causes. Also Martin Luther King Jr., "The solution to poverty is to abolish it directly by a now widely discussed measure: the guaranteed income." Democrats want prompt action to curtail global warming; a widely-endorsed approach is a carbon tax and dividend, and that's what this plan is, with the dividend first to win broad public support.

Republicans can refer to Ronald Reagan on freedom, free enterprise, individual initiative, and cutting government, presenting Citizen Dividends as a way to realize his vision. Most Republicans want to cut taxes, and many favor a flat tax. One way to make a flat tax practical, and the only way to make it popular, is to combine it with a basic income. An early, forceful, and persistent champion of the flat tax was economist Milton Friedman. He also wrote "We should replace the ragbag of specific welfare programs with a single comprehensive program of income supplements in cash — a negative income tax."

In general elections, suppose one candidate – only one – campaigns for this plan. Proponents can quote the other party's platform and promises: "If that's what you want, vote for me." Proponents might also denounce their opponent as an agent or tool of special interests. Landslide victories are likely.

A three-way race might have an independent proponent running against two major-party candidates with their usual policies. Independents can educate voters about the fact that moderate Democrats and moderate Republicans supported guaranteed income in the past. Then attack both parties for dropping the idea and betraying regular folks. The status quo is bipartisan. This plan is perfect for independent campaigns.

Smaller parties can craft versions as vehicles for their values. Some parties are religious, and can highlight biblical commandments to provide for the poor. Some parties are socialist, and might promote prospects for worker-owned businesses. The Green Party already endorses "livable income," in their platform since 2004. Libertarians can emphasize personal liberty, perhaps cite Friedrich Hayek's support for "the security of a minimum income." A current third party might soon be second or first.

Basic income activists from any party, or independents, can present themselves as the true voices for hope, change, reform, and progress, while calling on all Americans to work together as *We the People*.

Peaceful Democratic Revolution

The Declaration of Independence proclaims government's core purpose: to secure our unalienable rights to life, liberty, and the pursuit of happiness. But our government has become "destructive of these ends" and has subjected us to "a long train of abuses and usurpations, pursuing invariably the same object."

Our Constitution includes a mandate to promote the general welfare. But current policies are *specific*, not general, and mainly sustain the specific *wealthfare*, wealthy individuals and corporations and other special interests.

America today is a plutocracy, corporatocracy, or special-interest-ocracy. Maybe an elective autocracy.

The first American revolution was fought by regular citizens, uncountable thousands of unknown volunteers. They were pursuing justice, liberty, and happiness. They served and sacrificed. And they succeeded.

Now is our time to make history.

CHAPTER 12

Now

The Declaration of Independence concludes with these words:

> And for the support of this Declaration, with a firm reliance on the protection of divine providence, we mutually pledge to each other our lives, our fortunes, and our sacred honor.

Signers knew the risks. If captured by the British, they would have been executed for treason.

Sign on for Citizen Dividends, and know the rewards. Our lives will improve, our fortunes will increase, and our honor will flourish.

Attracting Allies

What is the America you want to live in, say in five or ten years? What are your dreams for your children and grandchildren? Would you like $1,000 a month, a guaranteed income, added to what you have or earn?

These are questions we can ask anyone, anywhere. Hope is attractive, and these questions inspire it, inviting all of us to envision a desired future. Questions are most compelling when we listen respectfully, with follow-up questions and dialogue.

Most politicians only pretend to listen. Instead of inspiring hope, they incite fear and distrust: "Be afraid if my opponent wins. Don't believe what he or she says." They're also mired in nostalgia. Democrats love New Deal and Great Society programs; Republicans revere Ronald Reagan, and Donald Trump promises to "make America great again." They're looking in the rearview mirror, driving with their foot on the brakes.

With this plan, we'll be driving confidently toward a peaceful, prosperous future. Confidence is attractive.

Attracting is different from convincing, persuading, or recruiting. Attracting is easier, even enjoyable. We can engage people through songs, stories, satire, and such, combined with respectful, encouraging questions. People will want to join us.

We can – indeed should, at least aspire to – view everyone as potential allies, likely to endorse basic income when they understand it. Understanding requires time. As Thomas Paine wrote in *Common Sense,* "Time makes more converts than reason."

We're laying the foundations for a healthy democracy, so we should start with friends, family, and neighbors — personal and local. Include young people, to inspire and motivate them to be active citizens. Also people who are turned off or turned away from politics, or were never turned on; they may be eager to overthrow the status quo.

To sustain our confidence, and to restore it after setbacks, we should meet occasionally with friends and allies to share stories, strategies, tactics, and hugs. Community is comforting and uplifting, and many of us experience that in religious services. Gathering together is valuable, even when we're preaching to the choir. Meetings are occasions to learn the words and the music, and to rehearse, so we can sing on key and make a joyful noise.

Likely allies are people whose jobs are threatened, endangered, or already lost to robots, computers, voice recognition, artificial intelligence, and related technologies. Autonomous vehicles will displace millions of jobs driving trucks, taxis, and buses. Jobs are also being disrupted and lost for lawyers, doctors, accountants, journalists, and other professionals; much of their work now performed with software or remotely, in India for instance.

One tactic for attracting allies is to question comments about left versus right, liberal versus conservative. When we encounter these concepts, we can present this plan as the best of both. Send emails, phone talk-radio shows, post on social media, speak-out at public events, write letters to the editors of newspapers and magazines, create and circulate songs and stories. Every contact is a potential ally.

In our emails, conversations, and other communications, we should emphasize the moral underpinnings of basic income. Moral arguments are central to the Declaration of Independence, and inspired the movements that abolished slavery, won the right for women to vote, enacted civil rights laws in the 1960s, and achieved marriage equality for gays and lesbians. The moral imperative with this plan is self-evident: basic human rights for everyone — justice, liberty, dignity, and a baseline of equality. Morality, for most of us, includes patriotism, so let's also highlight patriotic values.

Educating Ourselves

Through campaigning for this plan, we're learning that our government truly is ours. We're learning to act as citizens, not merely passive consumers, customers, clients, critics, or spectators. We're learning that politics is meaningful and can be satisfying.

Our learning can include reading about related ideas from Thomas Jefferson, Thomas Paine, the Progressive era, the origin of Social Security, the 1960s, and so on. Reviewing the history helps us stay motivated. Telling the story is a way to attract allies.*

One lesson is to postpone committing to the details. The Townsend Plan and Share Our Wealth called for sums that seemed excessive, imprudent, un-

---

* To assist with learning and telling the story, Appendix 1 is chronological and contains many quotes. When talking with liberals, start with Franklin Roosevelt, Lyndon Johnson, and Martin Luther King Jr. With conservatives, cite Friedrich Hayek, Milton Friedman, and other Nobel laureate economists. With CEOs and entrepreneurs, mention Peter Drucker, Jeremy Rifkin, and Silicon Valley billionaires. With religious people, talk about the Bible and its decrees to love and serve the poor. With secular folks, Robert Theobald, Erich Fromm, and Buckminster Fuller.

affordable. Critics could readily attack or ridicule the plans and proponents. Potential allies were deterred.

A second lesson is to compromise. Richard Nixon's Family Assistance Plan and George McGovern's Demogrants were fiscally sound, designed by respected economists, but blocked through political maneuvers. Nixon's plan was denounced by welfare rights groups, who insisted that the amount was too small; if activists had endorsed it, it would have passed, and they could have campaigned for increases or local supplements. McGovern's proposal was opposed by labor unions seeking job guarantees for their members; instead, unions might have underscored the universal benefits, and used that emphasis to expand their membership. Political maneuvers, though less public and more personal, also blocked Jimmy Carter's Program for Better Jobs and Income Support.

Third, a mass movement is imperative. Populists and Progressives achieved major reforms in the early 1900s, enacting policies we take for granted. Millions of Americans supported the Townsend Plan and Share Our Wealth in 1935, and they generated the political will to enact Social Security. Mass protests won big victories in the 1960s, and civil rights organizers were extending their efforts and demanding an end to poverty, until Martin Luther King Jr. was killed and the movement lost momentum. There were no marches, rallies, or demonstrations in support of Nixon's plan or McGovern's or Carter's.

The summary lesson: *We the People* win when we're smart, strategic, and resolute.

Educating ourselves can also start with issues or problems. Select health-care, say, or education or immigration, and consider the current situation. What's happening? Who's affected? Are you okay with that? Then contrast current policies with the basic income alternative, imagining and thinking about what we might gain. Benefits will be obvious, even if the basic income is local, not national, and the issue or problem is remote. For example, after any flood, wildfire, earthquake, hurricane, or tornado, people will have funds to help relatives and refugees.*

You might join or start a group, choose one issue each week or month, and discuss it at public meetings or potluck dinners. Talk about what's possible with a local basic income, and what to demand in a national plan. Consider the amount, program cuts, tax reforms, and other details. Review strategies and tactics. Say what you personally will do or contribute.

Organizing Actively

Public meetings and other events are opportunities to reach out to politicians, journalists, educators, clergy, and other potential allies. Invite them to share their ideas and opinions, or just to listen and learn.

Politicians, probably, will praise the plan and proponents, while refusing to commit; vague promises are a standard political practice. Our first goal is to get them to say the words *basic income* or *Citizen Dividends* (or UBI, guaranteed income, negative income tax, Freedom Dividend, or other term). They'll be on the record. We can quote them when we talk with our friends, on social media, and to journalists. If politicians won't commit, perhaps their opponents will be more courageous.

Some politicians will want to see polls, petitions, or other signs of public support, and some will conduct their own polls. Polls and petitions can be persuasive, though we have to read the fine print. Special interest opponents will also be polling and petitioning, and they'll inflate costs, distort details, and exaggerate the number of people who will quit jobs or misuse the money. Then they'll publicize their "data" to amplify doubts, disputes, and disagreements.

---

* Floods, etc., are reasons to act quickly; the next event might be tomorrow. With basic income, even the poorest will have money to prepare, to flee if necessary, and then to recover and move forward.

We've seen a huge surge in refugees over recent years, people fleeing floods, wars, and other disasters, and the numbers are forecast to increase significantly with global warming. Basic income will be the most cost-effective response. And the truly humane response.

Some politicians will propose pilot projects. That sounds positive and prudent, a way to assess possibilities and evaluate variations. Yet we already know the auspicious outcomes from the Income Maintenance Experiments in the 1960s and '70s. We can also be guided by past or current programs in Finland, Holland, Germany, India, and elsewhere, including privately-funded projects in the United States.[35]

Is another pilot project really necessary? Or is that a delaying tactic? When politicians call for studies, commissions, task forces, or "pilot projects," an underlying motive might be fear of losing support from special interests. Delay is costly. Millions of Americans are hungry, homeless, struggling. Calling for a pilot project, in effect, is telling those people that we don't trust them, don't respect them, and won't help them until someday later or never. In the time it would take to conduct a pilot project, we can be organizing, mobilizing, and possibly enacting this plan.

Organizing requires people who are willing to lead. Let's cultivate leaders among ourselves and our friends, becoming leaders. Leaders might also be elected officials who join our parade, earn our respect, and make their way to the front.

As potential leaders arise, emerge, or join us, we want them to be true public servants. Some would-be leaders are wannabe celebrities; some celebrities are wannabe leaders; and sometimes we confuse the two, mistaking celebrities for leaders while treating leaders as celebrities. True leaders seek to inspire and encourage everyone to act together as *We the People*. True public servants value personal dreams and goals.

Mobilizing Politically

Mobilizing is necessary mainly to elect or re-elect our allies. Beyond elections – before, during, and after – it's doing whatever is required to force government to act.

We can build on the efforts and successes of the Tea Party, Occupy, Black Lives Matter, and #MeToo. Regardless of whether we agree (or disagree) with their ideas, most of us can appreciate their anti-status-quo anger; most of us share it. Activists from each of these movements – and other groups too, on a wide range of issues – might endorse basic income to advance their causes. They may be eager to join us in organizing rallies, marches, sit-ins, and media alerts. They might be our champions as candidates in the next election.

The next election could be a special election to fill a vacant office. Special elections are great opportunities for us. Schedules are tight, turnout normally low. Campaigns can be referendums, basic income versus the status quo. With every election, special and general, we'll refine our strategies, tactics, and rhetoric as we prepare for future victories.

As we get closer to any election, we'll be less concerned with attracting politicians, more inclined to confront them: "Endorse Citizen Dividends, or we'll denounce you as an agent of special interests, an obstacle to progress." Maybe they'll join us. Maybe they'll refuse and lose, then reassess and reemerge as our allies.

We have to be willing to switch parties, at least one-time-only. Too many of us have been too loyal for too long, while the two major parties have been too self-serving, often taking supporters for granted. A readiness to switch parties, or to confront and change a party from within, is vital for a healthy democracy.

Every vote for any version is a step forward.

Writing the Bill

One way to attract and educate allies is to draft a bill or ballot initiative. Activists can highlight that term, draft, then invite open discussions and revisions. With the first draft and first bill, our main goals are to attract allies and build consensus.

A local bill can simply endorse the idea, perhaps call for a state or national plan. Or, more bold and ambitious, initiate a local program and instruct officials to act.

Ballot initiatives are powerful tools, perfect for our purposes. Activists can draft a proposal, collect signatures, and get their idea onto the ballot. If it passes, it's the law. This is an option in many cities, 24 states, and the

District of Columbia. With an initiative on the ballot, politicians, pundits, and interest groups are compelled to comment: for or against, they'll publicize the plan. If it wins, politicians who endorsed it are likely to also win. Any initiative, anywhere, even if it doesn't pass, can produce real gains for building our movement.*

Local bills and ballot initiatives may have to specify the sources of funds (program cuts, tax reforms, block grants from the jurisdiction(s) above), along with any required waivers, approvals, or enabling legislation from the jurisdiction(s) above. The basic income might be fairly small or only a goal. It might vary with economic conditions, like Alaska's PFD.

The first national bill can simply set an amount, say $500, $750, or $1,000 a month, and a flat tax rate, say 15, 20, 25, or 30 percent. This is the core plan. After we enact it, any version, *We the People* can focus on cutting programs, reforming other taxes, and so on.†

Passing the Law

One or two elected officials can introduce a bill in a city council, state legislature, or the U.S. Congress. We'll organize rallies and other public events to celebrate the bill, praising the sponsors, seeking cosponsors, and pressing party leaders to move it forward.

Candidates in diverse parties might offer distinct versions. Or similar versions, while emphasizing different goals, features, priorities, and possibilities.

---

* Millions of Americans first heard about basic income in October 2013, when activists in Switzerland submitted signatures for a ballot initiative. Their campaign was widely reported around the world.

† We might start even smaller, a basic income of $200 or $300 a month.

A small start can be a slight change in the tax code. The EITC can be "fully refundable," so folks with no income also receive it, ideally distributed monthly. (The child tax credit too, see Endnote 4.) Or change the standard deduction to a credit, and give it to everyone. A bill to do that, the Tax Cut for the Rest of Us Act of 2006, H.R. 5257, was introduced in Congress but never debated.

Then, step-by-step, consider further reforms. An incremental strategy for a gradual revolution.

- Democrats can focus on social, economic, and environmental justice, presenting this plan as a way to empower all Americans to work together for sustainability and peace.

- Republicans can highlight their continuing commitments to cutting taxes, shrinking government, rescinding regulations, and dethroning special interests. Drain the swamp.

- Greens, Libertarians, and independents can emphasize efforts to renew our political system, presenting themselves as the true agents of transformation.

Passing the law will be mostly straightforward where elected allies are a majority, though if they're in different parties we may have to mobilize to compel them to compromise. Where we have only a few elected allies, we'll employ greater force, with rallies, sit-ins, strikes, and such. Mass protests are most effective with specific demands, in our case to pass the law and implement it immediately. A rally or sit-in might surround a city council, state legislature, or the U.S. Capitol while officials are in session, blocking the exits so they can't leave until they vote for it.

★ ★ ★ ★ ★

Citizen Dividends will transform our politics. Every American will have monthly reminders that we are citizens, and equal; that we live in one country, united; and that we have reasons to act together, *We the People.*

Basic income is only a first step. Our political system has been failing for decades, our government is broken in multiple ways. Most of us are struggling with debt, worrying about our retirement prospects, worrying about our kids and how they'll manage. Most of us are upset or angry about crime, taxes, healthcare, education, immigration, global warming, national security, and other matters. We've got a lot of work to do.

We want and deserve – and can have – efficient, effective, responsive government at all levels.

We can have a politics of consensus and conviviality — a politics of common sense.

*   *   *   *   *

What do you think? Do you like these ideas? Should we enact some version?

You, your family, and every American might soon have a basic income, the money in our hands. A peaceful revolution for personal dignity, democracy, liberty, justice, and peace.

Are you ready to help make history?

We can start now.

From the Author

In the introduction, To the Reader, I asked you to pretend we're friends who haven't seen each other in a while, perhaps not since high school, and to imagine that this book was inspired by our shared concerns. That's how I've been thinking about you.

Before I began writing this book, *politics is personal* was abstract, a theory. It became concrete through seeing you as a friend and seeking to connect. I've been actively imagining multiple diverse versions of "you," unique individuals with distinct dreams, goals, and concerns. While reading, did you feel included and respected? I hope so.

To help you appreciate these ideas, I kept it brief. And I've been extra careful to be accurate with the economics, politics, history, and facts about recent events. If you believe I've been too brief – on an issue that affects you personally, perhaps – and if you find any errors or omissions or anything out-of-date, please publish your comments on blogs, social media, and other outlets. Then I and other folks can learn from you.

You might think I'm too optimistic – or naïve or foolish – and too quick to conjecture, leaping to conclusions without adequate evidence or analysis. Maybe you feel that I too often repeat myself. Optimism, conjecture, and repetition are necessary, I believe, to cut through the nonstop noise, nonsense, and negativity in the news. My optimism, in part, is cheerleading.

You've probably noticed that there's almost nothing about me, no narrative or anecdotes or personal information. One reason was to help you imagine that we're friends. Another reason, to keep the book short and straightforward. Third, to help me – force me, actually – to focus on *you*. Most important, to make it easier for you to consider these ideas directly, candidly, without biases or prejudices that might deter you, or anyone, from reading. I want everyone to feel welcome.

Our political system, today, is more partisan, polarized, and paralyzed than before the last election, and far worse than when I conceived this book in early 2011. Even so, writing it enhanced my faith in democracy. I'm now more confident that regular folks are capable of governing ourselves. And more certain that we must. Confident and certain, sincerely, though I'm also more aware of the challenges and obstacles.

I was completing a first draft when the 2016 election began, and I revised it while seeking to appreciate all sides, seeking to be truly nonpartisan or transpartisan. A major editing challenge was to identify my biases, and then to counter or delete statements that might be misinterpreted. That process continued throughout the 2018 election and into the impeachment hearings in the fall of 2019. I'm sure I still have blind spots, however, and I request your forbearance.

Friends have warned me to expect personal attacks. If that happens, online or direct, I hope you'll defend me. Please. Personal attacks, in my opinion, are evidence that the attacker is bound or blinded by self-interest, or an agent of some special interest. Personal attacks are a sign and a cause of dysfunctional politics.

I invite disagreements about details. Let's talk, debate, even argue – though always with mutual respect – while seeking possibilities to agree. Is there a version of this plan you might endorse? Are you willing to compromise?

When I mentioned high school in the introduction and above, I was recalling friends from those years. We wanted to create a better world, we weren't embarrassed to say so, and we believed we would succeed. I see similar idealism, ambition, and optimism today. Young people can lead the movement for basic income. Perhaps they must. They have the most to lose if the status quo persists, and the most to gain from our success.

Through writing, I learned to be more wary of everyday public or political discourse. As I discussed in Chapter 1, the political *we* is often deceptive, coercive, or self-serving. When public figures say "we," I now have an internal alarm, a voice that states, "There is no 'we.'" Then it asks several questions: Who, specifically, is the speaker talking about? Does that "we" include me? Did I consent? Do I consent? Did other folks consent? If there was no active consent, I discount, dismiss, or dispute whatever the person said.

Another alarm sounds when I hear "they." Politicians, when speaking to supporters, often refer to unspecified opponents as "they," "them," or "those people." That's common in casual speech, especially gossip, and it's generally okay. Though politicians occasionally go further, and my alarm gets louder, a warning siren. Some politicians denounce or denigrate opponents. Some demonize or dehumanize. Some are demagogues. And I sometimes wish the siren was audible, to alert us all.

I aspire to respect and connect with everyone, as unique individuals who can benefit with these ideas. This is why I avoid abstract terms and labels, including most forms of "identity politics." Two terms I particularly criticize are *the market* and *the economy,* and I discuss the reasons in Chapter 5, the section on "Economic Discourse."

In the final section of Chapter 10, I implied that corporate welfare, crony capitalism, and public-private partnerships are similar to the policies Britain imposed on the colonies before 1776. That's accurate, in my opinion. The colonists rebelled against both King George III and British corporations.*

Now, after repeatedly asking what you think and what you want, and after several years of considering you a friend, I feel obliged to share my an-

---

* Before they rebelled, the colonists endured years of abuse. The Declaration of Independence conceded that "mankind are more disposed to suffer, while evils are sufferable, than to right themselves by abolishing the forms to which they are accustomed."

I often think about that wisdom. We've had decades of government by special interests, for special interests. How much longer will we suffer? When will we rebel?

swers. I favor a fairly large basic income, $1,000 a month or more, with local supplements, plus a parallel program for children. Though I primarily want it soon, ASAP, even if it's only $100. Looking back at my life, I see many times when any amount would have freed me to make better choices, probably leading to greater success and more happiness. Thus, I haven't been focusing only on you. This book is also about, and for, me. It's personal.

I want to cut government deeply at the federal level, though only cautious cuts in local programs. Local governments are closest to the people they serve, and are therefore most able to ensure that no one is harmed. Children, seniors, and people with special needs must be protected as programs are cut.

A consensus rate for a flat tax seems likely to be between 15 and 30 percent, like the tables in Chapter 3, and I'd agree to 40 percent. Then, whether quickly or gradually, I want to cut income taxes and to implement a VAT, financial transaction taxes, and higher fossil fuel taxes with periodic increases. Local governments should be funded mainly through taxes on land values and related takings. I'm eager to see more analyses of the Payments Tax, which I briefly describe in Appendix 2.

On most other issues, however, aside from what I've already written, I prefer to be quiet. Issues are complicated, respected authorities disagree, decisions and policies ought to be local, and, frankly, in many cases I'm not yet sure what I think. Though I am ready to speak out on one topic: The best way to defend America, I'm positive, is to boldly pursue peace and disarmament — and to invite, entice, or pressure other countries to enact basic income programs.

Ideas aim to inspire action, I believe. Talking, writing, reading, and listening are valuable and often necessary for deciding what to do and preparing to do it. Yet ideas are most meaningful when we apply them, doing something new or different.

This movement requires thousands of leaders, maybe millions — maybe you. I want to live in a true democracy, without leaving the country. That means I'm counting on you. I hope we'll be allies and friends in the successful campaign for Citizen Dividends.

From the Author

Now is your time to say what you want for yourself, your family, your community, and your country. And our time to act together as *We the People*.

Appendix 1

Related Ideas and Efforts

Biblical Origins

The Bible commands us to do justice, to show mercy, and to provide for the poor. To do unto others as we would have them do unto us. And, in Leviticus, to forgive debts and redistribute property.

> You shall make the fiftieth year holy, and proclaim liberty throughout the land to all its inhabitants. It shall be a jubilee for you, and each of you shall return to his own property, and each of you shall return to his family. (Leviticus 25:10)

This passage expresses the link between liberty and property. For liberty, everyone needs property, at least food and shelter; therefore, property must sometimes be redistributed. "Proclaim liberty throughout the land" is inscribed on the Liberty Bell, which rang in Philadelphia to announce the signing of the Declaration of Independence.

The gospels include many parables of Jesus aiding and comforting the poor. He fed the masses through the miracle of the loaves and fishes, and didn't require people to dig ditches or wash dishes. He commanded us to follow his example and to love our neighbors.

In biblical times, and throughout most human history, people lived in extended families or clans and interacted with neighbors every day. Neighbors depended on each other.

We live in nuclear families, parents and kids only. Many of us live alone. Nearly all of us have neighbors we've never met.

One way to aid, comfort, and love our neighbors is to provide them with a basic income.*

Initial Ideas

Utopia (1516) by **Thomas More,** an English cleric, scholar, and counselor to King Henry VIII, imagined an island with an ideal society. Everyone is employed, men and women are mostly equal, and people and the rulers trust each other. "It would be far more to the point to provide everyone with some means of livelihood, so that nobody's under the frightful necessity of becoming, first a thief, and then a corpse."

In a 1525 essay, "On Assistance To The Poor," **Ludovico Vives** considered the role of the state in supporting residents. Public officials are in the best position to identify the poor who require help, he reasoned, so they should be the ones who deliver relief. He wrote the essay at the request of local officials in Bruges, Belgium, where he lived, and it influenced public policies in England and Germany.

He also wrote about learning, emotions, and memory, and has been called the "father of modern psychology."

---

* For a more theological discussion of the Bible and poverty, see *Always with Us? What Jesus Really Said about the Poor* (2017) by Rev. Dr. Liz Theoharis, codirector of the Kairos Center for Religions, Rights, and Social Justice. She's also cochair of the Poor People's Campaign: A National Call for Moral Revival, with Rev. Dr. William J. Barber II, who wrote a foreword to her book.

America's Founders

Thomas Jefferson, while serving in the Virginia legislature before writing the Declaration of Independence, proposed giving fifty acres of land to any propertyless individual willing to farm it. He discussed his reasons in a letter to James Madison on October 28, 1785,

> The earth is given as a common stock for man to labour and live on. … It is too soon yet in our country to say that every man who cannot find employment but who can find uncultivated land, shall be at liberty to cultivate it, paying a moderate rent. But it is not too soon to provide by every possible means that as few as possible shall be without a little portion of land. The small landholders are the most precious part of the state.

John Adams was on the committee that helped Jefferson draft the Declaration. In 1776, he wrote about the interconnections between liberty, equality, public virtue, and property.

> The only possible way, then, of preserving the balance of power on the side of equal liberty and public virtue, is to make the acquisition of land easy to every member of society … If the multitude is possessed of the balance of real estate, the multitude will have the balance of power, and in that case the multitude will take care of the liberty, virtue, and interest of the multitude, in all acts of government.

James Madison was the primary author of our U.S. Constitution, and the fourth president, after Jefferson. In a 1792 essay on the danger of political parties, he stated that democracy requires "establishing political equality among all." To achieve this, he endorsed

The silent operation of laws, which, without violating the rights of property, reduce extreme wealth to a state of mediocrity, and raise extreme indigence toward a state of comfort.*

Thomas Paine is most esteemed as the author of *Common Sense,* his 1776 pamphlet calling for American independence. In *Agrarian Justice* (1797), he described land as the "common heritage of mankind," and proposed to have landowners pay a "ground rent" into a "national fund." Every citizen would then receive a cash payment at age twenty-one and yearly payments starting at age fifty. "A right, and not a charity."

He summarized his plan on the title page,

Agrarian justice, opposed to agrarian law, and to agrarian monopoly. Being a plan for meliorating the conditions of man by creating in every nation, a national fund, to pay to every person, when arriving at the age of twenty-one years, the sum of fifteen pounds sterling, to enable him or her to begin the world! And also, ten pounds sterling per annum during life to every person now living of the age of fifty years, and to all others when they shall arrive at that age, to enable them to live in old age without wretchedness, and go decently out of the world.

Seniors will "see before them the certainty of escaping the miseries that under other governments accompany old age." Democracy will "have an advocate and an ally in the heart of all nations."

His plan anticipates Henry George and the land value tax, the Alaska Permanent Fund and Permanent Fund Dividend, and proposals from many modern economists, academics, and activists.

---

* Jefferson, Adams, and Madison, and these themes from American history are discussed in *The Crisis of the Middle-Class Constitution: Why Economic Inequality Threatens Our Republic* (2017) by Ganesh Sitaraman, a professor of law at Vanderbilt University.

Andrew Jackson was the seventh president. In his veto of an 1832 bill to renew the charter of the Second Bank of the United States,

> There are no necessary evils in government. Its evils exist only in its abuses. If it would confine itself to equal protection, and, as Heaven does its rains, shower its favors alike on the high and the low, the rich and the poor, it would be an unqualified blessing.

Mid and Late 1800s

English philosopher and economist **John Stuart Mill** published *Principles of Political Economy* in 1848. That was a year of revolutions in France, Germany, Denmark, Hungary, and other European countries; also the year Karl Marx published *The Communist Manifesto*. Partly in response to those events, Mill issued a second edition in 1849.

> I conceive it to be highly desirable that the certainty of subsistence should be held out by law to the destitute able-bodied, rather than that their relief should depend on voluntary charity. ... The state must act by general rules. It cannot undertake to discriminate between the deserving and undeserving indigent. ... The dispensers of public relief have no business to be inquisitors.
>
> What is needed, therefore, is neither private charity nor workhouses, but a legal guarantee of subsistence for all the destitute, whether able-bodied or not, whether deserving or not.

Writing about "the Socialist controversy," he praised a system that

> does not contemplate the abolition of private property, nor even of inheritance; on the contrary, it avowedly takes into consideration, as elements in the distribution of the produce, capital as well as labour. In the distribution, a certain minimum is first assigned for the subsistence of every member of the community, whether capable or not of labour. The remainder of

the produce is shared in certain proportions, to be determined beforehand, among the three elements, Labour, Capital, and Talent.

His book was used widely as an economics text for several decades.

Abraham Lincoln called for, and the federal government enacted, the National Homestead Act of 1862. It granted 160 acres of public land to any head of a family, twenty-one years of age or older, who agreed to reside upon the land and cultivate it for five years. About 720,000 homesteads were established under the law, and homesteads continued to be available in some states until the early 1900s.

The 1880s and '90s were marked by extreme inequality and widespread social unrest. A tiny percentage had vast wealth and enjoyed a "Gilded Age," while most Americans struggled and many starved. The **Populist** and **Progressive movements** provoked major reforms, and we still benefit from their efforts.

Two books were most inspiring. Each sold more than a million copies. (The U.S. population was about sixty million, so today's equivalent would be more than six million copies. Both also sold in huge numbers in other countries.) The authors were political economist **Henry George** and journalist **Edward Bellamy**.

In *Progress and Poverty* (1879), **Henry George** examined why poverty persists or increases as societies become wealthier. The main reason, he concluded, is that a few individuals own or control the land. "There is a fundamental and irreconcilable difference between property in things which are the product of labor and property in land." Society can end poverty, he argued, by removing all taxes on income, spending, buildings, and production, and replacing them with a "single tax" on land.

When Martin Luther King Jr. called for guaranteed income, he quoted *Progress and Poverty*,

The fact is that the work which improves the condition of mankind, the work which extends knowledge and increases power and enriches literature, and elevates thought, is not done to secure a living. ... It is the work of men who perform it for their own sake, and not that they may get more to eat or drink, or wear, or display. In a state of society where want is abolished, work of this sort could be enormously increased.

George published *The Land Question* in 1881, and proposed to tax back all the profits from speculation on land. When speculators profit, the gains are mainly due to public investments in roads, schools, transit, etc., combined with population growth. Those profits, therefore, should be returned to the community.

There would be at once a large surplus over and above what are now considered the legitimate expenses of government. We could divide this, if we wanted to, among the whole community, share and share alike.

George ran for mayor of New York City in 1886 as an independent and nearly won. Supporters claimed, and historians concur, that the election was stolen by the Democrats and their infamous Tammany Hall political machine. The Republican who finished third was Theodore Roosevelt, the future U.S. president.

Modern Georgists extend his ideas to include everything people take from nature: oil, coal, timber, metals, minerals, seafood, etc., along with electromagnetic spectrum and the burdens of pollution. Polluters are degrading our common property – air, water, and land that ought to be pristine – so they should compensate us for our losses.

An 1888 novel, *Looking Backward, 2000–1887,* was one of the most popular and influential books of the 19th century. The story is set in Boston, and mostly occurs in the year 2000. Author **Edward Bellamy** envisioned an ideal society where everyone has food, shelter, healthcare, and education. Men and women have opportunities to display their skills and rise to higher levels. All women have a full year of maternity leave with every child. Everyone from age twenty-one to forty-five has a job, and, as one character explains, "the worker is not a citizen because he works, but works because he is a citizen." People retire at age forty-five and enjoy real security for the rest of their lives. Bellamy foresaw a great increase in civility, creativity, solidarity, and happiness, with no crime and no social problems.

Readers around the United States were excited and motivated, and formed more than 162 "Bellamy clubs" to discuss his ideas and seek ways to implement them. Many readers ran for public office.

Early 20th Century England

Bertrand Russell was a philosopher, mathematician, and humanitarian activist. At the end of World War I, in 1918, he published *Proposed Roads to Freedom: Socialism, Anarchism and Syndicalism.*

> The plan we are advocating amounts essentially to this: that a certain small income, sufficient for necessaries, should be secured to all, whether they work or not, and that a larger income – as much larger as might be warranted by the total amount of commodities produced – should be given to those who are willing to engage in some work which the community recognizes as useful. ... When education is finished, no one should be compelled to work, and those who choose not to work should receive a bare livelihood and be left completely free.

"In Praise of Idleness," a 1932 essay, reasoned that everyone should work just four hours a day.

> I want to say, in all seriousness ... that the road to happiness and prosperity lies in an organized diminution of work.
> Above all, there will be happiness and joy of life, instead of frayed nerves, weariness, and dyspepsia. ... Ordinary men and women, having the opportunity of a happy life, will become more kindly. ... Modern methods of production have given us the possibility of ease and security for all; we

have chosen, instead, to have overwork for some and starvation for others.

... But there is no reason to go on being foolish forever.

He was awarded the Nobel Prize in Literature in 1950.

Scottish engineer and economist **C.H. "Major" Douglas** analyzed many big companies, and concluded that conventional concepts of money are flawed. And that those flaws are major factors in business failures. He was the author of *Economic Democracy* (1920), *Credit Power and Democracy* (1920), and *Social Credit* (1924).

Credit is a public good, he asserted, and access to credit ought to be a right. He proposed a National Credit Account based on all factors of production and consumption, and a **National Dividend** to provide "absolute economic security." The result, "democratic capitalism."

The Social Credit movement spread around the world, with electoral successes in England, Canada, Australia, and New Zealand.

The 1930s

Two national mass movements for guaranteed income, the **Townsend Plan** and **Share Our Wealth**, generated the political pressure to enact **Social Security.**

In 1933, the depth of the Great Depression, **Francis Townsend**, a 65-year-old family physician in Long Beach, CA, wrote a letter to the editor of his local newspaper. He then expanded it into a short pamphlet, the *Old Age Revolving Pension*.

The **Townsend Plan** sought "Liberal financial retirement for the aged with national recovery and permanent prosperity." Everyone aged 60 or older would get $200 a month (adjusted for inflation, roughly $3,500), funded through a 2 percent tax on all business transactions. There were three conditions. Recipients had to obey the law, quit any paid work, and spend the money. That spending would create jobs for younger workers, ending the Depression and producing "permanent prosperity" for society.

Over the following year, 2.2 million people joined Townsend Clubs, an estimated 7,000 clubs throughout the country, and they actively supported candidates in the 1934 election. Congress invited Townsend to present his ideas, which he did in February 1935. President Franklin Roosevelt signed the law creating Social Security on August 14, 1935. But the payments were much smaller than Townsend sought, so he denounced it.

Share Our Wealth called for $2,500 a year for every family (about $44,000 today), funded through taxes on the very rich. They claimed to have 7.7 million members in 1935, with groups in every state.

The founder and leader, **Huey Long,** was a Democratic U.S. Senator and former governor of Louisiana, and was preparing to run for president. But Long was murdered in September 1935, shot by the son of a political rival.

Many people describe Long as a "demagogue" or "populist" — though we should also and always consider the context. Supporters of Share Our Wealth were poor, struggling, often desperate, with valid grievances and meaningful demands.

Franklin Roosevelt established the **President's Committee on Economic Security** in June 1934. Secretary of Labor Frances Perkins, the first woman to serve in any president's cabinet, was the chairperson. Other members were Secretary of the Treasury Henry Morgenthau Jr., Attorney General Homer S. Cummings, Secretary of Agriculture Henry Wallace (who was vice president in Roosevelt's third term, 1941–5), and Federal Emergency Relief Administrator Harry L. Hopkins.

Their January 1935 report called for multiple programs and protections: employment assurance, unemployment compensation, old-age security, security for children, and protection for the risks arising out of ill health.

The one almost all-embracing measure of security is an assured income. A program of economic security, as we vision it, must have as its primary aim the assurance of an adequate income to each human being in childhood, youth, middle age, or old age — in sickness or in health. It must provide safeguards against all of the hazards leading to destitution and dependency. A piecemeal approach is dictated by practical considerations, but the broad objectives should never be forgotten. Whatever measures are deemed immediately expedient should be so designed that they can be embodied in the complete program which we must have ere long.

The Social Security Administration has the full report in the history section of their website: ssa.gov/history/reports/ces.html. (The quote above is at ssa.gov/history/reports/ces5.html.)

British economist **George D. H. Cole**, a professor at Oxford University, proposed a **social dividend** in 1935. All production involves public assets and our common heritage, he reasoned, so all citizens ought to receive a share of the profits.

James Meade, also at Oxford, endorsed the social dividend as a central element in a just society, and was awarded the Nobel Memorial Prize in Economic Sciences in 1977. American economist **Abba Lerner** expressed support in 1936. Polish economist **Oskar Lange** proposed a modified version in 1937. Both were on the faculty of the London School of Economics.

The 1940s and '50s

Franklin Roosevelt gave a State of the Union address on January 6, 1941, more than a year after World War II began in Europe, and eleven months before the United States entered the fighting. His theme was "Four Freedoms."

Freedom of speech and expression ... freedom of every person to worship God in his own way ... freedom from want — which, translated into world terms, means economic understandings which will secure to every nation a healthy peacetime life for its inhabitants — everywhere in the world ... freedom from fear ... .

"Freedom from want" seems unattainable without basic income. With it, the other freedoms may be inevitable.

In his State of the Union on January 11, 1944, and in a radio chat that evening, he proposed "a second Bill of Rights."

> We have come to a clear realization of the fact that true individual freedom cannot exist without economic security and independence. ... People who are hungry and out of a job are the stuff of which dictatorships are made. ... In our day these economic truths have become accepted as self-evident. We have accepted, so to speak, a second Bill of Rights under which a new basis of security and prosperity can be established for all—regardless of station, race, or creed.

Economist and social theorist **Friedrich Hayek** was a champion of free enterprise. *The Road to Serfdom* (1944), the most popular of his many books, condemned government programs because they encroach on markets and constrain people's freedom. Yet he endorsed the goal of providing "the security of a minimum income."

> There can be no doubt that some minimum of food, shelter, and clothing, sufficient to preserve health and the capacity to work, can be assured to everybody. ... [This is] no privilege but a legitimate object of desire ... [that] can be provided for all outside of and supplementary to the market system.

He shared the Nobel in economics in 1974. Five years later, in *Law, Legislation and Liberty, Vol. 3: the Political Order of a Free People* (1979),

> The assurance of a certain minimum income for everyone, or a sort of floor below which nobody need fall even when he is unable to provide for himself, appears not only to be a wholly legitimate protection against a risk common to all, but a necessary part of the Great Society in which the individual no longer has specific claims on the members of the particular small groups into which he was born.

The Great Transformation: the Political and Economic Origins of Our Time (1944), by economic historian **Karl Polanyi**, examined labor, land, money, markets, and the immense changes that occurred with the industrial revolution in England in the late 1700s. Wealthy landowners were enclosing their properties, forcing people off the land and into cities.

> Justices in the Speenhamland region, alarmed by a brutal increase in poverty, child labor, and general suffering, held a meeting in 1795, "a time of great distress" and decided that subsidies in aid of wage should be granted in accordance with a scale dependent upon the price of bread, so that a minimum income should be assured to the poor *irrespective of their earnings.*

Speenhamland "introduced no less a social and economic innovation than the 'right to live.'" Subsidies "became the law of the land over most of the countryside" and lasted for nearly 40 years, despite serious flaws and mounting problems, until the program was ended with the New Poor Law of 1834.

Markets are "embedded" in society, Polanyi showed, neither superior nor separate. For efficient, effective, successful markets, political oversight is necessary. When markets are allowed to self-regulate, personal freedom and democracy are diminished.

We're living through a great disruption, the digital revolution, with many parallels to the industrial revolution. Polanyi's ideas remain relevant, even prescient, and strongly affirm the core principles of basic income.

British writer and politician **Juliet Rhys-Williams** was the first to propose a **negative income tax**, in 1944.

American economist **George Stigler** endorsed it in 1946. He was on the faculty of the University of Chicago, with Milton Friedman, and a founding member of the Mont Pelerin Society with Friedman and Friedrich Hayek. Stigler was awarded the Nobel in economics in 1982.

Eleanor Roosevelt was world-renowned as an advocate for social justice, and in 1948 the newly-formed United Nations invited her to lead a commission on human rights and freedom. Their efforts produced the **Universal Declaration of Human Rights**. The General Assembly adopted it on December 10, 1948, with only eight countries abstaining and none voting against it.

Today, the **UDHR** is widely cited and respected around the world, and many countries have elements of it in their constitutions.

> Article 3: Everyone has the right to life, liberty and security of person.
> Article 25: Everyone has the right to a standard of living adequate for the health and well-being of himself and of his family, including food, clothing, housing and medical care and necessary social services, and the right to security in the event of unemployment, sickness, disability, widowhood, old age or other lack of livelihood in circumstances beyond his control.

In *The New Society* (1949), **Peter Drucker**, a pioneer in business management theory and practice, proposed a **predictable income** to "banish the uncertainty, the dread of the unknown and the deep feelings of insecurity under which the worker today lives." The predictable income would be minimal, and could be varied when economic conditions change.

Guaranteed income, he stated, is fundamentally different from any effort to guarantee jobs or wages. A job or wage guarantee "would not be worth the paper on which it is written. It would give the worker the illusion of security which is bound to be cruelly disappointed" during economic downturns. Such practices could also "freeze the economy ... subsidizing obsolescent industries and restricting, if not stopping, technological progress."

Basic income was first used in 1953, by British economist **George D. H. Cole**.

John Kenneth Galbraith, an economist at Harvard University, published *The Affluent Society* in 1958, and it was a bestseller. Familiar ideas are often flawed, in his view, and he urged readers to question "conventional wisdom" (a phrase he coined, intended as irony).

In a chapter on "The Divorce of Production from Security," he examined the problem of jobs, and concluded that

The answer is to find some way of diminishing the reliance now being placed on production as a source of income. ... to provide alternative sources of income, unrelated to production, to those whom the modern economy employs only with exceptional difficulty or unwisdom.

In 1966, after serving as an advisor to President Kennedy, Galbraith wrote an essay on "The Starvation of the Cities."

We need to consider the one prompt and effective solution for poverty, which is to provide everyone with a minimum income. The arguments against this proposal are numerous, but most of them are excuses for not thinking about a solution, even one that is so exceedingly plausible.

Idleness, we agree, is demoralizing. But even here there is a question: Why is leisure so uniformly bad for the poor and so uniformly good for the exceptionally well-to-do? ... We can easily afford an income floor. ... And there is no antidote for poverty that is quite so certain in its effects as the provision of income.

He revised *The Affluent Society* in 1969, and added a few sentences:

For those who are unemployable, employable only with difficulty, or who should not be working, the immediate solution is a source of income unrelated to production. This has come extensively into discussion under various proposals for a guaranteed income or a negative income tax. The principle common to these proposals is provision of a basic income as a matter of general right.

(He also added a footnote: "A discussion that has developed since the earlier editions of this book. I did not then think such ideas within the realm of practical political feasibility.")

"The Unfinished Business of the Century," a 1999 paper presented at the London School of Economics, focused on two concerns with "high visibility and urgency. The first is the very large number of the very poor even in the richest countries and notably in the United States."

The answer or part of the answer is rather clear: everybody should be guaranteed a decent basic income. A rich country such as the United States can well afford to keep everybody out of poverty. Some, it will be said, will seize upon the income and won't work. So it is now with more limited welfare, as it is called. ... Let us accept some resort to leisure by the poor as well as by the rich.

His second major concern was the need to abolish nuclear weapons. "The most urgent task now and of the new century is to bring to an end the threat of Armageddon."

The 1960s

The Challenge of Abundance (1961), by socio-economist and futurist **Robert Theobald,** examined automation and social trends. "Many changes will be necessary as we move from an economy of scarcity to an economy of abundance." We need "new principles specifically designed to break the link between jobs and income."

He elaborated on these principles and possibilities in a 1963 book, *Free Men and Free Markets.*

> The need is clear: the principle of an economic floor under each individual must be established. This principle would apply equally to every member of society and carry with it no connotation of personal inadequacy or implication that an undeserving income was being received from an over-generous government. ...
>
> Basic Economic Security can be best regarded as an extension of the present Social Security system to a world in which conventional job availability will steadily decline. ...
>
> *We will need to adopt the concept of an absolute constitutional right to an income. This would guarantee to every citizen of the United States ... the right to an income from the federal government sufficient to enable him to live with dignity.*

Basic Economic Security "would be very simple to operate compared to the present mosaic of measures ... which have been introduced at various times in the past to meet the same goal." He called for cutting other programs to pay for the guaranteed income.

Capitalism and Freedom, by economist **Milton Friedman**, was first published in 1962, and has been reprinted many times. In a chapter on the alleviation of poverty, he asserted that "the arrangement that recommends itself on purely mechanical grounds is a negative income tax."

> The advantages of this arrangement are clear. It is directed specifically at the problem of poverty. It gives help in the form most useful to the individual, namely, cash. It is general and could be substituted for the host of special measures now in effect. It makes explicit the cost borne by society. It operates outside the market.

He was an advisor to Barry Goldwater, the Republican candidate for president in 1964, served on President Richard Nixon's committee of economic advisors, and was awarded the Nobel in 1976.

From *Free to Choose* (1980), written with his wife **Rose**, and the basis for a PBS television series,

> We should replace the ragbag of specific welfare programs with a single comprehensive program of income supplements in cash — a negative income tax. It would provide an assured minimum to all persons in need, regardless of the reasons for their need, while doing as little harm as possible to their character, their independence, or their incentives to better their own conditions. ... A negative income tax provides comprehensive reform which would do more efficiently and humanely what our present welfare system does so inefficiently and inhumanely.

He continued to endorse these ideas until his death in 2006.

In his first State of the Union Address, on January 8, 1964, **Lyndon Johnson** declared an "unconditional war on poverty in America."

> Our chief weapons in a more pinpointed attack will be better schools, and better health, and better homes, and better training, and better job opportunities to help more Americans, especially young Americans, escape from squalor and misery and unemployment rolls where other citizens help to carry them.

The War on Poverty was a partial victory. During his administration, 1963-9, the official poverty rate fell from 22 percent to 13 percent. The rate has rarely been lower. (Over the years since then, it has fluctuated between 11 and 15 percent. In 2017, it was 12.3 percent. The poverty threshold that year was $13,064 for a single adult, $25,465 for a family of four; 39.7 million Americans were living on less than that amount. Many economists say the official rate and threshold are flawed, based on outdated measures, and much too low. Some classify 140 million Americans as poor.)

Johnson initiated three significant steps toward guaranteed income. He appointed a **National Commission on Technology, Automation, and Economic Progress** and a **National Commission on Income Maintenance Programs**. He also created the Office of Economic Opportunity, which funded and managed a series of **Income Maintenance Experiments** around the country.

In the spring of 1964, 35 prominent thinkers and political activists, the **Ad-Hoc Committee on the Triple Revolution**, published a 14-page report about three interrelated developments: "cybernation," their term for computers and automation; weaponry, particularly nuclear weapons; and the universal demand for full human rights.

> Gaining control of our future requires the conscious formation of the society we wish to have...
>
> We urge, therefore, that society ... undertake an unqualified commitment to provide every individual and every family with an adequate

income as a matter of right. ... The unqualified right to an income would take the place of the patchwork of welfare measures. ... the distribution of abundance in a cybernated society must be based on criteria strikingly different from those of an economic system based on scarcity.

The committee was convened by the Center for the Study of Democratic Institutions in Santa Barbara, CA. One member was Linus Pauling, recipient of the 1962 Nobel Peace Prize (and a 1954 Nobel Prize in Chemistry). Another was Gunnar Myrdal, who subsequently shared the 1974 Nobel in economics. Robert Theobald was a member. So was Bayard Rustin, a pioneering leader in the civil rights movement.

Their final paragraph:

Democracy, as we use the term, means a community of men and women who are able to understand, express, and determine their lives as dignified human beings. Democracy can only be rooted in a political and economic order in which wealth is distributed by and for people, and used for the widest social benefit. With the emergence of the era of abundance, we have the economic base for a true democracy of participation, in which men no longer need to feel themselves prisoners of social forces and decisions beyond their control or comprehension.

The Triple Revolution report influenced Martin Luther King Jr., and was featured in the award-winning 1967 science-fiction novella "Riders of the Purple Wage" by Philip José Farmer.

The Guaranteed Income: Next Step in Economic Evolution? (1966), edited by Robert Theobald, featured essays by ten renowned social scientists. **Erich Fromm**, an innovator in social and humanistic psychology and a bestselling author, wrote "The Psychological Aspects of the Guaranteed Income."

The principle prevailing throughout most of human history in the past and present is: "He who does not work shall not eat." This threat forced man not only to act in accordance with what was demanded of him but also to think and to feel in such a way that he would not even be tempted to act differently.

Guaranteed income would not only establish freedom as a reality rather than a slogan, it would also establish a principle deeply rooted in Western religious and humanist tradition: man has the right to live, regardless! This right to live, to have food, shelter, medical care, education, etc., is an intrinsic human right that cannot be restricted by any condition, not even the one that he must be socially 'useful.'

The shift from a psychology of scarcity to that of abundance is one of the most important steps in human development. … liberation from fear of starvation, would mark the transition from a prehuman to a truly human society.

Aside from the fact that there is already no work for an ever increasing sector of the population, and hence that the question of incentive for these people is irrelevant. … It can be demonstrated that material incentive is by no means the only incentive for work and effort. First of all there are other incentives: pride, social recognition, pleasure in work itself, etc. Secondly, it is a fact that man, by nature, is not lazy, but on the contrary suffers from the results of inactivity. People might prefer not to work for one or two months, but the vast majority would beg to work, even if they were not paid for it.

Another essay, "Guaranteed Income in the Electric Age," was written by **Marshall McLuhan**, a professor at the University of Toronto widely-known for examining the social impacts of technology and mass communication.

Guaranteed income must increasingly include the satisfaction we gain from effective involvement in meaningful work. "Leisure," which the artist always enjoys, is created by the fullest possible employment of the faculties in creative activity. … The guaranteed income that results from automation could therefore be understood to include that quite unquantifiable factor of joy and satisfaction that results from a free and full disclosure of one's powers in any task organized to permit such activity.

Technology and the American Economy was a 1966 report from the **National Commission on Technology, Automation, and Economic Progress**, appointed by Lyndon Johnson. One conclusion,

> Technological change and productivity are primary sources of our unprecedented wealth, but many persons have not shared in that abundance. We recommend that economic security be guaranteed by a floor under family income. That floor should include both improvements in wage-related benefits and a broader system of income maintenance for those families unable to provide for themselves.

Commission members were presidents of major corporations, presidents of labor unions, and prominent academics. They included Daniel Bell (chairman, Sociology Department, Columbia University); Patrick E. Haggerty (president, Texas Instruments); Edwin H. Land (president, Polaroid Corporation); Walter P. Reuther (president, United Automobile Workers); Robert M. Solow (professor of economics, MIT, and a 1987 Nobel laureate); and Thomas J. Watson Jr. (chairman of the board, IBM Corporation).

From June 1966 to January 1968, the **Ad Hoc Committee for a Guaranteed Income**, based at the University of Chicago School of Social Work, published a series of newsletters "to promote the adoption of a universal, adequate guaranteed income as a citizen's right." Some noteworthy items:

- A report on a conference they sponsored with Robert Theobald, Richard Cloward (professor at Columbia University School of Social Work), George Wiley (Director of the Poverty Rights Action Center), and James Bevel (Southern Christian Leadership Conference).

- Excerpts from a speech by the chairman of IBM, Thomas J. Watson Jr., describing his experience on the National Commission on Technology, Automation, and Economic Progress.

- A review of A *"Freedom Budget" for All Americans,* published by the A. Philip Randolph Institute.

- Notes from a U.S. Chamber of Commerce conference in Washington D.C. on December 9, 1966. Speakers included economists Milton Friedman, Henry Hazlitt, Robert Theobald, and James Tobin.

- Sociologist James W. Wilson's endorsement of income transfers to the poor: "I have found no compelling psychological or theoretical evidence that the souls of the poor are in greater danger than the souls of businessmen, intellectuals, and farmers, all of whom have been enjoying government largesse for some time."

- "A Strategy to End Poverty" from Richard Cloward and Frances Fox Piven (a professor at Columbia University School of Social Work).

One member of the group, **Irv Garfinkel**, is now dean of the Columbia University School of Social Work. He discussed the newsletter, which he helped edit, in an interview with Economic Security Project cofounder Chris Hughes. medium.com/economicsecproj/historical-q-a-irv-garfinkel-on-the-guaranteed-income-47260c585c20. (That page includes a link to pdfs of the newsletters.)

Martin Luther King Jr. called for a guaranteed income in his final book, *Where Do We Go From Here: Chaos or Community?* (1967). "Up to recently we have proceeded from a premise that poverty is a consequence of multiple evils." The proposed remedies are piecemeal, inadequate, uncoordinated, and "have another common failing — they are indirect. Each seeks to solve poverty by first solving something else."

I am now convinced that the simplest approach will prove to be the most effective — the solution to poverty is to abolish it directly by a now widely discussed measure: the guaranteed income. ... We are likely to find that the problems of housing and education, instead of preceding the elimination of poverty, will themselves be affected if poverty is first abolished.

Idleness and unemployment are serious concerns, he acknowledged, though he recognized that both are often a result of market dislocations, which trap many people against their will. With guaranteed income, everyone will have opportunities to pursue meaningful work.

He quoted from *Progress and Poverty* by Henry George, and cited economist John Kenneth Galbraith to show that guaranteed income is affordable. King was particularly concerned with personal dignity.

A host of positive psychological changes inevitably will result from widespread economic security. The dignity of the individual will flourish when the decisions concerning his life are in his hands, when he has the assurance that his income is stable and certain, and when he knows that he has the means to seek self-improvement.

There is nothing except shortsightedness to prevent us from guaranteeing an annual minimum – and livable – income for every American family.

Guaranteed income "is not a 'civil rights' program, in the sense that term is currently used," because "it would benefit all the poor, including the two-thirds of them who are white."

If democracy is to have breadth of meaning, it is necessary to adjust this inequity. It is not only moral, but it is also intelligent. We are wasting and degrading human life by clinging to archaic thinking.

The curse of poverty has no justification in our age. ... The time has come for us to civilize ourselves by the total, direct and immediate abolition of poverty.

Where Do We Go From Here is still relevant, and the concluding sentences are most eloquent:

In a real sense, all life is interrelated. The agony of the poor impoverishes the rich; the betterment of the poor enriches the rich. ... Whatever affects one directly, affects all indirectly.

A true revolution of values will soon cause us to question the fairness and justice of many of our past and present policies. ... A true revolution of values will soon look uneasily on the glaring contrast of poverty and wealth. ... America, the richest and most powerful nation in the world, can well lead the world in this revolution of values.

These are revolutionary times. ... We are confronted with the fierce urgency of *now.*

In early 1968, five prominent economists – **John Kenneth Galbraith**, **Paul Samuelson** (1970 Nobel laureate), **Robert Lampman**, **Harold Watts**, and **James Tobin** (1981 Nobel laureate) – published a letter calling on Congress "to adopt this year a national system of income guarantees and supplements."

Like all civilized nations in the twentieth century, this country has long recognized a public responsibility for the living standards of its citizens. Yet our present programs of public assistance and social insurance exclude the millions who are in need and meet inadequately the needs of millions more.

As economists we offer the professional opinion that income guarantees and supplements are feasible and compatible with our economic system. As citizens we feel strongly that the time for action is now.

They circulated the letter among economist colleagues, with an invitation to sign it. More than 1,200 signed.

Cultural anthropologist **Margaret Mead** was a prominent author and a regular contributor to *Redbook,* a popular magazine that mainly markets to married women. She discussed guaranteed income in a column in the spring of 1968.

The danger that we would be underwriting the failures is trivial compared with the benefits the guaranteed annual income would provide us. It would provide dignity for every citizen and choice for every citizen.

Philip Wogaman, a minister and professor of Christian social ethics, published *Guaranteed Annual Income: the Moral Issues* in 1968. His conclusion, after examining various concerns, disputes, and objections, is: "The case for guaranteed income is persuasive on both ethical and practical grounds."

> Man's right to be – his right to physical and social existence – is not something for his fellowmen to grant or withhold as an economic inducement or give as a gift. …
>
> Guaranteed income as a secure economic floor will make it possible for men to become what God intended them to become by free response. The fact that many will doubtless abuse this freedom is a risk which God has taken in creating man in the first place. … [T]his right to be is one which God has given to each of us regardless of our undeserving. Guaranteed income will be a recognition, in economic terms, of what God has done.

He also states that "Christians may have some unique contribution to make with respect to the guaranteed income issue." And with their passion for justice, they "may have a duty to endorse guaranteed income."

His appendix includes statements in support of guaranteed income from the National Council of Churches of Christ in the U.S.A., the United Methodist Church, and a special committee of the United Presbyterian Church in the U.S.A.

R. Buckminster Fuller was an architect, futurist, and design scientist. One of his many books was *Operating Manual for Spaceship Earth* (1969).

> Our labor world and all salaried workers … are now at least subconsciously if not consciously, afraid that automation will take away their jobs. …

[We] must give each human who is or becomes unemployed a life fellowship in research and development or in just simple thinking. Man must be able to dare to think truthfully and to act accordingly without fear of losing his franchise to live.

Through the universal research and development fellowships, we're going to start emancipating humanity from being muscle and reflex machines. We're going to give everybody a chance to develop their most powerful mental and intuitive faculties.

His universal fellowships proposal is also in *Utopia or Oblivion: the Prospects for Humanity* (1969). Society is on a critical path. To avert self-destruction, we must consciously and comprehensively design a world that works for 100 percent of humanity.

Grunch of Giants (1983), the last book he wrote, denounces giant corporations and finance capitalism. He compares giant corporations to pirates in the 15th to 18th centuries, plundering our planet to enrich themselves. That's *grunch:* "Gross Universal Cash Heist."

On August 8, 1969, seven months after taking office, President **Richard Nixon** gave a televised address on poverty and welfare.

We face an urban crisis, a social crisis — and at the same time, a crisis of confidence in the capacity of government to do its job. ... Nowhere has the failure of government been more apparent than in its efforts to help the poor and especially the system of public welfare.

That is why tonight I therefore propose that we abolish the present welfare system and that we adopt in its place a new family assistance system. Initially, this new system will cost more than welfare. But unlike welfare, it is designed to correct the condition it deals with and thus to lessen the long-range burden and cost.

For a family of four now on welfare, with no outside income, the basic Federal payment would be $1,600 a year. States could add to that amount and most states would add to it. In no case would anyone's present level of benefits be lowered.

This new system establishes a direct link between the government's willingness to help the needy and the willingness of the needy to help themselves. It removes the present incentive not to work and substitutes an incentive to work; it removes the present incentive for families to break apart and substitutes an incentive for families to stay together. It removes the blatant inequities, injustices, and indignities of the welfare system. It establishes a basic Federal floor so that children in any state have at least the minimum essentials of life.

Nixon's **Family Assistance Plan** was a guaranteed income or negative income tax. Its author, Daniel Patrick Moynihan, used both terms, though Nixon did not use either. (In a 1973 book, cited below, Moynihan quoted Nixon's speechwriter, William Safire, who said the address was crafted "to make a radical proposal seem conservative.")

In November 1969, after 22 months of hearings around the country, the **National Commission on Income Maintenance Programs** published its report. Appointed by Lyndon Johnson, the chairman was Ben W. Heineman (president of Northwest Industries). Members included Thomas J. Watson Jr. (chairman of IBM); David Sullivan (president of the Service Employees International Union); civil rights leader A. Philip Randolph; politicians Edmund G. Brown and Barbara Jordan; and economist Robert Solow (who was awarded the Nobel in 1987). The executive director was Robert A. Harris.

Their unanimous report, *Poverty Amid Plenty: the American Paradox,* called for "a new program of income supplementation for all Americans in need."

Our main recommendation is for the creation of a universal income supplement program financed and administered by the Federal Government, making cash payments to all members of the population with income needs. The payments would provide a base income for any needy family or individual.

Work requirements ... cannot be used effectively in determining eligibility for aid, and are undesirable in any case. ... Inevitably, any simple test designed to withhold aid from the voluntarily unemployed will deal harshly with some of those who cannot find work.

Our observations have convinced us that the poor are not unlike the non-poor. Most of the poor want to work. They want to improve their potential and to be trained for better jobs. Like most Americans, the poor would like to do something with their lives beyond merely subsisting. By providing them with a basic system of income support, we provide them with an opportunity to do these things.

We do not believe that work disincentive effects of the proposed program would be serious.

The 1970s

Nixon's **Family Assistance Plan** was popular, public opinion polls showed, and major newspapers endorsed it. On April 16, 1970, the House of Representatives passed it with a vote of 243 to 155. That vote was truly bipartisan: Democrats 141–83 in favor, Republicans 102–72.

In the Senate Finance Committee, extreme liberals wanted more generous assistance, while extreme conservatives opposed any increased aid to the poor. The committee stalled until after the election in November. Then extremists from both sides voted against it — and defeated the moderates. The full Senate never considered it.

The new Congress convened in January 1971, and a slightly revised and more generous version was introduced as H.R. 1, a designation that indicates a high priority bill. The House passed it again by nearly two-to-one. And the Senate blocked it again.

Daniel Patrick Moynihan, the plan's author, was a former Harvard professor and Nixon's principal domestic policy advisor; he later served as a Democratic senator from New York. In *The Politics of a Guaranteed*

Income: the Nixon Administration and the Family Assistance Plan (1973), he described in detail how the plan was conceived, presented, debated, and defeated. He blamed the defeat on several factors: Nixon's refusal to spend any political capital; the skillful maneuvering of conservative opponents in the Senate; the timidity of liberals in the Senate, combined with the ambitions of those who wanted to use the issue in their 1972 campaigns; and the misguided, shortsighted actions of the National Welfare Rights Organization, which demanded more generous benefits and organized against it.

(Nixon's chief of staff H.R. Haldeman wrote in his diary that Nixon "Wants to be sure it's killed by Democrats and that we make a big play for it, but don't let it pass, can't afford it.")

The **Income Maintenance Experiments** began in 1967 and continued until 1974, funded by the federal Office of Economic Opportunity. In New Jersey, Denver, Seattle, and elsewhere; in urban, suburban, and rural communities; in a series of programs with varied designs, a total of 8,500 people in poor families received guaranteed cash payments. Researchers tracked recipients' incomes, work hours, family situations, and other variables.

When the Senate debated the Family Assistance Plan in 1970, senators demanded information about the experiments. Preliminary data showed a decline in work hours and an increase in divorce. Conservative opponents cited both factors as reasons to reject the plan.

The final analyses were published several years later. The higher divorce rate was a statistical anomaly; there was no increase. The decline in total work hours was between 6 and 13 percent. That was mainly women who chose to stay home with their kids, and teens who stayed in school or went back to school. There were also men who left bad jobs, and were out of work temporarily while seeking better jobs. Thus, that decline was good for those individuals and families — and good for our whole society.

Because the experiments were publicized and politicized before they were fully analyzed, the results are often mischaracterized. Even today, opponents of basic income sometimes cite partial or preliminary "facts."

In 2002, the State University of New York at Stony Brook sponsored a conference that featured a panel of scholars who worked on the design, implementation, and evaluation of those experiments. They stated emphatically, unanimously, that the results clearly indicated the potential benefits of basic income.

That panel discussion is presented in "A Retrospective on the Negative Income Tax Experiments: Looking Back at the Most Innovative Field Studies in Social Policy" (2005) by Karl Widerquist, et al. Widerquist is also the author of "A Failure to Communicate: What (if anything) Can We Learn from the Negative Income Tax Experiments?" (2005). Both articles are at works. bepress.com/widerquist/.

"A national guaranteed income" was in the original 1970 platform of the **D.C. Statehood Party** in Washington, D.C., the first political party in the world to endorse this idea. The party is still active, now the **D.C. Statehood Green Party**.

George McGovern was a U.S. Senator from South Dakota, and the Democratic candidate for president in 1972. During his campaign, he called for universal **Demogrants** — guaranteed payments of $1,000 a year for every American, including children. (In today's dollars, approximately $5,000). The payments were to be phased-out or taxed-back from people with higher incomes.

The plan's author, **James Tobin**, was a member of President Kennedy's Council of Economic Advisors from 1961 to 1962, and was awarded the Nobel in economics in 1981.

McGovern first presented the plan during the California primary, and opponents promptly attacked it. Tobin later wrote that McGovern "botched the initial presentation," and cited that as a main reason the plan failed to attract wider support.

When the House of Representatives debated Nixon's Family Assistance Plan, the chief advocate was **Gerald Ford**, the Republican leader. He promoted it forcefully, resisted conservative objections, and succeeded twice in getting it passed with votes of nearly two-to-one. He became vice president in 1973. Nixon resigned the following summer, and Ford became president.

In 1975, Ford endorsed and signed the **Earned Income Tax Credit**, a direct cash subsidy for low-wage workers, though nothing for the unemployed, distributed yearly with tax refunds. Initially a compromise, afterthought, or fallback from the Family Assistance Plan, the **EITC** was and is truly bipartisan. Ronald Reagan proposed and signed a major expansion, and there have also been increases under George H.W. Bush, Bill Clinton, George W. Bush, and Barack Obama. More than 25 million workers benefitted in 2018, and, at $63 billion a year, it's now America's largest welfare program. Most states and many cities have parallel programs that supplement the federal payment.

In July 1975, the **National Urban League**, under executive director **Vernon E. Jordan Jr.**, called for a **Universal Refundable Credit Income Tax**, a reformed welfare system that sought to place a floor under all incomes. They identified five goals or principle characteristics:

I. The system should be adequate, equitable, and universal.

II. The system should be federally administered and funded.

III. The benefits should not be work conditioned.

IV. Benefits should be cash rather than in kind.

V. The goal of the new program should be income maintenance.

Only one southern governor endorsed the Family Assistance Plan, Georgia Democrat **Jimmy Carter**. While running for president in 1976, he called for comprehensive welfare reform. Two years later, President Carter presented his **Program for Better Jobs and Income Support**. Democrats controlled both houses of Congress, but the party was deeply divided. His plan was never debated.

The 1980s

Free Enterprise Without Poverty: a Bold Plan, Full-Fledged Capitalism with Economic Security for All (1981), is by **Leonard M. Greene**, an entrepreneur, economist, mathematician, and inventor. He proposed "a simple, universal cash grant of $1,000 a month for every American family of four," a **National Tax Rebate**, funded by cutting government programs.

A decade later, he set out to test it. As described in *The National Tax Rebate: a New America with Less Government* (1998), his Institute for SocioEconomic Studies ran ads in newspapers and on radio shows throughout the country:

> Tell us what you'd do with an extra $1,000 a month; and would you trade government benefits for a monthly check? To encourage individuals and families to respond, the institute broadcast that it would select three families from all those who wrote back, and award them a demonstration tax rebate of $1,000 a month for twenty years.

Thousands of people responded. His book presents the three selected families, with photos, and reports on how they were using the money. But although the project was supposed to continue for twenty years, Greene died in 2006 and the payments ended.

Alaska has a small basic income, the **Permanent Fund Dividend**. It began under **Jay Hammond**, the Republican governor from 1974 to 1982.

Oil was discovered in Alaska in 1969, and the state constitution was amended to create the **Alaska Permanent Fund**. A percentage of oil royalties goes into the Fund, which invests in a diversified portfolio for the benefit of current residents and future generations; that's what makes it permanent. The Fund began distributing dividends in 1982. Everyone who resides in the state for more than six months of the year, including children, receives an equal share.

The amount varies with oil prices, interest rates, investment markets, and other factors; between $1,000 and $2,100 a year. Payments are distributed in October.

The **PFD** was $1,606 in 2019. The largest dividend was $2,072 in 2015; that's $8,288 for a family of four.

The previous peak was in 2008, when it was $2,069. That year, as part of a deal to build a new pipeline, people also got a one-time bonus, an extra $1,200, so the total for a family of four was $13,076. The governor who campaigned for that bonus was Sarah Palin, a Republican, and it was a major reason for her popularity — therefore a significant factor in John McCain's selecting her to run for vice president. During the 2008 presidential campaign, though, national reporters didn't ask her about the PFD.

Alaskans love the PFD, and have rejected several attempts to curtail it. Research shows that people use the money responsibly, to pay debts, send kids to college, and save for retirement. Income inequality in Alaska is the lowest of the 50 states, and that's mainly – perhaps entirely – due to the PFD.

Perhaps they'll expand it: PFD Plus. Funds can come from higher oil royalties, taxes on other takings, reallocated money from the federal government, and a reinstated income tax. (Alaska abolished the income tax when they created the Permanent Fund. After he left office, Gov. Hammond said that was a mistake, and called for restoring it.)

Two books about the PFD are *Alaska's Permanent Fund Dividend: Examining its Suitability as a Model* (2012) and *Exploring the Alaska Model: Adapting the Permanent Fund Dividend for Reform Around the World* (2012). Each includes a number of short papers. Both were edited by basic income proponents **Karl Widerquist** and **Michael Howard**.

European journalist and social philosopher **André Gorz** endorsed basic income in several books, including *Farewell to the Working Class: an Essay on Post-Industrial Socialism* (1982) and *Critique of Economic Reason* (1989).

Allan Sheahen, an independent scholar-activist, published *Guaranteed Income: the Right to Economic Security* in 1983. He updated it thirty years later as *Basic Income Guarantee: Your Right to Economic Security* (2013).

At a meeting in Louvain, Belgium, in 1986, a group of economists, sociologists, political scientists, and philosophers founded the **Basic Income European Network**. Through publications, bi-annual congresses, and related activities, the idea spread and the network grew, attracting supporters from around the world. In 2004, members redefined the "E" — and **BIEN** became the **Basic Income Earth Network**.

BIEN welcomes everyone who's interested in related ideas, and does not endorse specific plans or proposals. Their formal definition of a basic income (as revised in 2016) has five core features: periodic, cash, individual, universal, unconditional.

> A basic income is a periodic cash payment unconditionally delivered to all on an individual basis, without means-test or work requirement.

The BIEN website, basicincome.org, publishes updates on activities around the world.

For the Common Good: Redirecting the Economy toward Community, the Environment, and a Sustainable Future (1989, and a 1994 second edition) is by economist **Herman E. Daly**, then at Louisiana State University and subsequently at the World Bank, and process theologian **John B. Cobb** of Claremont College. They call for a negative income tax, and strongly endorse Henry George's ideas about shifting property taxes off buildings and onto the full rental value of land.

The 1990s

In 1990, scholar-activists **Jeffrey J. Smith** and **Gary Flomenhoft** founded the **Geonomy Society** to advance the ideas of Henry George, plus **Citizen's**

Dividends. "Geonomy" or "geoism" emphasizes the fact that all economic activity – all life, in fact – starts with the earth.

Philippe Van Parijs, philosopher, political economist, and founding member of **BIEN**, is the author or editor of several books, including *Arguing for Basic Income: Ethical Foundations for a Radical Reform* (1992) and *Real Freedom for All: What (if Anything) Can Justify Capitalism?* (1997).

What's Wrong with a Free Lunch (2001) features a paper by Van Parijs, with responses from eminent social scientists, including Gar Alperovitz, Anne L. Alstott, Fred Block, Emma Rothschild, and Herbert Simon, a 1978 Nobel laureate in economics. The foreword is by economist Robert Solow, who served on the President's Commission on Income Maintenance and was awarded the Nobel in 1987.

Van Parijs also published a 2017 book with **Yannick Vanderborght**, *Basic Income: a Radical Proposal for a Free Society and a Sane Economy*.

Another **BIEN** founder is economist **Guy Standing**. He published several papers on basic income in the 1990s, and currently teaches at the University of London. He was the main organizer of the 2002 BIEN Congress, which was held at the headquarters of the International Labor Organization in Geneva, and he edited a book of papers from that Congress, *Promoting Income Security as a Right, Europe and North America* (2005).

The Precariat: the New Dangerous Class (2011) and *A Precariat Charter: from Denizens to Citizens* (2014) analyze the social dislocation and disengagement that's happening worldwide, and call for basic income as a necessary solution.

He was the lead economist in the pilot projects in Namibia and India, and is a coauthor, with Sarath Davala and others, of *Basic Income: a Transformative Policy for India* (2015).

His other books include *The Corruption of Capitalism: Why Rentiers Thrive and Work Does Not Pay* (2016) and *Basic Income: a Guide for the Open-Minded* (2017).

A former welfare mother and political organizer in New York City, **Theresa Funiciello**, published *Tyranny of Kindness: Dismantling the Welfare System to End Poverty in America* in 1992. After describing the abuses, indignities, disincentives, and inefficiencies in the welfare system, she endorses guaranteed income as the only viable solution.

James Robertson, a British author and activist, and a cofounder of the New Economics Foundation, is a long-time proponent of **Citizen's Income**. In a 1994 paper on "Benefits and Taxes: a Radical Strategy," he described it as

> A tax-free income paid by the state to every man, woman and child as a right of citizenship. It will be age-related, with more for adults than children and more for elderly people than "working-age" adults. ... The amount of a person's CI will be unaffected by their income or wealth, their work status, gender or marital status. The level of CI will be tied to the cost of living.

"The existing benefits system is socially ineffective and economically wasteful," he states, and "an aging population makes reform of the present system all the more urgent."

> CI would make part-time employment and self-employment more attractive. ... would allow a freer and more flexible labour market. ... help to reduce unemployment. ... make it easier for people to give time to useful unpaid work in the family, household and local community. ... contribute to national economic performance ... help to smooth the economic cycles. jamesrobertson.com/ne/benefitsandtaxes-1994.pdf.

The End of Work: the Decline of the Global Labor Force and the Dawn of the Post-Market Era (1995) is by **Jeremy Rifkin**, a professor at the Wharton School and a leading analyst of economic trends. As new technologies proliferated over recent decades, he observed major gains in productivity while jobs declined and workers were harmed. As a consequence,

Every country must ultimately grapple with an elementary question of economic justice. … Since the advances in technology are going to mean fewer and fewer jobs in the market economy, the only effective way to ensure those permanently displaced by machinery share the benefits of increased productivity is to provide some kind of government-guaranteed income. … With guaranteed income independent of their jobs, workers would be more free to set their own schedules and adapt to changing conditions. That adaptability would in turn allow greater flexibility for employers, plus many benefits for society as a whole.

David Korten holds a Ph.D. from Stanford Business School, taught at Harvard Business School, and worked for decades in international business and public policy. He published *When Corporations Rule the World* in 1995, with a second edition in 2001.

After reviewing ideas about poverty, equity, development, and economic growth, he presents a history of corporate power in the United States. Corporations, he concludes, because of the way they're chartered and managed, are inherently harmful.

He endorses guaranteed income as a way to empower workers and citizens.

Since earned income would not reduce the guaranteed payment, there would be little disincentive to work for pay, though employers might have to pay more to attract workers to unpleasant, menial tasks. If some choose not to work, this should not be a considered a problem in a labor surplus world.

To fund it, he calls for a financial transactions tax, a surtax on short-term capital gains, and shifting taxes onto resource extraction and other environmentally-harmful activities. His larger goals are "localizing the global system" and building a movement for "a living democracy."

Hazel Henderson, futurist, evolutionary economist, and founder of Ethical Markets Media, is a long-time supporter of a guaranteed income and negative income tax. She discusses these ideas in several books, including *Building a Win-Win World* (1996).

The $30,000 Solution: a Guaranteed Annual Income for Every American, (1996) is by **Robert Schutz**, who was a lecturer in economics and business administration at the University of California, Berkeley. His calculation of $30,000 for every adult was based on redistribution of all unearned income: rent, interest, capital gains, dividends, winnings, gifts, and inheritances.

The **Eastern Band of Cherokee Indians** in North Carolina opened a casino in 1997, and began distributing some of the profits directly to all members of the tribe, including children. (Money for children goes into a bank account until they graduate high school or reach 21.) Everyone gets about $4,000 a year, with a payment every six months.

Several years prior to that, researchers from Duke University initiated a study of children's mental health in western North Carolina. They randomly selected 1,420 children, and the group included 350 American Indians. One of the researchers, **Jane Costello**, a professor of medical psychology at Duke, described their research as an experiment on basic income — and uniquely meaningful because they started the study before the tribe began distributing money.

> Four years after the casino opened, Indian children had fewer behavioral and emotional problems than did neighboring children. Moreover, the effect continued into adulthood. At age 30, one in five of the American Indians had mental health or drug problems, compared with one in three of those in surrounding communities. The Indians had less depression, anxiety and alcohol dependence. ... The younger the participants were when their families started getting the casino payments, the stronger the effects on adult mental health.

Addressing concerns about people spending the money on drink or drugs, Costello noted that non-Indians also drink, take drugs, and waste money. "Most people used their income supplement wisely ... and there was no evidence that people worked fewer hours." With more than 20 years of evidence, the research "strongly suggests that on the whole, universal basic income works."

Her 2016 article is at salon.com/2016/06/21/many_countries_are_weighing_cash_payments_to_citizens_could_it_work_in_the_u_s/.

Charles M. A. Clark is a professor of economics at Fordham University and a past president of the Association for Evolutionary Economics. His books include *Pathways to a Basic Income* (1997, with John Healy); *Basic Income: Economic Security for all Canadians* (1999, with Sally Lerner and Robert Needham); *The Basic Income Guarantee: Ensuring Progress and Prosperity in the 21st Century* (2002); and *Rediscovering Abundance* (2006, with Helen Alford, Steve Cortright, and Mike Naughton).

Clark was a cofounder of the U.S. Basic Income Guarantee Network in 1999.

And Economic Justice for All: Welfare Reform for the 21st Century (1997) is by **Michael L. Murray**, a retired professor of insurance at Drake University in Iowa. He endorses a guaranteed adequate income combined with a flat income tax, and his book includes detailed budget analyses to show that it's affordable.

"How to make society civil and democracy strong" is the subject and subtitle of *A Place for Us* (1998) by social theorist **Benjamin R. Barber**. In the final chapter,

> We have to find new ways to distribute the fruits of nonlabor-based productivity to the general population, *whether or not they work for their living*. Otherwise, more and more citizens will become poor in economic and social terms ... [and the system itself] will be undermined and destroyed by political instability, new forms of class war, and – most ironic

of all – by not enough income-earning consumers to buy all the goods in this labor-free world.

The sooner we act, the greater the gains. "Once the political will is in place to decouple work and reward, many feasible innovations are possible."

Independent philosopher and activist **Steven Shafarman** published his first book about guaranteed income in 1998, *Healing Americans: a New Vision for Politics, Economics, and Pursuing Happiness.*

Over the following decade, he published three related books, each with a very different style and presentation: *Healing Politics: Citizen Policies and the Pursuit of Happiness* (2000); *We the People: Healing our Democracy and Saving our World* (2001); and *Peaceful, Positive Revolution: Economic Security for Every American* (2008).

His 2017 book, *Basic Income Imperative: for Peace, Justice, Liberty, and Personal Dignity*, is an early version of this one.

Bruce Ackerman and Anne Alstott are professors at Yale University Law School and authors of *The Stakeholder Society* (1999).

> We offer a practical plan for reaffirming the reality of a common citizenship. As each American reaches maturity, he or she will be guaranteed a stake of eighty thousand dollars. Our plan seeks justice by rooting it in capitalism's preeminent value: the importance of private property. It points the way to a society that is more democratic, more productive, and more free.

Their final chapter opens with a question: "Stakeholding sounds nice, but aren't there better and cheaper ways of fighting poverty?" Then, after reviewing tax reforms, education policies, welfare reform, national service, and expanded efforts to reward work – and criticizing all of these – they discuss "a bold initiative that is even closer in spirit to stakeholding": basic income.

> We urge its serious consideration in the United States. Like stakeholding, the basic income puts the emphasis on freedom. ... Some people would

continue to work just as hard and use their extra money to buy something: a better car, a better house, or perhaps private or parochial school for their child. Others would use the extra money to buy time: to go to school, to take care of young children, or just to take a month off. And others might use the extra income to take a risk on changing jobs or moving to a new community.

This extra freedom would have the greatest value for those in the bottom half of the income distribution. ...

Like stakeholding, the basic income grants this freedom and security without strings attached. It automatically supplements low wages without bureaucracy or complex wage subsides.

"Perhaps we will never completely realize the American dream of equal opportunity," they conclude. "But if we abandon that dream, we will surely lose our way."

They further examine both ideas in *Redesigning Distribution: Basic Income and Stakeholder Grants as Cornerstones for an Egalitarian Capitalism* (2006), written with Philippe Van Parijs.

The **U.S. Basic Income Guarantee Network** was founded in December 1999 by Fred Block, Charles M. A. Clark, Pam Donavan, Michael Lewis, and Karl Widerquist, social scientists at various universities. Other long-time leading members include Almaz Zelleke, Eri Noguchi, Michael Howard, and Jason Murphy. The first **USBIG** conference was in New York City in March 2002, sponsored by the State University of NY at Stony Brook. Yearly meetings have followed, cosponsored in recent years by Basic Income Canada and sometimes held in Canada. usbig.net.

The 2000s

Empire (2000), examines the decline in national sovereignties around the world, and the rise of "national and supranational organisms united under a single rule of logic." That unity, which they call Empire, now wields "enormous powers of oppression and destruction." The authors are **Michael Hardt**, Professor of Literature at Duke University, and independent scholar **Antonio Negri**, former Professor of Political Science at the University of Paris and the University of Padua.

Their final chapter, "The Multitude Against Empire," calls for *"a social wage and a guaranteed income for all."*

> The demand for a social wage extends to the entire population the demand that all activity necessary for the production of capital be recognized with an equal compensation such that the social wage is really a guaranteed income. Once citizenship is extended to all, we could call the guaranteed income a citizenship income, due each as a member of society.

When George W. Bush took office in 2001, the federal budget had a surplus – the first in several decades – though the U.S. economy was in recession after the bursting of a stock market bubble. The **Congressional Progressive Caucus**, comprising Representatives Bernie Sanders, Barbara Lee, Dennis Kucinich, Jerrold Nadler, and 50 other Democrats and independents, called for an **American People's Dividend**: $300 to every citizen, including children. The AFL-CIO and other groups endorsed it. Proponents sought to repeat the dividend yearly for ten years if surpluses continued, as economists expected. inthesetimes.com/issue/25/08/bleifuss2508.html.

That dividend was in the tax cut bill that passed in the House of Representatives, which Democrats controlled. But Republicans opposed it, and it was not in the Senate bill. The conference committee compromised on a one-time distribution to people who pay income taxes, nothing for children, nothing for people who have no income or incomes too low to be taxed. Bush signed that into law on June 7, 2001.

In July, the Bush administration sent a letter to every taxpayer, announcing the coming payment — and claiming credit. A week later, people got checks for $300, or $600 for couples who filed jointly. The recession was over in November.

Apart from those payments, that first Bush tax cut mainly reduced rates for high earners. Deficits returned in 2002, and deepened throughout his time in office, exacerbated by further tax cuts. If Congress had only enacted the Progressive Caucus plan, surpluses would have continued; dividends, too.

Socioeconomic Democracy: an Advanced Socioeconomic System (2002), by **Robley E. George**, the founder of the Center for the Study of Democratic Society, examines established economic models – capitalism, socialism, communism, and mixed economies – and finds serious flaws with each. A true democracy, he maintains, requires both a universal guaranteed income and maximum allowable personal wealth.

Marshall Brain created the website *How Stuff Works,* and teaches entrepreneurship at the University of North Carolina. In *Manna,* a 2003 novel, he proposed a guaranteed basic income of $25,000 for every U.S. citizen. This would simultaneously (1) "create the largest possible pool of consumers," (2) promote "maximum economic stability," (3) "create the largest possible pool of innovators," (4) encourage investment, and (5) provide people with "maximum freedom."

"Livable income" is in the platform of the **Green Party of the United States**, since June 2004.

> We call for a universal basic income (sometimes called a guaranteed income, negative income tax, citizen's income, or citizen dividend). This would go to every adult regardless of health, employment, or marital status, in order to minimize government bureaucracy and intrusiveness into people's lives. The amount should be sufficient so that anyone who is unemployed can afford basic food and shelter. State or local governments should supplement that amount from local revenues where the cost of living is high.
> gp.org/economic_justice_and_sustainability_2016.

Green parties around the world support basic income as a pillar in their commitment to social and economic justice.

Economist **Karl Widerquist**, a cofounder of USBIG and former cochair of BIEN, is an associate professor of philosophy at Georgetown University in Qatar. He has written or edited several books about basic income, including *The Ethics and Economics of the Basic Income Guarantee* (2005); *Alaska's Permanent Fund Dividend: Examining its Suitability as a Model* (2012); and *Exporting the Alaska Model: Adapting the Permanent Fund Dividend for Reform Around the World* (2012). (Both books on Alaska are coedited with **Michael Howard**, a professor of philosophy at the University of Maine.)

Stanley Aronowitz, a labor organizer and a professor at City University of New York Graduate Center, has endorsed a guaranteed basic income in several books, including *Left Turn: Forging a New Political Future* (2006).

Charles Murray is an emeritus scholar at the American Enterprise Institute and author of a number of influential books, including *In Our Hands: a Plan to Replace the Welfare State* (2006, with a 2nd edition in 2016). His plan would provide $10,000 a year to everyone age 21 and over, plus $3,000 for mandatory health insurance. (His ideas about health insurance are in a footnote on page 45.)

To pay for it, he wants to abolish all federal, state, and local programs that transfer funds to individuals or favored groups. In his 2016 edition, Appendix A lists the federal programs, with dollar amounts from 2014, along with estimates of state and local transfers; the total is $2.77 trillion. His plan's total cost would be $2.58 trillion, so there's a surplus of $200 billion. (More about his plan and the financing in Appendix 2.)

The **Tax Cut for the Rest of Us Act of 2006**, H.R. 5257, would have created a small basic income by transforming the standard tax deduction into a "fully refundable" tax credit of $2,000 for each adult and $1,000 for each child. Everyone who filed a tax form, even if they had no income, would have received that amount. **Allan Sheahen** and **Karl Widerquist** conceived the idea. The sponsor was Representative Bob Filner from San Diego. It was never debated.

The Earth Belongs to Everyone (2008), by **Alanna Hartzok**, is a collection of articles and essays from her decades of work as scholar, educator, and activist. A forceful proponent of Henry George, she also praises Thomas Paine's *Agrarian Justice*, particularly his idea that the earth is the "common heritage of mankind." Hartzok and other modern Georgists sometimes describe basic income as a "common heritage dividend."

Joseph V. Kennedy is an economist and attorney with experience in the public and private sectors, and was Chief Economist of the U.S. Department of Commerce under George W. Bush. In *Ending Poverty: Changing Behavior, Guaranteeing Income, and Transforming Government* (2008), he proposes

A bilateral, annual, and voluntary contract between the government and any citizen above the age of twenty-one who wishes to participate. The government would hopefully guarantee the individual a minimum income of at least $20,000.

We Hold These Truths: the Hope of Monetary Reform (2008) is by **Richard C. Cook**, who was a government budget analyst for 32 years, mostly at the U.S. Treasury Department and with NASA. An admirer of C.H. Douglas and the Social Credit movement, Cook is most concerned with flaws in America's monetary system. In the 19th century, the federal government simply issued money and spent it into circulation. When the Federal Reserve was created in 1913, he asserts, the real motives were to fund wars and to increase the wealth and power of the finance industry.

He wants to "abolish the Federal Reserve as a bank of issue," authorize "credit to be directly issued by the U.S. Treasury," and "issue an annual guaranteed basic income to all legal U.S. residents."

Barack Obama was elected president in the early months of the Great Recession of 2008–9, the worst financial crash since the Great Depression of the 1930s. His stimulus plan, the **American Recovery and Reinvestment Act of 2009**, included a temporary cut in the withholding rate for Social Security, from 6.2 to 4.2 percent. Every worker received extra money in our paychecks, an average of $1,000 a year for two years. Because it was tied to the payroll tax, it really was for all workers, even those who didn't earn enough to pay income taxes. People spent the money on goods and services, and that spending was a significant factor in the recovery.

Administration officials were concerned that people might save that money, instead of spending it. To encourage people to spend, and thus to expedite economic growth, they deliberately downplayed that element of the stimulus plan while touting other features, especially government spending on "shovel-ready projects." In other words: the Obama administration gave people money, a nearly-universal tax cut, but didn't seek acclaim. Has any other politician ever done that?

From 2010 through 2019

Envisioning Real Utopias (2010) by **Erik Olin Wright**, Professor of Sociology at the University of Wisconsin and past president of the American Sociological Society, considers the prospects for an "emancipatory social science" with a central moral purpose, "the creation of conditions for human flourishing."

The book is both empirical, examining existing institutions, and speculative or theoretical. Four ideas he discusses in detail, and endorses: participatory budgeting, Wikipedia, the Mondragon worker-owned cooperatives, and unconditional basic income.

In a 2019 book, *How to be an Anticapitalist in the 21st Century*,

> Unconditional basic income (UBI) constitutes a fundamental redesign of the mechanisms of income distribution. ... Taxes increase to pay for the UBI, so even though everyone gets the income, income earners above a certain threshold would be net contributors (their increase in taxes would

be larger than the UBI they receive). Existing public programs of income support would be eliminated, except those connected to special needs. ...

If a UBI is reasonably generous, it would constitute a significant step toward the egalitarian ideal of providing everyone with equal access to the material conditions needed to live a flourishing life. ... thus opens up an array of new possibilities for people. ...

UBI thus creates a potential alliance of poets and peasants, allowing them to engage in market and nonmarket activities from a base of security rather than vulnerability. ...

UBI would also be a way of supporting people who provide care work ... a component of an egalitarian, community-based needs-oriented solution to the problem of caring for the frail aged.

Unconditional basic income can thus be considered one of the core building blocks of a democratic socialist economy.

Mitch Daniels, a conservative Republican, is the author of *Keeping the Republic: Saving America by Trusting Americans* (2011). He directed the U.S. Office of Management and Budget under George W. Bush, was Governor of Indiana from 2005–2013, and is now the president of Purdue University.

His insights start with Milton Friedman and the negative income tax:

Central to the NIT concept is the idea that it replaces the vast array of social welfare programs we have today. ... Collectively, they cost more than what we would need to fund an adequate NIT. ...

Perhaps the greatest benefit of an NIT would be to reduce dependency — not eliminate it, obviously. This would produce a sharp shift away from a system that diminishes the citizenship of those who receive benefits. ...

By flattening and simplifying the U.S. tax code at both ends ... we can trigger and sustain the long boom that America must have to pay its bills. ... We can grow our economy and grow true citizenship at the same time. ...

It would also liberate an astonishing amount of human talent. ...

Fundamentally, the reason to consider an NIT, with all its imperfections, is that it would treat its beneficiaries as men and women of dignity.

How Much is Enough: Money and the Good Life (2012) maintains that "the state's *first* duty is to create the material conditions of a good life for all" and "no sane policy has growth itself as a final end." The authors are **Robert Skidelsky**, Emeritus Professor of Political Economy at the University of Warwick, and his son, **Edward Skidelsky**, a lecturer in philosophy at the University of Exeter.

Their concluding chapter, "Exits from the Rat Race," has several pages on basic income.

> An unconditional basic income would make part-time work a possibility for many who now have to work full-time; it would also start to give all workers the same choice as to how much work, and under what conditions, as is possessed now by owners of substantial capital.

Funds can come from various sources, including fossil fuel taxes and financial transaction taxes.

> Basic income schemes would not stop people working – in the sense now understood – as long and hard as they want to … . No doubt many would use their basic income merely to top up earnings from existing hours of paid work. But those who wanted to spend more time in unpaid activities … would have the option of doing so. …
>
> [If] basic income reduces the pressure for citizens or residents to work, it should help to lessen the fear of immigrants taking our jobs.

Robert Skidelsky is also the author of *Money and Government: the Past and Future of Economics* (2018).

> Workers displaced by machines will need to be guaranteed a replacement income. An unconditional basic income guarantee, financed by taxation, will probably be needed in the transition to a less work-intensive future.

Basic income is "an idea whose time has come here in the 21st century where technology is now forcing our hand," says freelance writer **Scott Santens**. In 2013, he became the moderator of a Reddit.com forum, r/basicincome. And he crowdfunded his own basic income through Patreon, freeing himself to be a full-time advocate. patreon.com/scottsantens.

Erik Brynjolfsson and **Andrew McAfee**, of the MIT Center for Digital Business, are coauthors of *The Second Machine Age: Work, Progress, and Prosperity in a Time of Brilliant Technologies* (2014).

Work is essential for individuals and society, they maintain. To "encourage and reward work,"

> We support turning the EITC into a full-fledged negative income tax by making it larger and making it universal. We also think claiming the EITC should be made easier and more obvious.

To fund it, they recommend "taxes on pollution and other negative externalities, consumption taxes, and the value-added tax (VAT)."

Income inequality was a major public concern in 2014, and *Capital in the Twenty-First Century* was a bestseller. **Thomas Piketty**, a professor at the Paris School of Economics, used historic data to show that inequality increases faster than economic growth. Thus, growth-stimulating policies cannot effectively reduce inequality, and normally make it worse. Government must intervene. He calls for wealth taxes, including a global wealth tax, to fund assistance for poor and working class folks.

He discusses basic income, and endorses it, in *The Economics of Inequality* (first published in French in 1997, and republished in 2015), and in recent articles and interviews.

Income inequality and global warming are normally viewed as separate problems, each immense and extremely complex. With a basic income funded through taxes on natural wealth, carbon taxes in particular, **Peter Barnes** maintains that we can achieve rapid, sustainable progress on both. A journalist and entrepreneur who has started and run several successful businesses, he discusses these ideas in *With Liberty and Dividends for All: How to Save Our Middle Class When Jobs Don't Pay Enough* (2014).

Rise of the Robots: Technology and the Threat of a Jobless Future (2015), by Silicon Valley entrepreneur **Martin Ford**, examines the massive social and economic disruptions that we're experiencing, and the many harmful consequences. His final chapter considers solutions, including "The Case for a Basic Guaranteed Income."

> The conservative argument for a basic income centers on the fact that it provides a safety net coupled with individual freedom of choice. Rather than having government intrude into personal economic decisions, or get into the business of directly providing products and services, the idea is to give everyone the means to go out and participate in the market. It is fundamentally a market-oriented approach to providing a minimal safety net, and its implementation would make other less efficient mechanisms – the minimum wage, food stamps, welfare, and housing assistance – unnecessary.

Envisioning the benefits,

> A guaranteed income might help increase marriage rates among lower-income groups, while helping to reverse the trend toward more children being raised in single-parent households. It would also, of course, make it more feasible for one parent to choose to stay at home with young children.

Examining the uncertainties,

> If some people work less or drop out entirely, then wages for those who are willing to work hard may rise somewhat. ... I don't see anything especially dystopian in offering some relatively unproductive people a minimal income as an incentive to leave the workforce, as long as the result is more

opportunity and higher incomes for those who do want to work hard and advance their situation. ...

The person who takes the income and drops out will become a paying customer for the hardworking entrepreneur who sets up a small business in the same neighborhood. And that businessperson will, of course, receive the same basic income. ...

A guaranteed income, unlike a job, would be mobile. Some people would be very likely to take their income and move away from expensive areas in search of a lower cost of living. ... A basic income program might help revitalize many of the small towns and rural areas that are losing population because jobs have evaporated. Indeed, I think the potential positive economic impact on rural areas might be one factor that could help make a guaranteed income policy attractive to conservatives in the United States.

Robin Chase, cofounder of Zipcar, is the author of *Peers Inc: How People and Platforms are Inventing the Collaborative Economy and Reinventing Capitalism* (2015). "When you can connect and share assets, people, and ideas" using the internet, "everything changes."

We need to create new social mechanisms to spread out the gains of the new platform economics — perhaps even a Basic Income allotted to every person. ... Without this, the social consequences could be dire. ... Basic income is the long-term answer to the increasing precariousness of ordinary people in a global economy that can shift their jobs to the other side of the world in a heartbeat.

To pay for it, she suggests a global wealth tax, citing Thomas Piketty, or

a value-added tax (VAT), a luxury tax, or, better yet, a carbon tax. The more you consume, the more you pay. It would be hard for either companies or individuals to hide from a global carbon tax, particularly if the tax was collected at the point where the carbon was mined or drilled rather than at the point of use.

"Social Security for All" is a chapter in *Inequality: What Can Be Done?* (2015), by economist **Anthony B. Atkinson**, a Fellow of Nuffield College, Oxford, and Centennial Professor at the London School of Economics and Political Science. He endorses a version of basic income that he calls a Participation Income. Two main features:

> First, it would complement existing social transfers rather than replace them. A retiree receiving a state pension would receive whichever amount was higher, the pension or the citizen's income. ...
>
> Second, the proposal is for the benefit to be paid on the basis not of citizenship but of "participation" ... defined broadly as making a social contribution.

Robert B. Reich was Secretary of Labor under Bill Clinton, and the author and star of the 2013 film *Inequality for All.* He's now on the faculty of the University of California, Berkeley.

Saving Capitalism: for the Many, not the Few (2015) examines major flaws in our political and economic system. "A Citizen's Bequest," his next-to-last chapter, endorses a "basic minimum income" and presents a brief history of related ideas. He has affirmed his support in blog posts, articles, and short videos.

"Demand full automation. Demand universal basic income. Demand the future." That's on the front cover of *Inventing the Future: Postcapitalism and a World Without Work* (2015, revised and updated in 2016) by **Nick Srnicek** and **Alex Williams**, lecturers at the City University of London.

They aspire to liberate "the utopian potentials inherent in twenty-first century technology," and view basic income as "an essential demand."

> The demand for UBI is a demand for a political transformation, not just an economic one. ...
>
> A basic income would necessitate a rethinking of the values attributed to different types of work. ... would not only transform the value of the

worst jobs, but also go some way towards recognizing the unpaid labour of most care work.

People Get Ready: the Fight Against a Jobless Economy and Citizenless Democracy (2016) is by **Robert W. McChesney**, a professor at the University of Illinois at Urbana-Champaign, and **John Nichols**, a columnist for *The Nation*. They mainly focus on the massive disruptions we're experiencing with automation. Their last chapter, "A Democratic Agenda for a Digital Age," considers ways to move forward.

> If we may generalize, the one solution that has currency, and that is promoted by scholars who have done so much to identify concerns outlined in this book, is the notion of a basic income or guaranteed annual income for all people in the nation.

Though it might be "a phony solution." A higher priority, they assert, is to invest in education. "Why not make it the national policy that *every* child in America gets the same caliber of education as the children of the wealthy?" We also have to "democratize the Constitution," "democratize journalism," "democratize planning," and "democratize the economy."

Andy Stern is a former president of SEIU, the Service Employees International Union, and was appointed by President Obama in 2010 to the National Commission on Fiscal Responsibility and Reform (known as Simpson-Bowles).

Raising the Floor: How a Universal Basic Income Can Renew Our Economy and Rebuild the American Dream (2016), written with **Lee Kravitz**, calls for "$1,000 per month for all adults between the age of eighteen and sixty-four and for all seniors who do not receive at least $1,000 per month in Social Security payments." The total cost would be "between $1.75 trillion and $2.5 trillion per year in government spending," and he shows that we can readily afford it. (His ideas for funding it are in Appendix 2.)

Another person who's thinking about basic income is **Barack Obama**. In June 2016, six months before he left office, he was asked about it in a long interview with *Bloomberg Businessweek*. *Business Insider* published a short excerpt with the title "President Obama hints at supporting unconditional free money because of a looming robot takeover." businessinsider.com/president-obama-support-basic-income-2016-6.

Wired asked him about the concept in an interview published in October 2016, and Obama responded,

> Now, whether a universal income is the right model – is it gonna be accepted by a broad base of people? – that's a debate that we'll having over the next 10 or 20 years. wired.com/2016/10/president-obama-mit-joi-ito-interview/.

He restated his interest in July 2018, in a speech in South Africa,

> Artificial intelligence is here, and it is accelerating. ... And the pace of change is going to require us to do more fundamental reimagining of our social and political arrangements. ... So, we're going to have to consider new ways of thinking about these problems, like a universal income. pbs.org/newshour/world/watch-live-barack-obama-delivers-speech-in-south-africa.

The **Movement for Black Lives** emerged from a gathering of more than 2,000 activists who were part of or inspired by **Black Lives Matter**. They conducted an extensive policy process, with input from hundreds of people and a wide range of organizations. In the summer of 2016, they published a demand for "Reparations ... in the form of a guaranteed minimum livable income for all Black people."

- No other social or economic policy solution today would be of sufficient scale to eradicate the profound and systemic economic inequities afflicting Black communities.

- As patterns and norms of "work" change rapidly and significantly in the decades to come – no matter how profound those changes are – it is likely that Black America and other populations that are already disadvantaged will bear the brunt of whatever economic insecurity and volatility results.

- A pro-rated additional amount included in a UBI for Black Americans over a specified period of time.

- UBI would then provide an individual-sustaining basic floor for people who are formerly incarcerated upon re-entry that does not currently exist.

- UBI would be an improvement on portions of today's current safety net and would benefit cash poor Black people the most. Some benefits, such as food stamps, are replete with paternalistic restrictions that rest on racist tropes about recipients and their consumption habits. Others, such as the Earned Income Tax Credit (EITC), are significantly tied to work, which is problematic when structural racism continues to create so many barriers to Black employment. UBI lacks these flaws.

This section of their platform is at policy.m4bl.org/reparations/.

Peter Frase is the editor of *Jacobin* magazine and the author of *Four Futures: Life after Capitalism* (2016). We're approaching the end of capitalism, he maintains; a precarious time. With basic income, we can prevent or avoid the worst outcomes, and potentially achieve the best.

No More Work: Why Full Employment is a Bad Idea (2016) by **James Livingston**, a professor of history at Rutgers University, is a spirited challenge to conventional notions about work, jobs, morality, and the meaning of life.

Either we detach income from work, or we kill ourselves, figuratively and literally. Either we guarantee everyone an income, regardless of their productivity, or we declare ourselves brain-dead.

Throughout 2016 and 2017, there was a surge of interest from venture investors and technology innovators, the extended community of Silicon Valley. That support continues:

- **Chris Hughes**, a cofounder of Facebook, launched the **Economic Security Project** "to support exploration and experimentation with unconditional cash stipends." economicsecurityproject.org/.

- **Sam Altman** of Y Combinator, a major start-up incubator, announced and funded a basic income experiment with 100 poor families in Oakland, CA. businessinsider.com/sam-altman-basic-income-gdp-profit-sharing-2017-12.

- **Al Wenger**, managing partner of Union Square Ventures, a technology investment firm, published *World After Capital,* which describes basic income as "economic freedom." He calls for it to be combined with "informational freedom" and "psychological freedom." worldaftercapital.org/.

- **Mark Zuckerberg** endorsed basic income in a 2017 commencement address at Harvard. news.harvard.edu/gazette/story/2017/05/mark-zuckerbergs-speech-as-written-for-harvards-class-of-2017/.

- **Elon Musk** praised the idea in several interviews. businessinsider.com/elon-musk-universal-basic-income-2017-2.

"Why We Should Give Free Money to Everyone" is Chapter 2 in *Utopia for Realists: How We Can Build the Ideal World* (2017, first published in Dutch in 2014) by historian **Rutger Bregman**. His reasons and evidence include the Family Assistance Plan; Alaska's Permanent Fund Dividend; the guaranteed income experiment in Dauphin, Canada; research with the Eastern Cherokee in North Carolina; and ongoing projects by GiveDirectly in Kenya and Uganda.

Juliana Bidadanure, an assistant professor of philosophy at Stanford University, founded the **Basic Income Lab** in early 2017. basicincome.stanford.edu.

Progressive journalist and college professor **Paul Buchheit**, in *Disposable Americans: Extreme Capitalism and the Case for a Guaranteed Income* (2017), calls for a basic income to be funded through a carbon tax, financial speculations tax, and other new revenues.

Doughnut Economics: Seven Ways to Think Like a 21st Century Economist (2017), by economist **Kate Raworth**, examines conventional economic models and exposes the underlying flaws. She also presents alternative models, theories, practices, and policies, with many examples.

> Contrary to concerns that a guaranteed basic income would make people lazy or even reckless, cross-country studies of cash transfer schemes show no such effect: if anything, people tend to work harder and seize more opportunities when they know they have a secure fallback. When it comes to delivering a basic income to the world's poorest people, the question is no longer 'how on Earth?' but 'why on Earth not?'

She teaches at Oxford University's Environmental Change Institute and is a senior associate of the Cambridge Institute for Sustainability Leadership.

Richard Florida, University Professor at the University of Toronto's Rotman School of Management, is the author of *The New Urban Crisis: How Our Cities are Increasing Inequality, Deepening Segregation, and Failing the Middle Class — and What We Can Do About It* (2017).

> Fundamentally, poverty is the absence of money. Providing every person with a guaranteed minimum income or universal basic income is the most straightforward way to combat it, … Such an approach is more cost-effective and less bureaucratically cumbersome way of mitigating poverty

than providing myriad direct-assistance programs for housing, food, child support, and the like.

A common criticism is that a basic income program like this would encourage slackers and slacking. But a negative income tax is designed to encourage work and entrepreneurial effort. ...

It would provide a mechanism to pay those who perform essential nonpaid work, such as raising children or taking care of sick relatives. ... could also function as a low-cost seed capital by giving people enough money to cover the bills while they develop and launch new businesses. This type of income redistribution could ultimately help limit inequality and boost economic growth.

He also favors a land value tax, as

The most effective approach to spurring denser and more clustered development is to switch from our current local reliance on the property tax to a land value tax. ... it creates significant incentives for property owners to put that land to its most intensive use. ...

[T]he rise in value of the land that occurs through these broader neighborhood improvements is also captured by the tax and returned to the public, where it can potentially be used to invest in needed services.

On May 5, 2017, the Hawaii legislature passed a law, House Concurrent Resolution No. 89, to establish a **Basic Economic Security Working Group** — the first state in the country to launch a formal study of universal basic income.

WHEREAS, while the United States is the wealthiest nation in the world, many families, individuals, and businesses in Hawaii have been struggling to keep pace, ...

WHEREAS, hundreds of thousands of Hawaii jobs may be replaced in the near future due to innovation, automation, and disruption; ...

WHEREAS, the concept of universal basic income is analogous to providing social security to every citizen at a level sufficient to cover their basic needs; and

WHEREAS, universal basic income would also allow more people to share part time work between the fewer number of jobs that may be available, while lifting burdens on businesses, and providing a more secure and substantial safety net for all people, ending extreme financial poverty, and providing for a more financially sustainable and equitable future for all citizens in spite of coming economic disruption; now, therefore,

BE IT RESOLVED by the House of Representatives of the Twenty-ninth Legislature of the State of Hawaii, Regular Session of 2017, the Senate concurring, that the Legislature declares that all families in Hawaii deserve basic financial security and that it is in the public interest to ensure economic sustainability for our people.

Representative **Chris Lee** was the author and lead sponsor.

The complete text is at capitol.hawaii.gov/session2017/bills/HCR89_.HTM.

For more information, see basicincome.org/topic/hawaii/. Also vox.com/policy-and-politics/2017/6/15/15806870/hawaii-universal-basic-income.

Scott Smith, a pioneer of structured finance on Wall Street and founder of multiple companies, is the author of a 2017 book, *The New Operating System for the American Economy: Instead of Paying Taxes, You Would Receive Dividends*. He seeks a basic income of $24,000 a year.

He proposes to fund it with a Payments Tax. Every financial transaction would have 0.1 to 0.2 percent deducted and removed from the money supply. "From the taxpayers' point of view, it would appear as a discount applied to the electronic clearing process." (Appendix 2 has more about his proposal.)

What Happened (2017), by **Hillary Rodham Clinton**, is her account of the 2016 presidential election and more, a blend of autobiography and public policy.

"Democrats should redouble our efforts to develop bold, creative ideas that offer broad-based benefits," and she offers an example: a national version of the Alaska Permanent Fund and Permanent Fund Dividend.

> Shared national resources include oil and gas extracted from public lands … the public airwaves … a financial transactions tax. … and carbon pricing. Once you capitalize the fund, you can provide every American with a modest basic income every year. Besides cash in people's pockets, it would also be a way of making every American feel more connected to our country and to one another — part of something bigger than ourselves.
>
> I was fascinated by this idea, as was my husband, … We would call it "Alaska for America."

Her policy team worked on the details for several weeks, but

> Unfortunately, we couldn't make the numbers work. … We decided it was exciting but not realistic, and left it in the shelf. … I wonder now whether we should have thrown caution to the wind and embraced "Alaska for America" as a long-term goal and figured out the details later.

George Monbiot, a British journalist and activist, endorses basic income in *Out of the Wreckage: a New Politics for an Age of Crisis* (2017).

> The idea is now moving into the mainstream partly because both employment and unemployment benefits are widely perceived to be failing. The insecurity and poverty experienced even by those who can find work, combined with a coercive and often draconian welfare state, has driven thinkers and politicians to explore alternatives.

To finance the UBI, he proposes "a national social wealth fund from the fees charged to those who use assets they did not create." That would include land value taxes and "income from common assets that are best administered nationally, such as licences to use parts of the electromagnetic spectrum."

> The fund could be supplemented with a tax on financial transactions …
> and taxes on other sources of unearned wealth, … The social wealth fund,
> by pooling these assets both spatially and temporally (smoothing fluc-
> tuations on income from one year to the next), would provide a steady,
> inflation-proofed basic income to every resident of the nation.

Tech entrepreneur and commentator **Andrew Keen** is the author of *How to Fix the Future* (2018). His final chapter notes that

> Everyone today, it seems, both inside and outside Silicon Valley, is talking
> about universal basic income as the fix to the looming joblessness crisis
> of our smart machine age in which we will all become members of what
> Yuval Noah Harari calls the "useless class."

He then presents a brief history of related ideas, and cites a range of current supporters, particularly in the tech sector.

The Divide: Global Inequality from Conquest to Free Markets (2018) is by **Jason Hickel**, a professor of anthropology at the London School of Economics. He calls for "ditching the GDP," "cancelling the debt" of poor nations, and implementing a basic income.

> A basic income could be funded in a variety of ways, including progres-
> sive taxes on commercial land use, like the land value tax made famous
> by American economist Henry George, or taxes on capital gains, foreign
> currency transactions, and financial transactions. … Another approach
> might be to tax the $32 trillion of private wealth that is presently hidden
> away in offshore tax havens, and use the proceeds for direct cash transfers.

Assistant Professor of Political Science at Mississippi State University **James A. Chamberlain** calls for a conscious restructuring of society — with a basic income to promote personal freedom, social justice, and healthy communities. His 2018 book is *Undoing Work, Rethinking Community: a Critique of the Social Function of Work*.

In a 2018 book, *Fair Shot: Rethinking Inequality and How We Earn*, **Chris Hughes** describes his small-town, working-class, religious upbringing, and how he earned a scholarship to Harvard, where his sophomore roommate was Mark Zuckerberg. After Facebook went public, Hughes, as a cofounder, had several hundred million dollars. Seeking to do the most good with his wealth, he began researching possibilities, and learned about basic income.

He's a cofounder of the **Economic Security Project**, with **Natalie Foster** of the Aspen Institute and **Dorian Warren** of Community Change. economicsecurityproject.org/.

Transaction costs are declining steeply, driven downward by smartphones, artificial intelligence, and changing lifestyle preferences. Economist **Michael Munger**, a professor at Duke University, views this decline as "the single key fact in explaining the disruption of the economic system of the past 20 years."

Tomorrow 3.0: Transaction Costs and the Sharing Economy (2018) concludes with endorsing basic income.

> Switching from the current system to a basic income system would save money on the spending side, increase the amount received by recipients, and increase the liberty and autonomy of the recipients at the same time. … While a BIG is not perfect, having a safety net that recognizes the general benefits and gives citizens a sense that they are insulated from the most unpredictable effects of the new economy will make the inevitability of the coming economic revolution less disruptive.

Entrepreneur **Andrew Yang**, a Democratic candidate for the presidential nomination in 2020, was the founder of Venture for America, which educates young people around the country to be entrepreneurs and launch businesses. In *The War on Normal People: the Truth About America's Disappearing Jobs and Why Universal Basic Income is Our Future* (2018), he calls for a "Freedom Dividend" of $1,000 a month for every adult American.

> The Freedom Dividend would replace the vast majority of existing welfare programs. ... The poverty line is currently $11,770. We would essentially be bringing all Americans to the poverty line and alleviate gross poverty.

His main funding recommendation is a value-added tax of 10 percent. A VAT would "extract more of the value from automation in order to pay for public goods and support displaced workers." And would "make it so that we'd all root for progress — the mechanic in Appalachia would feel like he's getting a stake every time someone gets rich."

David Graeber is a professor of anthropology at the London School of Economics, an anarchist who was active with Occupy Wall Street, and the author of *Bullshit Jobs: a Theory* (2018).

"Does your job make a meaningful contribution to the world?" In an essay published online in 2013, he discussed the nature of work and the fact that a significant percentage of people feel that their jobs are useless, superfluous, meaningless, bullshit. The original webpage received more than a million hits, and people translated the essay into many languages.

His book examines the structure of bullshit jobs, the "spiritual violence" they inflict, the reasons they're proliferating, why our society does not object, and the obstacles to meaningful change. Political reform efforts tend to add bullshit and bureaucracies, he notes, and that would surely occur with any guaranteed jobs program.

> I've only been able to identify one solution currently being promoted by social movements, that would reduce rather than increase the size and intrusiveness of government. That's Universal Basic Income.

"The main point of this book," he concludes, is "to start us thinking and arguing about what a genuine free society might actually be like."

The Future of Work: Robots, AI, and Automation (2018) is by **Darrell M. West**, vice president and director of governance studies at the Brookings Institution in Washington, D.C. Examining the rapid pace of technological change, he calls for "A New Social Contract," with multiple necessary political and economic reforms, including universal basic income.

Journalist **Sarah Kessler**, in *Gigged: the End of the Job and the Future of Work* (2018), surveys the problems that are occurring with the proliferation of contract, contingent, and temporary work. One possible solution is "a policy idea called 'Universal Basic Income' (UBI)."

Precarious finances are a fact of life for countless families today, and journalist **Alissa Quart** experienced "a few years of fiscal vertigo" after she and her husband had unexpected bills following the birth of their daughter. *Squeezed: Why Our Families Can't Afford America* (2018) recounts the struggles of many families, combined with her insights as Executive Editor of the Economic Hardship Reporting Project.

She also interviews people who "think that everything may be okay if we embrace universal basic income, or UBI (or the more catchy-sounding BIG, for basic income guarantee)."

> UBI might be of particular value to mothers caring for children and care-givers for elderly parents for all the difficult work they do free of charge. ... might give people who care for their loved ones for free a cushion that would economically and socially support their choice to nurture. That could well lead to a reframing of how we think of care overall. If UBI reigned, affection would be not just a sentiment but an ethical practice and also a form of accepted work: it would be legitimate that we could be paid to love.

Appendix 1

Annie Lowrey, a contributing editor for *The Atlantic*, takes readers on a world tour of basic income activity in her 2018 book, *Give People Money: How a Universal Basic Income Would End Poverty, Revolutionize Work, and Remake the World.*

Along the way, she introduces readers to people in many countries who are receiving some type of basic income, and she interviews activists and scholars who are spreading the word. She considers the potential downsides and the political obstacles. And she invites us to envision it as a possibility for ourselves. At the end of her journey,

> What I came to believe is this: A UBI is an ethos as much it is a technocratic policy proposal. It contains within it the principles of universality, unconditionality, inclusion, and simplicity, and it insists that every person is deserving of participation in the economy, freedom of choice, and a life without deprivation. Our government can and should choose to provide those things, whether through a $1,000-a-month stipend or not.

"How do computers and robots change the meaning of being human? How do we deal with the epidemic of fake news? Are nations and religions still relevant?" With these questions and others as a starting point, **Yuval Noah Harari** presents *21 Lessons for the 21st Century* (2018). He has a Ph.D. in history from the University of Oxford and lectures at the Hebrew University of Jerusalem.

His second chapter, "Work," opens by stating "When you grow up, you might not have a job." Universal basic income, therefore, may be imperative.

> UBI proposes that governments tax the billionaires and corporations controlling the algorithms and robots, and use that money to provide every person with a generous stipend covering his or her basic needs. This will cushion the poor against job loss and economic dislocation, while protecting the rich from populist rage. ...
>
> Alternatively, governments could subsidize universal basic *services*, ... free education, free healthcare, free transportation, and so forth. ...

It is debatable whether it is better to provide people with universal basic income (the capitalist paradise) or universal basic services (the communist paradise).

With either approach, "If we manage to combine a universal economic safety net with strong communities and meaningful pursuits, losing our jobs to algorithms might actually turn out to be a blessing."

Can American Capitalism Survive?: Why Greed is Not Good, Opportunity is Not Equal, and Fairness Won't Make us Poor (2018) is by **Steven Pearlstein**, a Pulitzer Prize-winning columnist for the *Washington Post* and the Robinson Professor of Public Affairs at George Mason University.

"A Better Capitalism," his final chapter, presents a range of policy prescriptions, including "Universal Service + Universal Basic Income."

> What I have in mind is a new compact between citizens and their government, one that commits all Americans to provide two or three years of national service in exchange for a commitment from the government to provide them with an annual "citizenship dividend" that guarantees they will be protected from deprivations and eases life's inevitable transitions.
>
> I won't elaborate too much on the national service aspect … other than to say we should be very flexible and not afraid to experiment. …
>
> Most significantly, national service would replenish social capital and reinforce not only our commitment to political and social equality but also our commitment to each other. A country that requires service from all citizens would have a political, economic and moral rationale for guaranteeing those citizens a basic income should they fall on hard times.

His proposed basic income is small, $3,000 a year that's truly universal. Plus "an additional $3,000 for everyone who works full-time, similar to the earned income tax credit," and for "everyone attending college or participating in an approved training program full time." Thus, half of the dividend is conditional. "Guaranteed income purists will hate this idea," yet he considers it "a political necessity."

The "citizen's dividend" would mainly be funded by "raising income taxes ... to claw back some of the dividend."

> For those in the top half of the income scale, the government would giveth with one hand and taketh away with the other. For those in the bottom half, some or all of the dividend would be retained.

Prosperity Now, a nonprofit organization that **Robert E. Friedman** founded in 1979, helps poor and working families "obtain assets that build wealth, like a house or education. ... [with] the opportunity to climb the economic ladder for a brighter future." He's the author of a 2018 book, *A Few Thousand Dollars: Sparking Prosperity for Everyone*.

Universal Basic Income, he states in Chapter 2, is "an obvious response to stagnating incomes and disappearing jobs." And "There is abundant evident that people make good decisions about how to use income, so unrestricted grants make sense."

But UBI is "unlikely to address or significantly reduce wealth inequality or the racial wealth divide" and "it will not generate asset effects."

To resolve these and other concerns, he says, "All Americans need and deserve universal savings accounts (USAs)." Such accounts would be designed and implemented with government support to mainly benefit the very poor. This approach has been tested around the country for many years, often called Child Development Accounts or "baby bonds."

In an afterword, **Senator Cory Booker**, who has introduced legislation for baby bonds and is a candidate for the Democratic presidential nomination in 2020, declares his personal commitment to "child savings accounts, so every child would have a reason to dream and the means to achieve."

America has a "National Jobs Disorder." That diagnosis – based on interviews with workers, teachers, CEOs, and social scientists – is from **Ellen Ruppel Shell**, a professor of journalism at Boston University, author of *The Job: Work and Its Future in a Time of Radical Change* (2018). The disorder, in part, is a failure to appreciate that "the drive to innovate is all but coded into our DNA." We have to "recognize a need to work as a fact of human nature." She prescribes a Basic Income Guarantee.

> The goal is to grant Americans an allowance, albeit a humble one, and the free time in which to spend it — thereby stimulating growth and creating more and better jobs. … In theory, this scheme would reduce competition for jobs, thereby giving those who chose to work more leverage to negotiate better wages, benefits, and working conditions, and perhaps even to decline the boring, demeaning, and underpaid gigs so many endure today. BIG would also presumably reduce public anxieties over automation, in the sense that low-paid or demeaning jobs better done by machines would be done by machines, for the benefit of all.

The **National League of Cities**, working with the Stanford Basic Income Lab, published "Basic Income in Cities: A Guide to City Experiments and Pilot Projects" in November 2018. nlc.org/resource/basic-income-in-cities-a-guide-to-city-experiments-and-pilot-projects.

The LIFT (Livable Incomes for Families Today) the Middle Class Act, proposed by **Senator Kamala Harris**, is close to a basic income. It would provide "middle class and working families with a tax credit up to $6,000 a year – or up to $500 a month – to address the rising cost of living." That's for families earning less than $100,000 a year; single taxpayers who earn less than $50,000 a year would get up to $250 a month. Eighty million Americans will benefit. harris.senate.gov/news/press-releases/harris-first-action-of-116th-congress-re-introducing-tax-cut-for-middle-class.

The tax credit is "refundable," which means it includes low-income taxpayers, though not people who have no incomes; she has other proposals to help them.

The LIFT+ Act, from **Representative Rashida Tlaib,** would be a true, though small, basic income — $250 a month for every adult. washingtonpost.

com/us-policy/2019/06/06/rep-rashida-tlaib-introduces-closest-plan-con-gress-universal-basic-income.

The **Stockton Economic Empowerment Demonstration** is a major basic income pilot project, now underway in Stockton, CA, funded by the Economic Security Project, other foundations, and individual donors. **Mayor Michael Tubbs** and the city government were involved from the outset in designing the program.

Starting in February 2019, and scheduled to continue for 18 months, 130 residents of poor neighborhoods are getting $500 a month, no strings attached.

Researchers will collect quantitative data, and will regularly interview the recipients.

For more information: sacbee.com/news/local/article226280230.html. Also latimes.com/local/california/la-pol-ca-basic-income-stockton-repara-tions-20190415-story.html. And nytimes.com/2018/05/30/business/stock-ton-basic-income.html.

Another current pilot project is the **Magnolia Mother's Trust** in Jackson, MS. Twenty single Black mothers, all of them extremely poor (average family incomes, $11,030) are receiving $1,000 a month for twelve months.

Springboard to Opportunities, a small nonprofit organization, is the project sponsor. springboardto.org/index.php/blog/story/introduc-ing-the-magnolia-mothers-trust.

Also see nytimes.com/2019/05/08/opinion/baby-steps-toward-guaran-teed-incomes-and-racial-justice.html.

Y Combinator Research is launching a much larger program, a basic income for 3,000 people, with 7,000 in comparison groups.

The gold standard for understanding a new social policy is a randomized controlled trial (RCT). By comparing a group of people who receive a basic income to an otherwise identical group of people who do not, we can isolate and quantify the effects of a basic income. We plan to randomly select individuals across two US states to participate in the study. Roughly half will receive $1,000 a month for up to five years; the rest will serve as a control group for comparison. basicincome.ycr.org/our-plan.

The founder and major funder of YCR is **Sam Altman**. The Research Director of the Basic Income Study is **Elizabeth Rhodes**.

Michael Lerner is a rabbi, the editor of *Tikkun* magazine, and the author of eleven books, most recently *Revolutionary Love: A Political Manifesto to Heal and Transform the World* (2019).

> We will establish a guaranteed basic income at a level sufficient to ensure families' basic needs for everyone regardless of whether they are employed or unemployed. ... [this] will give employers a strong incentive to make the work satisfying and enable working people to welcome new technologies that reduce unnecessary labor. ...
>
> In so doing, we affirm a new ethos in which people see their worth as human beings to be independent from their work status or income level. ...
>
> is a key element in social responsibility.

The 2019 Nobel Prize in Economics was awarded to Abhijit Banerjee and Esther Duflo from Massachusetts Institute of Technology, and Michael Kremer from Harvard, for pioneering research on ways to reduce poverty.

Abhijit Banerjee and **Esther Duflo** are also the coauthors of *Good Economics for Hard Times* (2019), which discusses basic income pilot projects and possibilities in Kenya, India, and the United States.

The Great Democracy: How to Fix Our Politics, Unrig the Economy, and Unite America (2019) by **Ganesh Sitaraman**, professor of law and director of the Program in Law and Government at Vanderbilt Law School, examines the flaws and failures of neoliberalism, and presents universal basic income as a potential alternative.

Appendix 2

Financial Matters

Potential allies may be deterred by doubts about funding: How do we pay for it? Where will the money come from? What about budget deficits and the national debt?

These questions mainly, though perhaps inadvertently, defend and strengthen the status quo. Today, because special interests are so dominant, the debt seems set to increase indefinitely.

With this plan, *We the People* will gain the power to demand cuts and reforms. If we're serious about fiscal responsibility, this plan may be the key — an indispensable first step.

In December 2017, the Trump administration and Republicans in Congress delivered $1.5 trillion in tax cuts, while merely asserting that it'll be funded by future economic growth. During the recession of 2008-9, Congress gave Wall Street an $800 billion bailout and gave the auto companies $80 billion; and the Federal Reserve created $4.1 trillion and gave that to Wall Street. Seven years before that, when launching the wars in Afghanistan and Iraq, there was minimal debate about how to pay for either; total spending now exceeds $5 trillion.

Decades earlier, government issued a vast amount of money – without raising taxes, or approving budgets, or estimating total costs; none of these until years later – to end the Great Depression in the 1930s and to win World War II in the 1940s. In both decades, creating that money, and then spending or distributing it, led to immediate gains: new jobs, less poverty, more private investment, and faster economic growth.

How did government fund all that?

It just did. Congress passed laws, presidents signed them, and the Federal Reserve created the funds.[36]

With basic income, too, our government will have the funds when *We the People* enforce our demands.*

Two recent books include budget numbers: *In Our Hands: a Plan to Replace the Welfare State* by Charles Murray (2016, updated from a first edition in 2006) and *Raising the Floor: How a Universal Basic Income can Renew Our Economy and Rebuild the American Dream* (also 2016) by Andy Stern with Lee Kravitz. Their analyses are especially noteworthy because the authors have opposite political orientations. Murray is a self-proclaimed libertarian, though some call him a conservative, an emeritus scholar at the American Enterprise Institute. Stern, an avowed progressive, was president of a major labor union, SEIU, Service Employees International Union. He also served on the National Commission on Fiscal Responsibility and Reform (Simpson-Bowles), appointed by President Obama.

Murray's plan is $10,000 a year for everyone age 21 and over, plus $3,000 for mandatory health insurance. To fund it, he wants to abolish all national, state, and local programs that transfer funds to individuals or favored groups. Appendix A includes two tables that list the federal transfer payments, using government data from 2014, plus a trendline graph of state and local transfers.

To summarize, here is where the money to fund the UBI would come from:

- Federal transfers to individuals ($2.22 trillion),
- Federal transfers to favored groups ($69 billion), and
- State and local transfers of all kinds ($477 billion).

---

* For a national plan, that is. State and local governments can't create money, so residents who want local programs will have to specify the sources of funds. One possibility is to create a public bank, like the Bank of North Dakota, which has been operating since 1919.[37]

Total cost of the programs to be eliminated, using rounded figures ($2.77 trillion).

That $2.77 trillion is entirely from eliminating current programs, no tax increases, no other reforms. His version of UBI would cost $2.58 trillion — so there's a surplus, $200 billion. And because transfer payments are projected to rise significantly, much faster than the basic income, the surpluses will increase year-by-year.

Stern is seeking $1,000 per month for all adults aged 18 to 64, and for all seniors who receive less than that in Social Security payments. The total cost would be "between $1.75 trillion and $2.5 trillion per year in government spending."

His "menu of funding possibilities"

- Cut 126 welfare programs, for a total of up to $1 trillion a year.

- Reduce expenditures through the tax code – credits, deductions, exemptions, and subsidies – yielding $1.2 trillion a year.

- A value added tax of 5 to 10 percent on the consumption of goods and services, for an estimated $650 billion to $1.3 trillion.

- A small financial transaction tax, adding $150 billion.

- Charge corporations for the use or taking of public assets, including air, water, data, and electromagnetic spectrum.

- A small wealth tax on the total value of personal assets beyond $1 million.

- Cut other government spending: the military budget, farm subsidies, subsidies to oil and gas companies, and so on.

Combined, Stern's and Murray's proposed funding sources total more than $4 trillion, potentially $5 trillion, while either version of basic income would cost $2.5 trillion. Other economists and budget experts have conducted similar analyses and agree. The funds are available.

One item on Stern's menu is a wealth tax, and that's something Senator Elizabeth Warren is promoting. Another option is a higher marginal tax rate, perhaps 70 percent on income over $10 million, as suggested by Representative Alexandria Ocasio-Cortez.[38]

Funds might also come from "universal basic *capital*." Nathan Gardels, a senior adviser to the Berggruen Institute and editor-in-chief of *The World-Post*, describes it as "an ownership stake in the robots and systems" that are displacing workers.

> All working-age citizens should hold an equity share in the growing wealth of companies where intelligent machines drive productivity gains. One way this can be done is through national savings accounts, in which all can participate, that are invested in mutual-fund type instruments mixed with diversified venture capital pools. …
>
> One can envision, to take but one example, a distributed share in ownership of self-driving Uber-like services for residents of the communities where they operate, self-administered through blockchain technology. Everyone online should also be compensated with royalty payments by the large information conglomerates that use their personal data.[39]

Another potential funding source is a "Payments Tax." Scott Smith, a pioneer in structured finance on Wall Street, and a founder of companies in finance, education, and technology, presents this proposal in a 2017 book, *The New Operating System for the American Economy: Instead of Paying Taxes You Would Receive Dividends*. He wants to abolish the income tax, which he considers obsolete. The Payments Tax would be a small amount, 0.1 to 0.2 percent, deducted from every financial transaction. "Instead of taking the money deducted from a payment and crediting it to an account for transfer to the Treasury Department," the funds would simply be removed from the money supply. "From the taxpayers' point of view, it would appear as a discount applied to the electronic clearing process." His proposed basic income is $24,000 a year. More information is at thefinancialfreedomact.com.

Economists at the Roosevelt Institute examined several versions of basic income, and found that $12,000 a year for every adult would

> permanently grow the economy by 12.56 to 13.10 percent – or about $2.5 trillion by 2025 – and it would increase the labor force by 4.5 to 4.7 million people. Putting money into people's hands and keeping it there would be a perpetual boost and support to job growth and the economy.[40]

Economic growth will increase. The labor force will increase. Productivity will increase. Therefore, government tax revenues will also increase.

These analyses are only the beginning. We'll see major financial gains from better health, reduced crime, improved education, greater social justice, and a healthier environment. There's also the money we'll save by cutting waste and excess from military spending, plus potentially huge savings through vigorously promoting peace.

Let's put everything on the table, consider our options, seek consensus, and compromise. The first step is to enact any version of this plan. Everyone will then have incentives to work together to cut programs, reform the tax code, balance budgets, and reduce the national debt.

We can positively afford a basic income. We cannot afford status quo policies. We must mobilize the political will.

Financial matters are reasons to act promptly.

Appendix 3

International Activities

Iraq, the Debate About Rebuilding

On April 9, 2003, three weeks after the U.S. launched the war to oust Saddam Hussein, the *New York Times* published an op-ed, "Sharing, Alaska-Style," by Steven C. Clemons, executive vice president of New America, a prominent think tank.

> Most revolutions that produce stable democracies expand the number of stakeholders in the nation's economy. ... Iraq's annual oil revenue comes to approximately $20 billion. A postwar government could invest $12 billion a year in infrastructure to rebuild the nation. The other $8 billion could anchor an Iraq Permanent Fund. ... The resulting income would go directly to Iraq's six million households.
>
> Establishing this fund would show a skeptical world that America will make sure Iraq's oil revenues directly benefit Iraqi citizens. By spreading capital broadly among new stakeholders, the plan would also prevent a sliver of Iraq's elite from becoming a new kleptocracy. Finally, the creation of an Iraqi oil fund could begin to help repair America's damaged image abroad — itself no small dividend at a time when many people remain suspicious about American motives in the Middle East. nytimes.com/2003/04/09/opinion/sharing-alaska-style.html.

In the summer of 2003, Senators Lisa Murkowski, a Republican from Alaska, and Mary Landrieu, a Democrat from Louisiana, introduced a Senate resolution calling for an "Iraqi Freedom Fund." Secretary of State Colin Powell testified in favor. Trustees from the Alaska Permanent Fund lobbied for it. latimes.com/archives/la-xpm-2003-may-01-war-iraqoil1-story.html.

"THE STRUGGLE FOR IRAQ: IRAQ'S WEALTH; a Popular Idea: Give Oil Money to the People Rather Than the Despots," by *New York Times* columnist John Tierney, was published on September 10, 2003.

> The notion of diverting oil wealth directly to citizens, perhaps through annual payments like Alaska's, has become that political rarity: a wonky idea with mass appeal, from the laborers in Tayeran Square to Iraq's leaders. ... The concept is also popular with some Kurdish politicians in the north and Shiite Muslim politicians in the south, who have complained for decades of being shortchanged by politicians in Baghdad. nytimes.com/2003/09/10/world/struggle-for-iraq-iraq-s-wealth-popular-idea-give-oil-money-people-rather-than.html.

Then, however, with no news or explanation, the idea disappeared.

Canada

Canada conducted several income maintenance experiments in the 1970s. The most significant was in Dauphin, Manitoba. Nearly 1,000 residents of the rural town, total population 10,000, received unconditional cash payments from 1974–1979. Then a newly-elected government promised to cut spending; it ended the program, the research and other documents were put in storage.

Decades later, economist Evelyn Forget, a professor at the University of Manitoba, heard about Dauphin and found the files. After reconstructing and analyzing the data, she showed that the program cut poverty, increased employment, improved education outcomes, and produced major gains in public health.

"A Canadian City Once Eliminated Poverty and Nearly Everyone Forgot About It," one of the first popular articles about Dauphin and Forget, appeared in the *Huffington Post* in 2014. huffingtonpost.ca/2014/12/23/mincome-in-dauphin-manitoba_n_6335682.html.

Public radio's *Marketplace* featured the story in 2016. marketplace.org/2016/12/20/world/dauphin.

Dauphin is often cited by basic income advocates around the world.

In 2017, the premier of Ontario, Kathleen Wynne, announced plans for a three-year pilot program with 4,000 participants. The aim, she states, was "to find out whether a basic income makes a positive difference in people's lives," and gives them "the ability to begin to achieve their potential." theguardian.com/world/2017/apr/24/canada-basic-income-trial-ontario-summer.

Payments began in 2018. Ontario then elected a new premier, Doug Ford. While campaigning, he promised to maintain the program, but he broke his promise and ended it. fortune.com/2018/08/03/universal-basic-income-ontario-canada/. Also businessinsider.com/ontario-basic-income-recipients-react-to-program-cancellation-2018-8.

Mexico, Conditional Cash Transfers

Mexico started providing cash to poor residents in 1997, initially to help people who were harmed by NAFTA (the North America Free Trade Agreement). They expanded the policy in 2002, and it now helps nearly half of all families in the poorest states.

A 2014 World Bank article discussed Mexico's program, and how it has been a model for the world. Brazil, Colombia, Peru, and dozens of other countries now have conditional cash transfers. Research shows that people use the money responsibly, with significant gains in health, education, and employment. Poverty declines; tax revenues increase. worldbank.org/en/news/feature/2014/11/19/un-modelo-de-mexico-para-el-mundo.

Brazil

Brazil began a conditional cash program in 2001; payments to poor parents so children can attend school. They added health outcomes in 2003, and named it the Bolsa Familia (Family Grant).

On the tenth anniversary, 2013, a World Bank opinion article summarized the gains.

> [Bolsa Familia] has been key to help Brazil more than halve its extreme poverty – from 9.7 to 4.3% of the population. Most impressively, and in contrast to other countries, income inequality also fell markedly. ... Equally important, qualitative studies have highlighted how the regular cash transfers from the program have helped promote the dignity and autonomy of the poor. This is particularly true for women, who account for over 90% of the beneficiaries.
>
> The ultimate goal of any welfare program is for its success to render it redundant. Brazil is well placed to sustain the achievements over the last decade and is close to reaching the amazing feat of eradicating poverty and hunger for all Brazilians, a true reason to celebrate. worldbank.org/en/news/opinion/2013/11/04/bolsa-familia-Brazil-quiet-revolution.

Brazilians now have a legal right to a minimum income. Their senate passed that law unanimously, and President Luiz Inácio Lula da Silva signed it in January 2004. The law's author, Senator Eduardo Matarazzo Suplicy, learned about guaranteed income while living in the United States in the late 1960s, earning his Ph.D. in economics. en.wikipedia.org/wiki/Basic_income_in_Brazil.

More than 60 million Brazilians received monthly Bolsa Familia payments in 2019. That's 30 percent of the population of 200 million.

Namibia

In late 2007 through 2009, 930 residents of Otjivero-Omitara, a poor rural village, received monthly payments of 100 Namibian dollars (equal to about

U.S. \$13). The project was privately funded, with money from people in Germany, England, the United States, and elsewhere.

As summarized by Spanish economist Daniel Raventos, a lecturer at the University of Barcelona, and his colleague, Julie Wark, the payments

> reduced poverty from 76% to 16%; child malnutrition fell from 42% to 10%; school dropout rates plummeted from 40% to almost 0%; average family debt dropped by 36%; local police reported that delinquency figures were 42% lower; and the number of small businesses increased, as did the purchasing power of the inhabitants, thereby creating a market for new products. counterpunch.org/2015/08/21/the-basic-income-debate-political-philosophical-and-economic-issues/.

"A New Approach to Aid: How a Basic Income Program Saved a Namibian Village" was published in the German magazine *Der Spiegel* in 2009. spiegel.de/international/world/a-new-approach-to-aid-how-a-basic-income-program-saved-a-namibian-village-a-642310.html.

Namibians want a national program, opinion polls indicate, and elected officials are on record in support. But Namibia is a poor country, and would require outside funding.

India

In a project organized by the Self-Employed Women's Association of India, SEWA, in 2011-2013, eight poor rural villages, with a total population of 6,000, were randomly chosen from a group of twenty. (The other twelve were a control for research purposes.) Every adult resident received a monthly grant of 200 rupees (equal to about U.S. \$3.50), which increased to 300 rupees after the first year. Children received half that amount (paid to the mother). Payments continued for between 12 and 17 months. The project was funded by UNICEF (United Nations Children's Fund) India.

"Rupees in Your Pocket" appeared in the French journal *Le Monde Diplomatique*, with the subtitle "An experiment in paying villagers in one of

India's poorest states an unconditional basic income has been successful enough to change the government's thinking."

> The hypothesis was that direct financial payments would change behaviour and improve family living conditions, especially children's nutrition and health.
>
> Studies at the beginning, mid-point and end of the project confirmed that, in villages receiving payments, people spent more on eggs, meat and fish, and on healthcare. Children's school marks improved in 68% of families, and the time they spent at school nearly tripled. Saving also tripled, and twice as many people were able to start a new business. mondediplo.com/2013/05/04income.

Recipients worked more hours than people in the comparison villages. And the benefits continued even after the payments stopped — with better sanitation, more education, new businesses, and, especially among women, greater personal dignity.

SEWA also conducted an urban pilot project in Delhi — and it also had remarkably positive outcomes.

Basic Income: A Transformative Policy for India (2015) is by Sarath Davala, Renana Jhabvala, Guy Standing, and Soumya Kapoor Mehta, the organizers and researchers of the SEWA program.

"Why India is Ready for a Universal Basic Income: How it Could Cut Poverty and Bureaucracy" was in *Foreign Affairs* in April 2017. foreignaffairs.com/articles/india/2017-04-06/why-india-ready-universal-basic-income.

In January 2019, the ruling party in Sikkim, a small northern state, proposed a basic income. washingtonpost.com/world/2019/01/17/tiny-indian-state-proposes-worlds-biggest-experiment-with-guaranteed-income/?utm_term=.c19ce74ae093.

Also in January 2019, the leader of India's major opposition party, Rahul Gandhi of the Congress Party, announced plans for a "Minimum Income Guarantee," declaring that "We have taken a decision that every poor person in India … will be guaranteed minimum income. … There will be no

more hunger or poverty." vox.com/future-perfect/2019/1/29/18202061/
rahul-gandhi-basic-income-indian-election.

But his party lost in April 2019. Prime Minister Narendra Modi and the
Bharatiya Janata Party were reelected.

Kenya, Uganda, and Rwanda

Eight, a nonprofit organization based in Belgium, launched and funded a
two-year pilot project in 2017. They found that cash distribution was effective,
efficient, and empowering. eight.world.

GiveDirectly, a New York nonprofit, is "leading the world's largest and
longest term experiment to date studying the effects of a Universal Basic Income."

> As part of this $30M project, we have already distributed millions of dollars
> to 20,000 individuals living across 197 villages, and an additional 100 villages
> have been surveyed as a control group. Some individuals will receive payments for 12 years, and the full study will last at least that long, but initial
> results are expected in 2020. givedirectly.org/ubi-study/.

European Activities

In October 2013, Swiss basic income activists submitted signatures for a national ballot initiative. To mark the occasion and attract greater support, they
dumped eight million 5-cent coins, one for each Swiss citizen, in the plaza
outside the Federal Palace in Bern. And they invited people to play, picnic, or
stay overnight on the coins. They also created the world's largest poster (as
certified by Guinness World Records): "What would you do if your income
were taken care of?"

See basicincome.org/news/2013/10/switzerland-national-referendum-will-be-held-on-basic-income/. Also see cnbc.com/2016/06/02/what-you-need-to-know-about-the-swiss-basic-income-vote.html.

The activists knew from the start that such bold initiatives are normally defeated, the first time. The vote was on June 5, 2016, and it lost. Yet they succeeded, hugely, in moving the idea forward around the world. When they relaunch their campaign, they'll be able to cite results from pilot projects in other European countries and beyond; several countries might already have national programs.

Finland initiated a pilot project in 2017.

The government chose 2,000 unemployed citizens at random and gave them a check of 560 euros ($635) every month for two years. ... recipients reported less stress than the control group. That was true even for recipients who felt they were still struggling to make ends meet. ...

The recipients also reported that they felt more trust toward other people and social institutions — from political parties to the police to the courts — than they did before getting a basic income.

... made recipients happier without making them any less likely to join the workforce. Although this wasn't everything the Finnish government was hoping for – its stated goal was to boost employment – it still offered an important counter to critics of basic income, who often claim getting free money will induce people to work less. The evidence does not support that. vox.com/2019/4/6/18297452/finland-basic-income-free-money-canada.

Holland, Scotland, Spain, Israel, and several other countries are planning or conducting pilot projects. interestingengineering.com/the-15-most-promising-universal-basic-income-trials.

Italy has a coalition government. The largest party is the Five Star Movement, which initially campaigned for a "citizens' income." bloomberg.com/opinion/articles/2019-01-28/italy-s-populists-hand-out-some-free-money.

★ ★ ★ ★ ★

The Pilot Project We Need Now is a Whole Country

Or a whole city, state, or region within a country.

Canada, Switzerland, Finland, etc., are wealthy democracies. If their citizens demand it, their governments can launch local or national programs.

Mexico, Brazil, and other countries with conditional cash transfers could remove the conditions. They might have true, though small, basic incomes within a few years.

Namibia, India, Kenya, and so on are relatively or extremely poor. They may be eager to have some form of basic income — if they get help with outside funds.

Activists in wealthy countries can press our governments to fund poor countries' programs; redirect foreign aid, perhaps increase it. We can also lobby for funding from the World Bank, International Monetary Fund, and other multinational institutions. Philanthropists and private foundations might offer funds. Many foundations have charters that mandate spending on health, hunger, poverty, education, women's rights, racism, the environment, and other goals that are sure to gain with this approach. Multiple foundations can combine or coordinate their efforts.

Who will be first?

Appendix 4

For More Information

The **Basic Income Earth Network, BIEN,** was founded in 1986 and holds a congress every year or two in a different location. The website has regular news updates from around the world, with links to national and transnational affiliates. basicincome.org.

The **U.S. Basic Income Guarantee Network** launched in 1999 as an informal association of academics and activists, and became a nonprofit organization in 2016. **USBIG** has a yearly conference, alternating between the U.S. and Canada (and cosponsored by Basic Income Canada). usbig.net.

The **Economic Security Project**, since 2016, coordinates activities that involve "learning how we can use cash to end poverty and rebuild the middle class in America." The website has links to various projects and resources: economicsecurityproject.org/.

OurFutureUBI.com is Steven Shafarman's website for this book, with a blog, articles, videos, and more, plus opportunities for readers to connect on their concerns and campaigns.

Basic income is also featured on many other websites, Facebook pages, Twitter feeds, and such, with several forthcoming films.

Endnotes

1. Chapter 1, page 6. Note the comma and dash in "pursuit of happiness, —
that to secure these rights ... ." A period is standard, sometimes with the dash,
but the period appears to be a mistake, a slight error in an early copy. This
is a recent discovery. The National Archives in Washington, D.C., examined
it in a June 2015 forum with Danielle Allen, a professor of government at
Harvard University, and other scholars. She initiated the inquiry with her
2014 book, *Our Declaration: A Reading of the Declaration of Independence
in Defense of Equality.*

(Thomas Jefferson used semi-colons in his drafts. He also capitalized
words in the middle of sentences, which was common at the time, and those
capitals confound questions about the punctuation.)

With a comma, Allen saw, the sentence is a syllogism, a form of logic
with a first premise, second premise, and conclusion. The classic example,
from Aristotle: All men are mortal; Socrates is a man; therefore, Socrates is
mortal. In the Declaration: All men are created equal with unalienable rights;
to secure our rights, governments are instituted by consent; therefore, if
government is destructive, instituting new government is a right.

With a period, that logic is lost or hidden. The period separates the opening clauses from everything that follows. Readers reach the period, pause,
then often only skim the rest.

The first premise is about individual rights:

We hold these truths to be self-evident, that all men are created equal, that they are endowed by their creator with certain unalienable rights, that among these are life, liberty, and the pursuit of happiness, ...

The second premise proclaims the reciprocity between people and governments. The dash distinguishes it, especially when there's also a dash at the end:

— that to secure these rights, governments are instituted among men, deriving their just powers from the consent of the governed, —

The conclusion starts with "that," like the second premise and three clauses in the first premise. With a comma, all five "that" statements are self-evident truths:

that whenever any form of government becomes destructive of these ends, it is the right of the people to alter or to abolish it, and to institute new government, laying its foundations on such principles, and organizing its powers in such form, as to them shall seem most likely to effect their safety and happiness.

More evidence of the original intent: The first premise includes Aristotle's opening words, "all men are." Also, the first premise and the conclusion have the same last word, "happiness," a parallel to Aristotle's "mortal." Furthermore, the premises use similar phrases, "men are created" and "are endowed," and "governments are instituted." The conclusion shifts to active language and proffers guidance about how to institute new government.

Jefferson wrote with editing assistance from John Adams, Benjamin Franklin, Robert R. Livingston, and Roger Sherman, the drafting committee appointed by the Continental Congress. Four were lawyers; all five would have known Aristotle's syllogism. They also knew theories of government from Locke, Spinoza, Montesquieu, Hume, Rousseau, and other Enlightenment thinkers. They worked together for two-and-a-half weeks, and presumably debated every word, comma, colon, semi-colon, and period — and, more important, the core principles and self-evident truths.

The complete 110-word sentence is a coherent logical argument, a syllogism, that declares our sovereignty with a clear, concise, compelling demand for democracy.

This punctuation – a comma, plus two dashes to mark the syllogism – might become the new standard. I hope so. I believe this small change can make a big difference in helping Americans recognize our roles, rights, and responsibilities as citizens.

Danielle Allen discusses this sentence and its logic in a short video: the-atlantic.com/video/index/574750/danielle-allen/.

2. Chapter 2, page 14. Basic income, as defined by the Basic Income Earth Network, has five core features: periodic, cash, individual, universal, unconditional.

> A periodic cash payment unconditionally delivered to all on an individual
> basis, without means-test or work requirement.

This definition is on the homepage of the BIEN website, basicincome.org, with a link to an article that discusses the reasons for it.

I'm campaigning for the core concept, and calling for compromise on details and features. Most versions are for citizens only; others include legal residents. Most are for adults only; others add a smaller amount for children, or call for a parallel program of universal child benefits. Some are not quite universal or are partly conditional.

Proponents have used various terms for theoretical reasons or political purposes. Early terms include *national dividend,* from C.H. Douglas in 1920; *social dividend,* from George D. H. Cole and James Meade in 1935; *negative income tax,* from Juliet Rhys-Williams in 1944; *predictable income,* from Peter Drucker in 1949; and *basic income,* from George D. H. Cole in 1953.

Basic Economic Security is from Robert Theobald in 1963, and he also used *guaranteed income.* That was a year after Milton Friedman endorsed a *negative income tax,* and conservatives continue to favor that term. Liberals, then and now, prefer *guaranteed income,* sometimes *guaranteed adequate income, guaranteed annual income, guaranteed livable income, or guaranteed minimum income.*

The *Family Assistance Plan* of 1969 was a guaranteed income or negative income tax; Daniel Patrick Moynihan, the plan's author, used both terms, though Richard Nixon avoided both.

Demogrants is from James Tobin, economic policy advisor to George McGovern, Democratic candidate for president in 1972. After Nixon defeated McGovern, both major parties mostly abandoned these ideas. (Two exceptions: Gerald Ford, while in Congress as leader of the Republican party, was the chief advocate for the Family Assistance Plan, and might have reintroduced it if he had been re-elected president in 1976. Jimmy Carter presented his Program for Better Jobs and Income Support in 1978, but his Democratic party did not support him.)

Basic income became the common term after 1986, with the founding of BIEN, the Basic Income European Network. (They changed the "E" to Earth in 2004.) Many people expand it to *universal basic income* or *unconditional basic income,* or abbreviate it as *UBI.* People also use *basic income grant* or *basic income guarantee,* sometimes abbreviated as *BIG.*

Citizen's Income and *Citizen Dividends* emerged in the late 1980s or early '90s, and emphasize that this is for citizens, though some versions include all legal residents.

Common heritage dividend honors Thomas Paine's principle that land is "the common heritage of mankind." *Social Security for All* echoes Robert Theobald's idea that "Basic Economic Security can be best regarded as an extension of the present Social Security system."

Other terms include *Assured Income, Basic Grant, Dividends for All, Freedom Dividend, Livable Income, National Tax Rebate, Participation Income, State Bonus, State Grants, Subsistence Income, Universal Allocation, Universal Benefit,* and *Universal Refundable Credit Income Tax.* Translations vary and new terms may emerge.

3. Chapter 3, page 29. The quote and the 6.1 billion hour figure are from January 2013 story in the *New York Times*. nytimes.com/2013/01/09/business/irss-taxpayer-advocate-calls-for-a-tax-code-overhaul.html.

"In the United States, filing taxes is painful by design," Monica Prasad, a professor of sociology at Northwestern University, states in a 2019 article in *The Atlantic*.

> The tax-collection system as we know it is the outcome of three forces: corporate lobbying, a stubborn resistance to borrowing good ideas from other Western nations, and the Republican Party's decades-long campaign against taxation itself. theatlantic.com/ideas/archive/2019/04/american-tax-returns-dont-need-be-painful/586369/.

4. Chapter 3, page 33. Many countries provide direct cash support for children, and that includes Canada, England, France, Germany, Denmark, Finland, Israel, Japan, and Australia. The United States is wealthier, yet our child poverty rates are much higher.

The Niskanen Center, a libertarian think tank, has been a leader on this issue. Their 2016 plan for Universal Child Benefits is "$2,000 per child under the age of 18, phased out for high income households," and they describe it as "a guaranteed minimum income for kids." They estimate that it "could be paid for several times over by consolidating some existing child programs and streamlining the complex and fragmented bureaucracy." niskanencenter.org/wp-content/uploads/2016/10/UniversalChildBenefit_final.pdf.

In autumn 2017, two Republican senators, Mike Lee of Utah and Marco Rubio of Florida, called for expanded child tax credits, including direct payments to the poor. Their proposal, though in a reduced form, was included in the Trump-Republican tax cut, and is now the law. Parents get up to $1,400 per child. The amount varies with earnings, and it's paid yearly, with tax refunds. sunshinestatenews.com/story/marco-rubio-showcases-child-tax-credit-expansion.

Two Democratic senators, Michael Bennet of Colorado and Sherrod Brown of Ohio, introduced The American Family Act in 2017 and reintroduced it in March 2019. All poor and middle-class parents, even those with no income, would receive at least $3,000 a year for each child, monthly payments of $250. The Senate Bill is S. 690. A companion bill in the House is H.R. 1560, sponsored by Democratic Representatives Rosa DeLauro of Connecticut and Suzan DelBene of Washington.

5. Chapter 3, page 33. "Class warfare," normally, is mere rhetoric, typically an attack or counterattack. In this case, though, we can cite a widely-respected authority, billionaire investor Warren Buffett: "There's class warfare, all right, but it's my class, the rich class, that's making the war, and we're winning." nytimes.com/2006/11/26/business/yourmoney/26every.html.

Buffett's class scored a big win with the 2017 Trump-Republican tax cut.

Many in his class have declared their willingness to pay higher taxes. They even have an organization, Patriotic Millionaires. As stated on their website:

> Proud "traitors to their class," members of the Patriotic Millionaires are high-net worth Americans, business leaders, and investors who are united in their concern about the destabilizing concentration of wealth and power in America. The mission of The Patriotic Millionaires organization is to build a more stable, prosperous, and inclusive nation by promoting public policies based on the "first principles" ...
>
> All citizens should enjoy political power equal to that enjoyed by millionaires;
>
> All citizens who work full time should be able to afford their basic needs;
>
> Tax receipts from millionaires, billionaires and corporations should comprise a greater proportion of federal tax receipts. patrioticmillionaires.org/about/.

6. Chapter 4, page 43. The Earned Income Tax Credit was enacted in 1975, several years after the Senate blocked the Family Assistance Plan. The EITC

was a compromise, afterthought, or fallback, and it's truly bipartisan. Ronald Reagan, George H.W. Bush, Bill Clinton, George W. Bush, and Barack Obama endorsed and increased it.

To get the EITC, people have to file an extra tax form. Many eligible workers – 20 percent, by some estimates – miss out because they fail to file or make mistakes. Another flaw is that it renders low-wage workers more afraid of losing their jobs, therefore afraid to ask for sick leave, higher pay, better hours, family leave, or a union. And it reduces pressure on employers to raise pay or improve working conditions. Consequently, perhaps deliberately, the EITC indirectly subsidizes companies that pay the lowest wages — covert corporate welfare for Walmart and McDonald's.

Even so, one way to implement a small basic income would be to expand and extend the EITC to include everyone who files a tax form, even if they have no income. Child tax credits can also be expanded and extended. Dylan Matthews, a writer at *Vox*, discusses these possibilities at vox.com/future-perfect/2019/6/27/18744563/gavin-newsom-california-earned-income-tax-credit

7. Chapter 4, page 43. The flaws, fallacies, and absurdities of corporate welfare were on display in 2018, with Amazon and Foxconn. Derek Thomson, a senior editor at *The Atlantic*, examines both in "Amazon's HQ2 Spectacle Isn't Just Shameful — It Should be Illegal." theatlantic.com/ideas/archive/2018/11/amazons-hq2-spectacle-should-be-illegal/575539/.

After Amazon announced in 2016 that it was seeking bids for a second headquarters, 238 cities entered the competition, and many offered multi-billion dollar subsidies. Those cities, all of them, spent significant taxpayer money on preparing their proposals, and they gave the company valuable data it can use for marketing and future expansions. Yet nearly all had zero chance of winning.

Foxconn got a great deal.

Wisconsin Governor Scott Walker lured Foxconn with a subsidy plan totaling more than $3 billion. (For the same amount, you could give every household in Wisconsin about $1,700.)

8. Chapter 5, page 55. In *For the Common Good: Redirecting the Economy Toward Community, the Environment, and a Sustainable Future* (1989, and a 1994 second edition), economist Herman Daly and theologian John B. Cobb examine the flaws in GDP and conclude that economic welfare peaked in the early 1970s. Since then, most "growth" has been in activities that harm society and our environment. One remedy they endorse is a negative income tax. Another is to replace the GDP with an Index of Sustainable Economic Welfare. Daly elaborates on these themes in *Beyond Growth: the Economics of Sustainable Development* (1996).

"The Trouble with GDP," in *The Economist* on April 30, 2016, argues that GDP is "a poor measure of prosperity" and "not even a reliable gauge of production." economist.com/briefing/2016/04/30/the-trouble-with-gdp.

Kate Raworth, an economist and research associate at Oxford University's Environmental Change Institute, seeks a "regenerative and distributive economy" that, functionally, is the opposite of GDP. Instead of pursuing perpetual growth, public policies must aim for "a safe and just space for humanity." She's the author of *Doughnut Economics: Seven Ways to Think Like a 21st Century Economist* (2017).

The Divide: Global Inequality from Conquest to Free Markets (2017) is by Jason Hickel, a professor of anthropology at the London School of Economics. His concluding chapter calls for "ditching the GDP" and shifting to GPI, the Genuine Progress Indicator (which is similar to Daly's proposal). He also endorses basic income.

In Bhutan, the King has declared that "Happiness is more important than Gross Domestic Product." Bhutan added Gross National Happiness to their constitution in 2008. vox.com/future-perfect/2019/6/8/18656710/new-zealand-wellbeing-budget-bhutan-happiness.

In New Zealand, Prime Minister Jacinda Ardern released a "wellbeing budget" in May 2019, with a personal letter.

Growth alone does not lead to a great country. So it's time to focus on those things that do.

We have broadened our definition of success for our country to one that incorporates not just the health of our finances, but also of our natural resources, people and communities. treasury.govt.nz/publications/wellbeing-budget/wellbeing-budget-2019-html#section-2.

9. Chapter 7, page 75. Democracy, as these phrases indicate, involves much more than elections. Yet people tend to overemphasize elections, and often overlook other elements.

That overemphasis is a problem. Autocrats, authoritarians, and military rulers use elections to legitimize their regimes; that's routine, their standard playbook. After "winning" the election, they claim popular mandates for themselves and their policies. And they almost always get away with it, even when elections are brazenly stolen, and the abuses, crimes, and lies are documented. Protests subside or are repressed. The regime stays in power.

Overemphasis on elections was also a factor in prolonging the wars in Afghanistan and Iraq. In both countries, the Bush administration pushed for early national elections. Elections were held, and U.S. officials declared the countries to be democracies, asserting that those governments would succeed. If, instead, there was appropriate respect for rule of law, equal rights, etc. – and local elections first, before national ones – Afghanistan and Iraq might have become stable and peaceful within a few years.

Rule of law, equal rights, etc., are indispensable for democracy. Elections are not. An alternative is sortition, selecting officials at random for a limited term, like a grand jury. Ideally, officials are diverse and anonymous, and act as groups through consensus. Officials have compelling reasons to legislate responsibly: their term ends, and then they have to live under the laws and policies they devised.

The world's first democracy, ancient Athens, used sortition. They viewed it as superior to elections, possibly imperative for true democracy.

10. Chapter 7, page 76. Thom Hartmann, author, entrepreneur, and television host, examined the *Santa Clara* decision in *Unequal Protection: the Rise of*

Corporate Dominance and the Theft of Human Rights (2002). When the Court created corporate personhood, it,

> was not a formal ruling ...
>
> - There was no Supreme Court decision to the effect that corporations are equal to natural persons and not artificial persons.
> - There were no opinions issued to that effect, and therefore no dissenting opinions on this immensely important constitutional issue.

Corporations Are Not People: Why They Have More Rights Than You Do and What You Can Do About It (2012), by Jeffrey D. Clements, reviews that history and focuses on the Supreme Court's 2010 ruling in *Citizens United*. He's a lawyer and cofounder of American Promise, americanpromise. net, one of the groups working to end corporate personhood with a 28th amendment to our Constitution.

Adam Winkler, a professor of constitutional law at UCLA, is the author of *We the Corporations: How American Businesses Won Their Civil Rights* (2018), a comprehensive history and analysis of these issues from colonial times until today. He notes that Thomas Jefferson denounced "the aristocracy of our monied corporations which dare already to challenge our government." For James Madison, "the indefinite accumulation of property" was "an evil which ought to be guarded against," and "the power of all corporations ought to be limited in this respect." James Wilson, who signed the Declaration of Independence and our U.S. Constitution, and was one of the first six justices on the Supreme Court, counselled that corporations "should be erected with caution, and inspected with care."

Corporate personhood was created through fraud. In the *Santa Clara* lawsuit, Southern Pacific Railroad was represented by Roscoe Conkling, a former senator. Conkling was on the committee that drafted the Fourteenth Amendment, and had twice turned down appointments to the Court.

As Winkler describes it,

[Conkling claimed that] the drafters had inserted the word *persons* instead of *citizens* with the goal of covering corporations but never told anyone of their purpose or of the effect of the word choice. ...

[But] Conkling's account of the drafting history was fanciful. There was no conspiracy by the drafters of the Fourteenth Amendment to sneak broad new protections for corporations into the Constitution. ... the fraud was Conkling, who purposefully misled the justices about the original meaning and intent of the Fourteenth Amendment.

Winkler sees two stages of corporations attaining greater legal status, first property rights then liberty rights. Today, he maintains, corporations' property rights are fully established, pervading our economy and therefore difficult or impossible to change. But we must reverse or restrict their liberty rights, to reject their claims to freedom of speech, freedom of religion, and so on. We have to exclude them from our democracy.

(Endnote 22 has more about *Citizens United*. Endnote 33 cites additional groups that are working to overturn it.)

11. Chapter 8, page 83. Before the 1990s, both parties worked to protect our environment.

Republican Richard Nixon signed the Clean Air Act, Clean Water Act, Endangered Species Act, and the law that established the Environmental Protection Agency. Republican Ronald Reagan was a leader in negotiating and implementing the Montreal Protocol, a strict international agreement to phase out ozone-depleting chemicals. Republican George H. W. Bush declared himself the "environmental president," updated the Clean Air Act, and enacted a cap-and-trade program that reduced sulfur dioxide emissions that cause acid rain.

The partisan split began while Democrat Bill Clinton was president. Since then, Republican politicians – led by George W. Bush, Mitch McConnell, and Donald Trump – have zealously proclaimed their desire to dig coal, drill for oil, rescind regulations, and repeal legislation.

12. Chapter 8, page 84. Carbon tax supporters got a major boost in February 2017. As described in the *New York Times*, "A group of Republican elder statesmen is calling for a tax on carbon emissions to fight climate change."

The group, led by former Secretary of State James A. Baker III, with former Secretary of State George P. Shultz and Henry M. Paulson Jr., a former secretary of the Treasury, says that taxing carbon pollution produced by burning fossil fuels is "a conservative climate solution" based on free-market principles. nytimes.com/2017/02/07/science/a-conservative-climate-solution-republican-group-calls-for-carbon-tax.html.

That group is the **Climate Leadership Council**, and they also endorse a dividend. Their plan is "pro-growth, pro-competitiveness and pro-working class, which aligns perfectly with President Trump's stated agenda," according to three members, Martin S. Feldstein, Ted Halstead, and N. Gregory Mankiw. nytimes.com/2017/02/08/opinion/a-conservative-case-for-climate-action.html.

An "Economists' Statement on Carbon Dividends," published in January 2019, stated that a carbon tax is "the most cost-effective lever to reduce carbon emissions at the scale and speed that is necessary." Signers include 27 Nobel laureate economists, 15 former chairs of the Council of Economic Advisors, and 4 former chairs of the Federal Reserve. Their final recommendation:

> To maximize the fairness and political viability of a rising carbon tax, all the revenue should be returned directly to U.S. citizens through equal lump-sum rebates. The majority of American families, including the most vulnerable, will benefit financially by receiving more in "carbon dividends" than they pay in increased energy prices. clcouncil.org/economists-statement/.

The **Intergovernmental Panel on Climate Change**, the world's top scientists on this topic, recommends a carbon tax in their October 2018 report. nytimes.com/2018/10/07/climate/ipcc-climate-report-2040.html.

The 2018 Nobel in economics went to two Americans, William Nordhaus and Paul Romer. From the *New York Times*:

The Yale economist William D. Nordhaus has spent the better part of four decades trying to persuade governments to address climate change, preferably by imposing a tax on carbon emissions. His careful work has long since convinced most members of his own profession.

Professor Nordhaus shared the prize with Paul M. Romer, an economist at New York University whose work has demonstrated that government policy plays a critical role in fostering technological innovation. nytimes.com/2018/10/08/business/economic-science-nobel-prize.html.

A tax-and-dividend bill, the **Energy Innovation and Carbon Dividend Act**, H.R. 763, was introduced in 2019. It aims to "drive down America's carbon pollution and bring climate change under control, while unleashing American technology innovation and ingenuity." Proponents describe it as "Effective. Good for people. Good for the economy. Bipartisan. Revenue Neutral." energyinnovationact.org.

Supporters are organizing nationwide through the **Citizens Climate Lobby.** citizensclimatelobby.org/.

With Citizen Dividends, dividend-then-tax, a carbon tax might be hugely popular.

13. Chapter 8, page 86. Roads, bridges, sewers, etc., are normally described as *infrastructure*. The term is recent. In the early 1980s, the *New York Times* and other newspapers used it with quotation marks. Engineer and scholar Henry Petroski cites this fact in *The Road Taken: The History and Future of America's Infrastructure* (2016). A prior term, now mostly forgotten, is *public works*.

This shift is noteworthy for its timing. Ronald Reagan was president in the 1980s. In his first inaugural address, he declared that "In this present crisis, government is not the solution to our problem; government is the problem." His administration cut funding for public works, public transit, public services, etc., particularly programs that serve the poor. He equated *public* with *socialism*.

These views and policies express neoliberalism, the dominant ideology of recent decades. Neoliberal Republicans routinely denounce *public* and promote privatization. Neoliberal Democrats praise public-private partnerships, though the outcomes are similar.

Post-neoliberal citizens ought to reclaim *public* and *public works.* The public is us, *We the People.*

14. Chapter 8, page 88. The benefits of land value taxes are most evident in Japan, Taiwan, and Hong Kong. Japan and Taiwan were poor countries prior to World War II. After the war, both instituted land value taxation, and the decline in land speculation helped transform both into economic powers. Hong Kong land is owned by the public. Buildings are privately owned, and owners pay a ground rent. When government invests in schools, parks, transit, etc., nearby locations and buildings become more valuable. Those gains are taxed and returned to society.

In the United States, many cities have a "split-rate" property tax that mainly taxes land values, with a lower rate on building values. Although this is not a full land value tax "experience in Pennsylvania and Maryland has shown that ... [it] lowers property taxes on homeowners and vastly increases new construction and infill construction in urban areas," according to R. Joshua Vincent at the Center for the Study of Economics, a Philadelphia think-tank. urbantoolsconsult.org.

Land Value Taxation: Theory, Evidence, and Practice (2009), edited by Richard F. Dye and Richard W. England, associates of the Lincoln Institute of Land Policy in Cambridge, MA.

Rent as Public Revenue: Issues and Methods (2018), edited by Lindy Davies, a former Program Director of the Henry George Institute.

15. Chapter 8, page 89. Taxes on takings have many forms. In Bristol Bay, Alaska, in the early 1970s, Mayor Jay Hammond, alarmed by a steep increase in Japanese commercial fishing, persuaded residents to tax the taking of

salmon. Although local fisherman opposed the tax, it brought in significant revenues from the Japanese, with benefits for the whole community.

Hammond was elected governor in 1974, and was a leader in creating the Alaska Permanent Fund and the Permanent Fund Dividend.

16. Chapter 8, page 92. E. G. Vallianotos was an analyst at the Environmental Protection Agency for 25 years, mostly in the Office of Pesticides Programs. In *Poison Spring: the Secret History of Pollution and the EPA* (2014), he and coauthor McKay Jenkins document how the EPA was captured by the chemical, petroleum, and agribusiness industries.

The EPA, they say, mainly functions as a "polluters' protection agency."

17. Chapter 8, page 92. Glyphosate, according to *Poison Spring,* is correlated with "cancer, endocrine disruption, damage to DNA, and deleterious malformations of the reproductive, neurological, and developmental systems of animals and humans." Monsanto is now owned by Bayer, and they've lost or settled several big lawsuits over glyphosate.

When debating GMOs, typically, people on each side talk past or over the other side. Supporters tout golden rice, which has an added gene that produces vitamin A. Critics warn about salmon modified for faster growth and greater size, "Frankenfish," and the risks to wild salmon and other species.

With GMO corn, soybeans, etc., modified genes have spread to weeds. Monsanto, Bayer, and their competitors are developing a next round of GMO seeds, engineered to resist herbicides that are more potent than glyphosate. Scientists now have a technology, Crispr, that can modify genes rapidly, at low cost. European governments ban most GMOs.

We, as individuals and our government, should assess all GMOs carefully, scientifically, applying the precautionary principle while seeking long-term public benefits.

18. Chapter 8, page 92. A peer-reviewed scientific paper on Corexit and the Deepwater Horizon disaster: journals.plos.org/plosone/article?id=10.1371/journal.pone.0045574.

On the science and the politics, from *Mother Jones* magazine, mother-jones.com/environment/2010/09/bp-ocean-dispersant-corexit.

19. Chapter 8, page 92. Plastic trash in the oceans has been widely reported over many years. *National Geographic* published a long article in January 2015, news.nationalgeographic.com/news/2015/01/150109-oceans-plastic-ea-trash-science-marine-debris/.

20. Chapter 9, page 102. Worldwide weapon sales totaled $80 billion in 2015. Half was sold by the United States; France was second at only $15 billion. Major buyers that year were Qatar, Egypt, Saudi Arabia, South Korea, and Pakistan. nytimes.com/2016/12/26/us/politics/united-states-global-weapons-sales.html.

21. Chapter 10, page 114. Efforts to end gerrymandering are bipartisan. On the Republican side, a leading proponent is Arnold Schwarzenegger, former governor of California. Among Democrats, former attorney general Eric Holder and his former boss, Barack Obama.

Nonpartisan redistricting is proving effective in Arizona, California, Iowa, and Washington. Ohio voters enacted it with a constitutional amendment in May 2018, by a margin of 75–25. Colorado, Michigan, Missouri, and Utah passed redistricting reform initiatives in November 2018.

22. Chapter 10, page 114. Nearly all elected officials say they support full disclosure. But it won't happen until *We the People* force them to act.

A master in thwarting disclosure is Senator Mitch McConnell, the Republican leader. The U.S. Senate for many years was the only major legislature that required paper forms for campaign finance reports. Electronic filing is faster, simpler, and cheaper. Also more searchable by journalists, activists, and political opponents. The House of Representatives began electronic filing in 2001, as did most states around the same time.

McConnell blocked it in the Senate until September 2018. His often-stated reasons were to protect donors' privacy and freedom of speech. Perhaps. Though big donors are superrich, the 0.1 percent and 0.01 percent, and McConnell is in the 0.1 percent.

Congress has enacted various laws that require disclosure or limit donations, and the Supreme Court has upheld them. The first was the Tillman Act, a response to the Great Wall Street Scandal of 1905; it banned all donations by corporations, and President Theodore Roosevelt signed it in 1907. A recent law was the Bipartisan Campaign Reform Act of 2002 (BCRA or "McCain-Feingold," for its lead sponsors in the Senate, Republican John McCain and Democrat Russ Feingold). McConnell sued to overturn it, *McConnell v. Federal Election Commission.* The Court ruled it constitutional in 2003.

In *Citizens United*, 2010, the Court cited the First Amendment and freedom of speech, and ruled that government cannot prohibit corporations from donating to PACs (Political Action Committees), Super-PACs, and 501(c)(4) groups. Those are supposed to be independent of political campaigns, but that's a pretense, an impractical joke; groups are funded and controlled by friends of the candidates. And they can conceal donors or defer disclosure until after elections. *Citizens United* led to a surge in unreported "dark money."

Full disclosure is vital for a healthy democracy. Our government must equally protect the rights of all citizens, including non-donors and non-voters.

(Endnote 10 has more about *Citizens United*. Endnote 33 has the names of various groups that are working to overturn it, to require full disclosure, and to get money out of politics.)

23. Chapter 10, page 114. Small donor public financing has proved successful in cities around the country, and for state offices in Arizona, Connecticut, Maine, and Minnesota. Small donations are multiplied by 4 to 1, 6 to 1, or other formula, while outside fundraising is banned or limited. Programs are voluntary and fully constitutional. Participating candidates can focus on

talking with, and listening to, regular folks, instead of constantly seeking dollars from big donors.

Vouchers are used in Seattle, and were approved by both the city council and a voter referendum. In the 2017 election for city council, the first one with the program, voters received four $25 vouchers they could assign to the candidate(s) they favored. It was a success. Voter turnout increased from prior elections, and candidates were more diverse and representative of their communities. seattle.gov/democracyvoucher.

Legal scholar Richard L. Hasen, a professor of law and political science at the University of California Irvine School of Law, calls for vouchers in *Plutocrats United: Campaign Money, the Supreme Court, and the Distortion of American Elections* (2016).

Richard Painter was chief ethics officer in the George W. Bush administration, and proposes a federal tax rebate of $200 that people can allocate to selected campaigns. His book is *Taxation Only with Representation: The Conservative Conscience and Campaign Finance Reform* (2016).

24. Chapter 10, page 115. Ranked Choice Voting, sometimes called Preference Voting, Alternative Voting, or Instant Runoff Voting, has proven effective in cities across the country. Other countries and many private entities also use it.

RCV, in addition to encouraging positive campaigns and ensuring that winners have majority support, opens the door for small parties, independent candidates, and new ideas. Today, routinely, Democrats and Republicans attack small parties and independent candidates as "spoilers." "Don't waste your vote," they tell their supporters. "If you vote for a small party or independent, the other big party might win — and it'll be your fault." Both big parties work actively, sometimes jointly, to keep or kick small parties and independents off polls, debates, and ballots.

Maine has RCV for state offices and the U.S. Congress. Voters enacted it in 2016, through a ballot initiative. In June 2018, a few days before the primary election that was the first with RCV, the *New York Times* endorsed it. nytimes.com/2018/06/09/opinion/ranked-choice-voting-maine-san-francisco.html.

Two of those primaries were decided through RCV, both on the Democratic side, for governor and one of Maine's congressional districts. There was also a ballot question about whether to retain it. Voters said "yes" by a large margin.

In November 2018, in Maine's second congressional district, the top two candidates each received 46 percent of the vote, with the Republican incumbent slightly ahead. The other 8 percent voted for an independent or a Green Party candidate; those voters had their second choices counted — and Democrat Jared Golden won.

New York City voters approved a ballot question on RCV in November 2019, by a margin of 3 to 1. They'll use it in primary and special elections starting in 2021. businessinsider.com/new-york-just-embraced-a-revolutionary-ranked-choice-voting-system-2019-11.

RCV can be especially useful for party primaries, particularly for president. Representative Jamie Raskin presents this idea in an article written with Rob Ritchie, President and CEO of FairVote.org, and Adam Eichen of EqualCitizens.us.

> [RCV] will help any party gain stronger nominees and provide more clarity about what voters really want going into conventions. Because voters' backup choices matter, candidates with RCV tend to run more positive campaigns, seek common ground, and respect their opponents' supporters. That means primaries will see less of the divisive rhetoric that can weaken nominees in the general election. thehill.com/blogs/congress-blog/politics/426982-a-crowded-2020-presidential-primary-field-calls-for-ranked.

Election scientists and mathematicians say our usual voting method – plurality voting, "first past the post," even if the one with the most votes has less than 40 percent – is the worst in many ways. RCV is only one alternative. Another is Approval Voting. Voters select each candidate they approve of, perhaps score each on a scale of 0 to 5, then whoever has the greatest approval is elected. Three advocacy groups are the Center for Election Science, electionscience.org; Unsplit the Vote, unsplitthevote.org; and Star Voting, "Score Then Automatic Runoff," starvoting.us.

25. Chapter 10, page 115. California instituted top-two open primaries in 2012. Since then, general elections have often been two Democrats, including for the U.S. Senate in 2016 and 2018. Democrats hold all statewide offices in 2019, with supermajorities in both branches of the state legislature. Top-four with RCV will be far more democratic.

26. Chapter 10, page 115. Elections are run by partisan secretaries of state. (Also local officials, though some are nonpartisan.) That's like a football game with a referee who's on one of the teams — unacceptable in every sport, and we should eliminate it from our democracy.

In Kansas and Georgia in 2018, secretaries of state ran the elections while campaigning for governor. Both were asked to resign or recuse, and both refused. In Kansas, Kris Kobach lost to Laura Kelly. In Georgia, with Brian Kemp, there were multiple lawsuits over voter purges, voter suppression, mishandling of ballots, and racial bias. The outcome was close; counting required ten days. Kemp was elected over Stacey Abrams.

Election integrity is imperative and priceless. We could employ non-partisan professionals; that's common sense, it's how other democracies operate, and whatever it costs will be a wise investment. Also paper ballots that voters can verify and officials can audit or recount. And equipment and software that's fully testable and tested, not proprietary, and never connected to the internet.

We should also reform the Federal Election Commission. It was created in 1974 as a response to corrupt fundraising by Richard Nixon. The FEC has six members, normally three from each party, so it's often deadlocked, impotent. About 40 percent of Americans are independent or unaffiliated. For proper checks and balances and representation, the FEC could have seven members: two Democrats, two Republicans, and three who are neither. The three members might be vetted and nominated by a Nonpartisan Commission, created for that purpose, comprised of people who are publicly unaffiliated or members of smaller parties.

This nonpartisan model might also make sense for other government agencies and commissions, national, state, and local.

27. Chapter 10, page 115. Because this paragraph focuses on election reforms, it omits other ideas, such as term limits. We can realize most of the gains of term limits, and avoid the flaws, by ending the unfair advantages of incumbents. When the playing field is level for challengers, we'll have natural term limits: truly fair elections.

Proportional representation with multimember districts has large districts; voters elect several officials, normally diverse ones, so that all voters feel represented. Ten states have multimember districts for at least one house of their state legislatures, and that includes Arizona, Maryland, New Jersey, and South Dakota. ballotpedia.org/Multi-member_district.

The National Popular Vote Interstate Compact is an agreement among states to allocate all of their electoral votes to the winner of the nationwide popular vote. It'll go into effect when approved by enough states to make an electoral vote majority — and it's getting close to that. nationalpopularvote.com and makingeveryvotecount.com.

Current campaign laws, rules, and regulations are an incumbent protection racket. Challengers, especially small parties and independent candidates, have to spend substantial sums on lawyers and consultants for help with avoiding the obstacles. The system is rigged. We have to unrig it.

Political campaigns, particularly debates, are job interviews. *We the People* are the employers. We should set the rules.

Initial suggestions: Debates should be hosted by groups that are truly nonpartisan, with the hosts deciding the format, schedule, and other details. Debates should be mandatory, or nearly so, with massive shaming of any candidate who tries to avoid or evade them. We should also compress or curtail campaigns; citizens deserve a break, please, and we want our representatives to focus on governing – the jobs we elect them to do – not constant campaigning. Primaries for most offices can be in September, open primaries that advance the top four, then general elections with RCV. For president, state primaries might be in the summer, party conventions in September. (And RCV, though first we may have to abolish the electoral college or bypass it with the National Popular Vote.)

Also: Let's urge, encourage, and support the news media to focus more on issues and policies, and much less on personalities and polls.

Countless news stories cover politics like a game or sport, who's up or down, favored or fading, the odds and the point spread, the "horse race." States and districts, and issues and voters, are routinely labeled red or blue, left or right, liberal or conservative. When reporters interview regular folks, typically, the first or only question is "Who do you support?"

Those polls, labels, and practices exacerbate dysfunctional tribalism. When people choose one side or candidate, and whenever we use or accept the labels, tribal identities are strengthened and cemented; we tend to defend our choice, seeking or making-up facts, reasons, explanations, and rationalizations.

(Psychologists call that motivated reasoning, confirmation bias, or cognitive dissonance. We believe what we want to believe, in effect, and we knee-jerk deny or dismiss evidence that conflicts with our beliefs. That's normal, nearly universal. We've all seen it in other people, most obviously when someone disagrees with us about sports or politics, though we're usually unaware when we do it. One way to avoid or overcome it is to deliberately, even stubbornly, remain undecided until after seeking and evaluating facts from multiple perspectives.)

Reporters can help renew our democracy by asking us *What do you want?* or *What do you think?* regarding specific issues. What do you want – or think about – regarding crime, taxes, healthcare, education, immigration, global warming, or other matters. Ask people to rank their priorities: what do you want most, or more, or less, or least. Ask people what they know about each candidate's plans, policies, and promises, and how those fit with your personal priorities. Then, if appropriate, conclude by asking people which candidate they support.

These questions are constructive, irrespective of the answers, because they invite people to think actively about the issues. And, more importantly, about our roles, rights, and responsibilities as citizens.

Let's also urge and encourage reporters to focus more on local concerns. We can do that by supporting local newspapers, radio stations, and news websites — reading, listening, and subscribing, especially to those that are independent and truly local.

28. Chapter 10, page 115. Calls for expanding the House of Representatives gained renewed attention a week after the 2018 election. Based on comparisons with other democracies, and a mathematical formula, the editorial board of the *New York Times* presented a proposal for 593 members. nytimes.com/interactive/2018/11/09/opinion/expanded-house-representatives-size.html.

In a follow-up piece, they endorse multimember districts, show how the 593 members might be distributed, and consider how this would strengthen our democracy.

> The result of all this is that the vast majority of voters, whether they live in cities, in suburbs, or in rural areas, would have someone in power who represents them. This could help foster bipartisanship and compromise, as members of different parties would need to work together on behalf of their district's voters. After all, both Democrats and Republicans need the potholes to be fixed. nytimes.com/interactive/2018/11/10/opinion/house-representatives-size-multi-member.html.

29. Chapter 10, page 116. The plenary power doctrine was established in *United States v. Rogers*, and that 1846 opinion was written by Chief Justice Roger Taney. He was also the author of the *Dred Scott* ruling, 1857, which stated that the U.S. Constitution did not protect African-Americans, neither slaves nor the free. *Dred Scott* is universally condemned as one of the Court's

worst decisions, and it was superseded by the Thirteenth and Fourteenth Amendments in 1868.

But the plenary power doctrine is still the law. And the Trump administration has cited it as the authorization for confining immigrants and separating immigrant children from their parents. nytimes.com/2019/05/26/opinion/american-indian-law-trump.html.

30. Chapter 10, page 118. Figures are from a March 2017 *New York Times* article about the size, cost, reach, and power of the U.S. military. nytimes.com/interactive/2017/03/22/us/is-americas-military-big-enough.html.

In April 2019, the Stockholm International Peace Research Institute reported that

> Total world military expenditure rose to $1822 billion in 2018, representing an increase of 2.6 per cent from 2017, … The five biggest spenders in 2018 were the United States, China, Saudi Arabia, India and France, which together accounted for 60 per cent of global military spending. sipri.org/media/press-release/2019/world-military-expenditure-grows-18-trillion-2018.

31. Chapter 10, page 121. Of the two that were not ratified, one is now the Twenty-Seventh Amendment. It was added in 1992, after being dormant for 200 years. "No law, varying the compensation for the services of the Senators and Representatives, shall take effect, until an election of representatives shall have intervened."

32. Chapter 10, page 123. Modern Tea Party supporters – if they fully embrace the goals, ideals, and values of the original – ought to demand sovereignty over corporations.

33. Chapter 10, page 124. Activists from across the political spectrum are working to overturn *Citizens United* and get corporate money out of our political system. That may require us to amend the U.S. Constitution. By the

summer of 2019, more than 100 cities and 20 states had passed resolutions calling for a 28th amendment.

Campaign organizations include American Promise, americanpromise. net; End Citizens United, endcitizensunited.org; Issue One, issueone.org; Represent Us, represent.us; Take Back Our Republic, takeback.org; and Wolf Pac, wolf-pac.com. Groups have distinct strategies, tactics, and priorities, though they're generally aligned and mutually supportive.

Allied groups have been active for decades on multiple issues, and include Common Cause, commoncause.org; People for the American Way, pfaw.org; and Public Citizen, citizen.org.

(For more about corporate personhood, see Endnote 10. For more about campaign finance and disclosure, see Endnote 22.)

34. Chapter 11, page 127. "Inverted" is from Sheldon Wolin, who was a professor emeritus of politics at Princeton University. In *Democracy Incorporated: Managed Democracy and the Specter of Inverted Totalitarianism* (2008), he examines economic power and how it shapes our politics. Wealthy corporations, today, are both the agents of our government and its masters — managing it, and us, to serve their interests.

America is becoming, or already is, a new type of totalitarian state, "inverted" because there's minimal overt coercion. We, a large majority of us, readily comply with corporations' requests and demands, and rarely question their power. We're consumers, primarily, not true citizens.

Democracy is "about the conditions that make it possible for ordinary people to better their lives by becoming political beings and by making power responsive to their hopes and needs."

35. Chapter 12, page 138. The stated reason for pilot projects, almost always, is concern about people quitting their jobs or misusing the money, with a secondary focus on how to design the program to encourage responsible behaviors. Yet the research clearly shows that regular folks, including the extremely poor, make good decisions and use their basic income responsibly.

Numerous pilots and experiments are reviewed in Appendices 1 and 3. None has revealed significant problems. All have demonstrated substantial, immediate benefits.

36. Appendix 2, page 220. The conventional notion is that government has to raise taxes before spending money, or must do both at the same time, as if taxing and spending are inseparable, like two sides of a coin.

That's wrong, economist Stephanie Kelton insists. And it's harmful, an obstacle to enacting desired popular programs. Special interests can hijack progress by opposing the taxes. And because special interests are focused, organized, and mobilized, they usually prevail.

Taxing and spending are separate. Taxes have two main purposes: to halt or prevent inflation by reducing the money supply, removing money from circulation, and/or to create incentives or disincentives for specific behaviors, such as excise taxes on tobacco, alcohol, imports, or fossil fuels.

Questions about funding – "How are you going to pay for it?" "Who's going to pay for it?" – Kelton states, are

> designed to stop any meaningful policy debate by dividing us up, and get us fighting over where the money is going to come from. Since none of the headline politicians has really figured out how to respond ... they all end up trying to answer it by pointing to some new revenue source.
>
> And then there are self-imposed constraints, like PAYGO, that require lawmakers to offset any new spending with higher taxes or cuts to some other part of the budget. That means you can't even get a piece of legislation to the floor for a vote if isn't fully "paid for." It also makes passing anything that much harder, since it requires politicians to raise taxes or carve out money from other programs.

Our top priority should be investing in social and environmental programs that provide lasting benefits. *Investing*, in the strict, literal meaning of that term, as distinct from *spending*. Smart investments lead to a better future and higher tax revenues.

We get good-paying jobs, a cleaner world and more safe assets (Treasuries) for everyone, including wealthier taxpayers. ... without treating the super-rich as a piggy bank. bloomberg.com/opinion/articles/2019-02-01/rich-must-embrace-deficits-to-escape-taxes.

Kelton is a Professor of Public Policy and Economics at Stony Brook University, and former chief economist for the U.S. Senate Budget Committee. She's a leading advocate of Modern Monetary Theory, MMT.

37. Appendix 2, page 220. Public banks are "operated in the public interest, through institutions owned by the people through their representative governments." Many cities and states are looking to launch their own banks, their efforts coordinated by the Public Banking Institute. publicbankinginstitute.org/.

Public banks could facilitate local basic income programs by managing the money flow, working with local and state governments.

Ellen Brown, author of *The Public Bank Solution: From Austerity to Prosperity* (2013) and founder of the Public Banking Institute, discusses these possibilities in several blog posts, "How to Fund a Universal Basic Income Without Increasing Taxes or Inflation" and "Universal Basic Income Is Easier Than It Looks." Both are at ellenbrown.com/tag/universal-basic-income/.

38. Appendix 2, page 222. Andy Stern's proposed wealth tax is "1.5 percent ... on all personal assets over $1 million," and would generate "over $600 billion in new revenue." He states that wealthy Americans might find that "less onerous" than higher income tax rates.

Senator Elizabeth Warren's "Ultra-Millionaire Tax" would only affect the wealthiest Americans, the top 0.1 percent, fewer than 80,000 households. "Households would pay an annual 2% tax on every dollar of net worth above $50 million, and a 3% tax on every dollar of net worth about $1 billion." It would raise an estimated $2.75 trillion over ten years. She talks about it in her campaign for the 2020 Democratic nomination. warren.senate.gov/

newsroom/press-releases/senator-warren-unveils-proposal-to-tax-wealth-of-ultra-rich-americans.

(A prominent billionaire proposed a much larger wealth tax in 1999, while talking about possibly running for president, "a one-time 14.25 percent net-worth tax on the wealthiest members of our society." That was Donald Trump. He wanted to eliminate the national debt, fund middle class tax cuts, and safeguard Social Security. "Personally this plan would cost me hundreds of millions of dollars, but in all honesty, it's worth it." cnn.com/ALLPOLITICS/stories/1999/11/09/trump.rich/index.html.

In 2018, *USA Today* published an opinion piece stating that "Trump should revive the wealth tax he called for in 1999. America needs it more than ever." Author Darrell M. West is director of governance studies at the Brookings Institution. usatoday.com/story/opinion/2018/07/31/trump-1999-wealth-tax-lower-deficits-reduce-inequality-column/826224002/.)

When Warren announced her plan in January 2019, several billionaires responded immediately: "socialism," "ridiculous," "punitive," "it's called Venezuela." Billionaires and pundits launched similar attacks when Representative Alexandria Ocasio-Cortez called for a 70 percent marginal rate on incomes over $10 million.

Those attacks ignore the facts. The top marginal tax rate was 91 percent in the 1950s, above 70 percent until 1981, and estate taxes were much higher than today. The United States was not Venezuela, and not socialist. The 1950s and '60s was a golden age of capitalism.

First, though, we should end their tax breaks. That's "A Better Way to Tax the Rich," Steven Rattner suggests in a *New York Times* piece, responding to Ocasio-Cortez's proposal.

> There are other, better ways to raise revenue — in particular, by increasing the tax rate on capital gains and dividends and closing loopholes.
>
> At present, a beneficiary of long-term capital gains or dividends pays 23.8 percent of the profit to Washington. That's already a good bit less than the 37 percent top rate on so-called ordinary income. ...

Proponents of huge increases in the top marginal tax rates argue that they were once even higher than 70 percent and applied to lower levels of income. Yes, the "sticker prices" in the past went up to just over 90 percent, but few people actually paid them. Instead, they took advantage of tax shelters and tax-avoidance schemes to keep their bill as low as possible.

… I'm not opposed to a reasonable increase in the top marginal rate, but when it comes to getting the richest Americans to pay more, there are much better ideas than Ms. Ocasio-Cortez's plan. nytimes. com/2019/01/28/opinion/aoc-wealth-tax.html.

Rattner cites several specific tax breaks and loopholes to eliminate, including provisions in the 2017 Trump-Republican tax cut that "allow many real estate guys (including President Trump) to pay little, if any tax."

Rattner is a journalist and Wall Street executive, and very rich; he's proposing to raise his own taxes. Many wealthy Americans say their taxes should be higher. They even have an organization, Patriotic Millionaires. (Endnote 5 has an excerpt from their website.)

We might start with a tax like the charts in Chapter 3, a flat rate of 15, 25, or 35 percent. Then, if we want to do more to reduce inequality, perhaps a 40 percent rate above $1 million and 70 percent above $10 million. Or a 10 percent surtax on all income above $2 million. Or increase the estate tax. Or enact a wealth tax. Or all of these.

For a healthy democracy, *New York Times* columnist Farhad Manjoo suggests, we may have to "Abolish Billionaires." nytimes.com/2019/02/06/opinion/abolish-billionaires-tax.html.

Wealth taxes can also be indirect, and that might be best. Millionaires and billionaires have bigger homes, fancier cars, more vacations, and more stuff. Tax consumption – with a VAT, carbon taxes, land value taxes, etc. – and the wealthy will pay much more than regular folks.

Land value taxes may be most effective. The Federal Housing Finance Agency published a study in January 2019 showing that land values vary – by 7,500 to 1 – between prime urban locations and rural regions. As reported in the *Washington Post,*

Nationwide, land values are rising faster than home values, according to an analysis of more than 16 million appraisals across almost 40,000 U.S. neighborhoods. ...

It's not just the distribution of land wealth that's unequal, it's the growth in that wealth. The areas with the most valuable lots also saw their land values grow fastest, even after adjusting for current value. And those differences are responsible for many of the trends in inequality which have defined our era.

"Generally, land tends to appreciate faster than structures," said the study's lead author, William Larson, "because when housing demand changes, you can build more structures but you can't build more land." The *Post* also quoted economist Joseph Stiglitz of Columbia University, "There can be an increase in the value of land without any increase in the productive potential of the economy."

The *Post* article is "Detailed Data Show the Value of Land Under Homes across the Country." washingtonpost.com/us-policy/2019/01/23/why-its-problem-that-dirt-brooklyn-is-so-much-more-expensive-than-dirt-arkansas/.

The complete study: fhfa.gov/PolicyProgramsResearch/Research/Pages/wp1901.aspx.

39. Appendix 2, page 222. Universal basic capital, Nathan Gardels states, "is a far deeper response to the challenges ahead than 'universal basic income.'" To emphasize that idea, the title of his opinion piece is "Alexandria Ocasio-Cortez is not Radical Enough." washingtonpost.com/news/theworld-post/wp/2019/01/25/alexandria-ocasio-cortez/.

Capital accounts will require years to accumulate, maybe a decade or two. Proponents of universal basic capital might want to start with a small basic income. Then, when capital accounts are adequate, use those assets to increase the amount.

40. Appendix 2, page 223. This short summary is from Andrew Yang in *The War on Normal People: the Truth About Disappearing Jobs and Why Universal Basic Income is our Future* (2018).

The full report is at rooseveltinstitute.org/modeling-macroeconomic-effects-ubi/.

Acknowledgments

The core of this book, for me, is the way of thinking that led to these ideas and the reader-centered presentation. I especially esteem two mentors, though both are no longer alive. Moshe Feldenkrais was an engineer, mathematician, neuroscientist, judo master, and the creator of the Feldenkrais Method of somatic education. I view him primarily as a philosopher. Thinking, he avowed, is more fundamental than language; words often thwart, distort, or distract us from thinking; and "real thinking leads to new ways of acting." He acted to "make the abstract concrete." He aspired to "say yes and no at the same time."

Robert Fitzgerald was a "recovering attorney," devoted environmentalist, and steadfast advocate for system science and rigorous thinking. Bob insisted on refining or distilling ideas first, before crafting any presentation. "There is no 'we'" is his phrase, and I heard it often. When I wrote my first book about basic income, in 1997, he was my first reader, and his advice was always valuable. While writing this book, I often wished he was available.

Moshe and Bob were true mentors, as distinct from teachers. They encouraged me to trust my insights, to question abstract concepts, and to think functionally and constructively. Their influence is throughout this book.

I've talked about these ideas with thousands of people over more than three decades, and I'd like to thank everyone. Through your listening and your questions – even if you doubted, objected, or bluntly rejected what I was saying – you helped me refine my thinking and my skills in communicating.

From my years in Santa Barbara, I thank Jeffrey J. Smith, Gary Flomenhoft, and J.W. Ballard.

Thanks to everyone who attended any meeting of USBIG or BIEN, especially Allan Sheahen, Karl Widerquist, Eri Noguchi, Michael Lewis, Almaz Zelleke, Michael Howard, Diane Pagen, and Jason Murphy. Also Guy Standing and Philippe Van Parijs.

I began writing this book in early 2011, initially as two distinct books, one for liberals, the other for conservatives, then merged them in 2014. I revised that draft throughout the 2016 election, and self-published a version in the summer of 2017, *Basic Income Imperative: For Peace, Justice, Liberty, and Personal Dignity.*

That book was immensely improved by a superb, professional, anonymous editor. Thanks for indirectly making this one much better. (She edits for politicians and other public figures, and insists on anonymity with non-fiction projects.)

I compiled Appendix 1 over three decades, and have previously published several iterations. This is the most comprehensive, by far. Thanks to Philippe Van Parijs and Yannick Vanderborght for a few items from your 2017 book. Also to Dorian Warren and Bill Arnone.

Thanks to Alanna Hartzok and Rick Rybeck for responding to questions about the land value tax. Thanks to Rob Ritchie and Cynthia Terrell at FairVote.

Amplify and RealClear Publishing have been great; I was most fortunate to find them when I did, thanks to Neal Simon for referring me. Editor Kristin Clark Taylor was a joy to work with, smart, thoughtful, and always respectful of me and the book. Thanks to publishers Naren Aryal and Carl Cannon, and to Nina Spahn, Erin Weston, Lauren Kanne, and the rest of the team. Thanks to John Dreyfuss for the cover design.

I also want to thank the friends and family members who sustained me over the years of feeling driven to complete this book, when I was often absent or inattentive, and I'll do that in person. One I must mention is my mother, Janis Shafarman, for expressing her love in many ways, including financial support, even while urging me to set this project aside and focus on my other career.

Enthusiastic thanks, in advance, to everyone who helps move these ideas forward. If you decide to run for political office, I'll do what I can to assist your campaign.

Let's make history!

Index

#MeToo, 9, 138
9/11, 46

A. Philip Randolph Institute, 170
abortion, 10, 66–7, 71
Ackerman, Bruce, 188–9
Ad Hoc Committee for a Guaranteed
Income, 169–70
Ad Hoc Committee on the Triple
Revolution, 166–7
Adams, John, 19, 151, 152, 238
Affordable Care Act (Obamacare), 45,
48–9
Afghanistan, 27, 103, 109–11, 118–9,
128, 219, 245
agriculture, 90–4
Alaska Permanent Fund Dividend
(PFD), 14, 35, 104, 105, 125, 126,
152, 180–1, 192, 208, 226, 251
Alford, Helen, 187
Allen, Danielle, 237–9
Alperovitz, Gar, 183
Alstott, Anne L., 183, 188–9
alternative voting, see ranked choice
voting
Altman, Sam, 204, 218
American Family Act, 242
American People's Dividend, 190
American Promise, 246, 261
American Recovery and Reinvestment
Act of 2009, 194

America's Founders, 6, 19, 74, 76-8,
113, 116, 120-1, 151, 153, 237-9
approval voting, 255–6
Ardern, Jacinda, 244–5
Aronowitz, Stanley, 192
Atkinson, Anthony B., 200
automation, 78–9, 134, 164–5, 166,
168, 169, 173, 196, 200–1, 206, 211,
212, 216, 222

baby bonds, 215 see also universal
child benefits
Baker, James A. III, 248
Banerjee, Abhijit, 218
Barber, Benjamin R., 187–8
Barber, William J. II, 150
Barnes, Peter, 197–8
basic income, core concepts, 14,
135,182, 239
international efforts, 3, 14, 150, 157,
228–33, 241
local programs, 15, 40, 80, 87–9,
125–7
pilot projects and experiments, 90,
100, 126, 138, 177, 180, 186–7, 204,
216, 227–33, 261–2
Basic Income Earth Network (BIEN),
1, 182, 183, 192, 235, 239, 240, 270
basic income grant/guarantee (BIG),
see basic income
Basic Income Lab, 205, 216
Bell, Daniel, 169

Index

Bellamy, Edward, 154–6
Bennet, Michael, 242
Bevel, James, 169
Bhutan, 244
Bible, 14, 135, 149–50
Bidadanure, Juliana, 205
Bill of Rights, 113, 121–3
  First Amendment, 8, 77, 121, 253
  Fourteenth Amendment, 76, 116,
    123, 246–7, 260
  Twenty-Eighth Amendment, 246,
    261
Bipartisan Campaign Reform Act of
  2002 (BCRA), 253
Black Lives Matter, 9, 118, 138, 202
Block, Fred, 183, 189
Boehner, John, 99
Bolsa Familia (Brazil), 106, 228
Booker, Cory, 215
Border Security, Economic
  Opportunity, and Immigration
  Modernization Act, 99
Boston Tea Party, 123
Brain, Marshall, 191
Brazil, 100, 106, 227–8, 233
Bregman, Rutger, 204
Brown, Edmund G., 175
Brown, Ellen, 263
Brown, Sherrod, 242
Brynjolfsson, Erik, 197
Buchheit, Paul, 205
Buffett, Warren, 242
Bush, George H.W., see Bush (George
  H.W.) administration
Bush, George W., see Bush (George
  W.) administration
Bush (George H.W.) administration,
  179, 243, 247
Bush (George W.) administration, 53,
  54, 118, 179, 190–1, 193, 195, 243,
  245, 247, 254

campaign finance reform, 101, 114,
  252–4, 260–1
carbon tax, see taxes, carbon
Carter, Jimmy, see Carter
  administration
Carter administration, 136, 179, 240
Center for Election Science, 256

Chamberlain, James A., 210
Chase, Robin, 199
Chile, 95, 100
China, 47, 92, 95, 101–2, 119, 260,
Citizen Dividends, see basic income
Citizens Climate Lobby, 249
Citizen's Income, see basic income
*Citizens United v. Federal Election
  Commission*, 77, 124, 246–7, 253,
  260–1
Civil War (U.S.), 76, 116, 123
Clark, Charles M. A., 187, 189
class war, 33, 37, 187–8, 242
Clean Air Act, 247
Clean Water Act, 247
Clements, Jeffrey D., 246
Clemons, Steven C., 225–6
climate change, 35, 84, 93, 248–9 *see
  also* global warming
Climate Leadership Council, 248
Clinton, Bill, see Clinton
  administration
Clinton, Hillary Rodham, 208
Clinton administration, 179, 200, 243,
  247
Cloward, Richard, 169, 170
Cobb, John B., 182, 244
Cole, George D. H., 159, 162, 239
Colombia, 100, 227
Common Cause, 261
common heritage dividend, 35, 152,
  159, 193, 240 *see also* basic
  income; Paine, Thomas
conditional cash transfers, 100, 106,
  227–8, 233
Conkling, Roscoe, 246–7
Constitution, see U.S. Constitution
Cook, Richard C., 193
Corexit, 92, 252
Coronavirus, 98, 110
corporations, 54–7, 59, 81, 86, 128
corporate personhood, 76–8, 80, 123,
  246–7
corporate welfare, 14, 19, 23, 43, 47–8,
  57, 78, 84, 123, 128, 145, 218, 242–3
Cortright, Steve, 187
Costello, Jane, 186–7
COVID–19, 98, 110

crime and criminal justice, 7, 17, 25, 65–6, 69–70, 81, 89, 116, 122
crony capitalism, 43–4, 46, 48, 49, 123, 145
Cummings, Homer S., 158

Daly, Herman E., 182, 244
Daniels, Mitch, 195
dark money, 114, 253 *see also* campaign finance reform
Dauphin, Manitoba, Canada, 126, 204, 226–7
Davala, Sarath, 183, 230
Davies, Lindy, 250
debt, individual, 64
    international, 47, 209
    national, 16, 47, 218
Declaration of Independence, 19, 73, 78, 113, 130, 133, 135, 145, 149,151, 237–9, 246
Deepwater Horizon, 92, 252
DeLauro, Rosa, 242
DelBene, Suzan, 242
Demogrants, 136, 178, 240 *see also* basic income
discrimination and diversity, 64, 69, 74–5, 87, 118
dividend-then-tax, 84, 249
Dodd-Frank, 57
Donavan, Pam, 189
Douglas, C.H. "Major", 157, 193, 239
Dred Scott (*Dred Scott v. Sandford*), 259–60
Drucker, Peter, 135, 162, 239
Duflo, Esther, 218
Dye, Richard F., 250

Earned Income Tax Credit (EITC), 43, 140, 179, 197, 203, 214, 242–3
Eastern Band of Cherokee Indians in North Carolina, 90, 126, 186–7, 204
Eichen, Adam, 255
Eight, 231
Economic Security Project, 170, 204, 210, 217, 235
education, 26, 67–71, 126
election reform, 11, 80–1, 114–5, 245, 256–7, 259 *see also* campaign finance reform

End Citizens United, 261
Endangered Species Act, 247
England, Richard W., 250
entitlements, 18–9
environment, 83–9, 104, 247
Environmental Protection Agency (EPA), 247, 251
EqualCitizens.us, 255

FairVote.org, 255
Family Assistance Plan, 14, 136, 175, 176–7, 178–9, 204 *see also* Nixon administration
family issues and values, 65–8, 71, 126
Federal Election Commission (FEC), 77, 124, 253, 256
Federal Reserve, 21, 52–4, 57, 193, 219, 248
Feingold, Russ, 253
Feldstein, Martin S., 248
Filner, Bob, 193
financial transaction tax, *see* taxes, financial transaction
Finland, 107, 126, 138, 232–3, 241
fiscal policy, 21, 53
Five Star Movement (Italy), 232
Flomenhoft, Gary, 182–3
Florida, Richard, 205
food stamps, *see* welfare
Ford, Doug, 227
Ford, Gerald, *see* Ford administration
Ford, Martin, 198–9
Ford administration, 178–9, 240
Forget, Evelyn, 226–7
Foster, Natalie, 210
Founders, *see* America's Founders
Franklin, Benjamin, 19, 238
Frase, Peter, 203
Freedom Dividend, 2, 14, 137, 211, 240 *see also* basic income
Friedman, Milton, 14, 32, 36, 129, 135, 161, 165, 170, 195, 239–40
Friedman, Robert E., 215
Fromm, Erich, 135, 167–8
Fuller, R. Buckminster, 135, 173–4
Funiciello, Theresa, 184

Galbraith, John Kenneth, 162–4, 171–2
Gandhi, Rahul, 230–1

Gardels, Nathan, 222, 266
Garfinkel, Irv, 170
genetically-modified crops (GMOs), 92–3, 95, 251
genuine progress indicator (GPI), 244
Geonomy Society, 182–3
George, Henry, 152, 154–5, 171, 182, 193, 209
George, Robley E., 191
Germany, 34, 102, 107, 138, 150, 153, 229, 241
GiveDirectly, 204, 231
global warming, 25, 26, 84–5, 91, 93, 95, 109, 129, 137, 197 see also climate change
Gorz, André, 181
Great Britain, 34, 107, 111, 121, 123, 133, 145, 150, 156–7, 161, 229, 232, 241
Great Depression, 44, 78, 157–8, 194, 219
Great Recession, 53–4, 194, 219
Great Society, 129, 134, 160 see also Johnson administration
Green New Deal, 84
Green Party, 24, 130, 141, 178, 191–2, 255
Greene, Leonard M., 180
gross domestic product (GDP), 54–5, 58–9, 84, 101, 127, 209, 244
gross national happiness, 244
Graeber, David, 211
guaranteed income, see basic income
guns, 10, 118, 121

Haggerty, Patrick E., 169
Halstead, Ted, 248
Hammond, Jay, 180–1, 250–1
Harari, Yuval Noah, 209, 213
Hardt, Michael, 190
Harris, Kamala, 216
Harris, Robert A., 175
Hartmann, Thom, 245–6
Hartzok, Alanna, 193
Hasen, Richard L., 254
Hawaii Basic Economic Security Working Group, 206–7
Hayek, Friedrich, 130, 135, 160–1
Hazlitt, Henry, 170

health and healthcare, 22, 25–6, 88, 90–1, 98, 117, 186–7, 192
Healy, John, 187
Heineman, Ben W., 175
Henderson, Hazel, 185–6
Hickel, Jason, 209, 244
Holder, Eric, 252
Hopkins, Harry L., 158
Howard, Michael, 181, 189, 192
Hughes, Chris, 170, 204, 210

immigration, 26, 89, 98–100, 108–9, 110–1, 137, 260
income inequality, 64, 70, 125, 197–8
Income Maintenance Experiments, 126, 138, 166, 177
Index of Sustainable Economic Welfare, 244
India, 107, 111, 126, 134, 138, 183, 204, 218, 229–31, 233
inflation, 15, 20–1, 42, 52–3, 54, 59–60, 209, 262
infrastructure, see public works and assets
instant runoff voting, see ranked choice voting
Intergovernmental Panel on Climate Change, 248
Iraq, 27, 104–5, 107, 109, 118–9, 128, 219, 225–6, 245
Iraqi Freedom Fund, 105, 226
Islam, 46, 101, 104–5, 118
Issue One, 261

Jackson, Andrew, 153
Jefferson, Thomas, 14, 19, 135, 151, 152, 237–8, 246
Jenkins, McKay, 251
Jhabvala, Renana, 230
Johnson, Lyndon, see Johnson administration
Johnson administration, 129, 135, 166, 169, 175
Jordan, Barbara, 175
Jordan, Vernon E. Jr., 179

Kairos Center for Religions, Rights, and Social Justice, 150
Keen, Andrew, 209

Index

Kelton, Stephanie, 262–3
Kemp, Brian, 256
Kennedy, John, *see* Kennedy
    administration
Kennedy, Joseph V., 193
Kennedy administration, 163, 178
Kenya, 126, 204, 218, 231, 233
Kessler, Sarah, 212
King, Martin Luther Jr., 14, 69, 87, 129,
    135, 136, 154–5, 167, 170–2
Kobach, Kris, 256
Korten, David, 185
Kravitz, Lee, 201, 220
Kremer, Michael, 218
Kucinich, Dennis, 190
Kuznets, Simon, 55

Lampman, Robert, 172
Land, Edwin H., 169
land value taxes, *see* taxes, land value
    and property
Landrieu, Mary, 105, 226
Lange, Oskar, 159
Lee, Barbara, 190
Lee, Chris, 207
Lee, Mike, 241
Lerner, Abba, 159
Lerner, Michael, 218
Lerner, Sally, 187
Lewis, Michael, 189
Libertarian Party, 24, 130, 141
LIFT+ Act, 216
LIFT (Livable Incomes for Families
    Today) the Middle Class Act, 216
Lincoln, Abraham, 14, 154
Livingston, James, 203
Livingston, Robert R., 19, 238
Long, Huey, 158
Lowrey, Annie, 213

Madison, James, 19, 151, 152, 246
Magnolia Mother's Trust, 217
Mankiw, N. Gregory, 248
McAfee, Andrew, 197
McCain, John, 181, 253
McCain-Feingold, *see* Bipartisan
    Campaign Reform Act of 2002
McChesney, Robert W., 201
McConnell, Mitch, 10, 247, 252–3

*McConnell v. Federal Election
    Commission*, 253
McGovern, George, 136, 178, 240
McLuhan, Marshall, 168
Mead, Margaret, 172–3
Meade, James, 159, 239
Medicare/Medicaid, 18, 23, 24, 36–7,
    42, 45–6, 48, 49, 128
Medicare for All, 46
Mehta, Soumya Kapoor, 230
Mexico, 34, 97, 100, 227, 233
military spending, 23, 46–8, 100–3, 100,
    102, 108–9, 118, 252, 260
Mill, John Stuart, 153
Modern Monetary Theory (MMT),
    263
Monbiot, George, 208–9
Montreal Protocol, 247
More, Thomas, 150
Morgenthau, Henry Jr., 158
Movement for Black Lives, 202–3
Moynihan, Daniel Patrick, 175–7, 240
Munger, Michael, 210
Murkowski, Lisa, 105, 226
Murphy, Jason, 189
Murray, Charles, 45–6, 192, 220–1
Murray, Michael L., 187
Musk, Elon, 204
Myrdal, Gunnar, 167

Nadler, Jerrold, 190
National Climate Assessment, 84
National Commission on Income
    Maintenance Programs, 64, 166,
    175–6, 183
National Commission on Technology,
    Automation, and Economic
    Progress, 166, 169
National Council of Churches of
    Christ in the U.S.A., 173
national dividend, *see* basic income
National Homestead Act of 1862, 154
National League of Cities, 216
National Popular Vote, 115, 257–8
National Tax Rebate, 180, 240
National Urban League, 179
Native Americans, 64, 90, 99, 116–7
Naughton, Mike, 187
Needham, Robert, 187

negative income tax, 32, 129, 161, 165, 206, 240 *see also* basic income
Negri, Antonio, 190
neoconservative, 128
neoliberal, 128, 218, 250
New Deal, 134 *see also* Roosevelt (Franklin) administration
New Zealand, 107, 157, 244–5
Nichols, John, 201
Niskanen Center, 241
Nixon, Richard, *see* Nixon administration
Nixon administration, 14, 136, 165, 174–9, 204, 240, 247, 256
Noguchi, Eri, 189
Nordhaus, William, 248–9

Obama, Barack, *see* Obama administration
Obama administration, 45, 53–4, 179, 194, 201–2, 220, 243, 252
Obamacare, *see* Affordable Care Act
Ocasio-Cortez, Alexandria, 222, 264–5, 266
Occupy Wall Street, 9, 24, 31, 138, 211
Office of Economic Opportunity, 126, 166, 177
Ontario, Canada, 227
Otjivero-Omitara, Namibia, 106–7, 109, 126, 183, 228–9, 233

Paine, Thomas, 14, 35, 86, 134–5, 152, 193, 240
Painter, Richard, 254
Palin, Sarah, 181
Paris Agreement, 85–6
participation income, *see* basic income
Patriotic Millionaires, 242, 265
Pauling, Linus, 167
Paulson, Henry M. Jr, 248
Payments Tax, 35, 146, 207, 222–3
Pearlstein, Steven, 214–5
Pelosi, Nancy, 10
People for the American Way, 261
Perkins, Frances, 158
Peru, 100, 227
Petroski, Henry, 249
Piketty, Thomas, 197, 199

Piven, Frances Fox, 170
plenary power doctrine, 116, 259–60
Polanyi, Karl, 161
political campaigns, 7–8, 86–7, 257–9
political discourse, 8–9, 11, 58–9
pollution, 26, 54, 85, 89, 92–4, 248, 249, 251–2 *see also* environment
Poor People's Campaign, 150
poverty, 22–3, 25, 43, 88–9, 109, 162–5, 187–8, 205, 211, 215, 218, 241
Powell, Colin, 105, 226
predictable income, 162, 239 *see also* basic income
preference voting, *see* ranked choice voting
President's Committee on Economic Security, 158
Program for Better Jobs and Income Support, 136, 179, 240 *see also* Carter administration
Prosperity Now, 215
Public Banking Institute, 263
public banks, 220, 263
Public Citizen, 261
public works and assets, 17, 47, 78, 84, 86–7, 249–50

Quart, Alissa, 212

Randolph, A. Philip, 175
ranked choice voting (RCV), 254–6, 258 *see also* election reform
Raskin, Jamie, 255
Rattner, Steven, 264–5
Raworth, Kate, 127, 205, 244
Reagan, Ronald, *see* Reagan administration
Reagan administration, 129, 134, 179, 243, 247, 249
recessions, 15, 20–1, 53–4, 59–60, 190
Reich, Robert B., 200
reparations, 69, 202–3
Represent Us, 261
resource curse, 104–5, 109
Reuther, Walter P., 169
Revolutionary War (U.S.), 113, 123, 130–1, 133, 145
Rhodes, Elizabeth, 218
Rhys-Williams, Juliet, 161, 239

Rifkin, Jeremy, 135, 184
Ritchie, Rob, 255
Robertson, James, 184
Romer, Paul, 248–9
Roosevelt, Eleanor, 161–2
Roosevelt, Franklin, *see* Roosevelt (Franklin) administration
Roosevelt, Theodore, 155, 253
Roosevelt (Franklin) administration, 78–9, 129, 135, 158–60
Rothschild, Emma, 183
Rubio, Marco, 241
Russell, Bertrand, 156–7
Russia, 101–2, 104, 107, 119
Rustin, Bayard, 167
Rwanda, 231

Samuelson, Paul, 172
Sanders, Bernie, 10, 190
Santa Clara County v. Southern Pacific Railroad, 76, 123, 245–7
Santens, Scott, 197
Schumer, Chuck, 10
Schutz, Robert, 186
Schwarzenegger, Arnold, 252
second Bill of Rights, 79, 129, 160
  see also Roosevelt (Franklin) administration
Self-Employed Women's Association of India (SEWA), 229–30
Seneca Falls Women's Rights Convention, 116
Shafarman, Steven, 188, 235
Share Our Wealth, 44, 135–6, 157–8
Sheahen, Allan, 182, 192–3
Shell, Ellen Ruppel, 215–6
Sherman, Roger, 19, 238
Shultz, George P., 248
Silva, Luiz Inácio Lula da, 228
Simon, Herbert, 183
Sitaraman, Ganesh, 152, 218
Skidelsky, Edward, 196
Skidelsky, Robert, 196
Smith, Adam, 56
Smith, Jeffrey J., 182–3
Smith, Scott, 35, 207, 222–3
Social Credit movement, 157, 193
social dividend, *see* basic income

Social Security, 18, 23–4, 36–7, 44–5, 48, 54, 128, 135–6, 157–8, 164, 194, 201, 207, 221
Social Security for All, 14, 45, 200, 240
Solow, Robert, 169, 175, 183
Springboard to Opportunities, 217
Srnicek, Nick, 200–1
Standing, Guy, 183, 230
Star Voting, 256
Stern, Andy, 201, 220–2, 263
Stigler, George, 161
Stiglitz, Joseph, 36, 266
Stockton Economic Empowerment Demonstration, 217
Sullivan, David, 175–6
Suplicy, Eduardo Matarazzo, 228
Supplemental Nutrition Assistance Program (SNAP), *see* welfare
Switzerland, 140, 231–3
Syria, 104, 107, 111, 118–9

Take Back Our Republic, 261
Tax Cut for the Rest of Us Act of 2006, 140, 192–3
taxes, 15, 25, 29–31, 33, 35–7, 43, 70, 140, 264–5
  carbon or fossil fuel, 35–6, 38–9, 53, 84–6, 88–9, 91, 93, 129, 146, 196–7, 199, 205, 208, 248–9, 262, 265
  corporate, 36–7, 185, 264–5
  financial transaction, 35, 38–9, 57, 146, 157, 185, 196, 207–9, 221, 222
  income, 30–1, 37–9, 59, 129, 146, 179, 187, 214–5, 240
  land value and property, 35–6, 88–9, 91, 93, 146, 153–5, 182, 208–9, 250, 265–6
  payroll, 34, 36, 44–5, 54, 194
  value-added, 34, 39, 146, 197, 199, 211, 265
  wealth, 33–4, 197, 199, 222, 242, 263–5
Taxpayer Advocate Service, 29
Tea Party, 9, 24, 31, 138, 260
Temporary Assistance for Needy Families (TANF), *see* welfare
term limits, 257
terrorists and militants, 46–7, 97–8, 101–3, 105–8, 117–8

Theobald, Robert, 135, 164, 167, 169–70, 239, 240
Theoharis, Liz, 150
Tillman Act, 253
Tlaib, Rashida, 216
Tobin, James, 35, 170, 172, 178, 240
Tobin tax, *see* taxes, financial transaction
Townsend, Francis, *see* Townsend Plan
Townsend Plan, 44, 135–6, 157–8
Trump administration, 10, 37, 84–5, 91, 99, 134, 219, 241–2, 247, 248, 260, 264, 265
Trump, Donald, *see* Trump administration
Tubbs, Michael, 217

Uganda, 204, 231
Ultra-Millionaire Tax, *see* taxes, wealth; Warren, Elizabeth
unconditional basic income (UBI), *see* basic income
unemployment, 20–1, 51–2, 59–60, 79, 126, 209
United Methodist Church, 173
United Nations, 161–2
United Nations Children's Fund (UNICEF), 229–30
United Presbyterian Church, 173
United States v. Rogers, 259–60
universal basic capital, 222, 266
universal basic income (UBI), *see* basic income
universal child benefits, 23, 33, 42, 65, 68–71, 126, 140, 212, 215, 241–3
Universal Declaration of Human Rights (UDHR), 162
Universal Refundable Credit Income Tax, 179, 240
universal savings accounts (USAs), 215
Unsplit the Vote, 256
U.S. Basic Income Guarantee Network (USBIG), 1, 187, 189, 192, 235
U.S. Constitution, 6, 8, 75–8, 80, 113, 115–6, 118, 120–3, 130, 151, 201, 246–7, 253, 259, 260

Vallianotos, E. G., 251
value-added tax (VAT), *see* taxes, value-added
Van Parijs, Philippe, 183, 188
Vanderborght, Yannick, 183
Vives, Ludovico, 150

Wallace, Henry, 158
War on Poverty, 129, 166 *see also* Johnson administration
Warren, Dorian, 210
Warren, Elizabeth, 222, 263–4
Washington, George, 118
Watson, Thomas J. Jr., 169, 175
Watts, Harold, 172
wealth tax, *see* taxes, wealth
welfare, 14, 16, 19, 23, 41–3, 47, 93, 120, 129, 165, 167, 174–5, 179, 184, 195, 198, 211, 221, 228
Wenger, Al, 204
West, Darrell M., 212, 264
Widerquist, Karl, 178, 181, 189, 192, 193
Wiley, George, 169
Williams, Alex, 200–1
Wilson, James W., 170, 246
Winkler, Adam, 246–7
Wogaman, Philip, 173
Wolf Pac, 261
Wolin, Sheldon, 261
Wright, Erik Olin, 194
Wynne, Kathleen, 227

Y Combinator, 204, 217–8
Yang, Andrew, 34, 211, 267

Zelleke, Almaz, 189
Zuckerberg, Mark, 204, 210